HUMAN RESOURCE DEVELOPMENT QUARTERLY

Sponsored by ASTD and the
Academy of Human Reso·

T0340158

Editor

Tim Hatcher
North Carolina State University

Baiyin Yang
University of Minnesota

Editorial Board

Michael Beer
Harvard Business School

Laura Bierema
University of Georgia

Wayne Cascio
University of Colorado

Neal Chalofsky
George Washington University

Andrea D. Ellinger
*University of Illinois,
Urbana-Champaign*

K. Peter Kuchinke
University of Illinois

Michael Leimbach
Wilson Learning

Michael Scriven
Western Michigan University

David Ulrich
University of Michigan

Frederick Nafukho
University of Arkansas

Tony O'Driscoll
IBM

Qualitative Methods Editor

Tonette Rocco
Florida International University

Quantitative Methods Editor

Reid Bates
Louisiana State University

Ex Officio

Darlene F. Russ-Eft
Oregon State University

Larry Dooley
Texas A&M University

Rich Torraco
University of Nebraska

Brenda Sugrue
ASTD

Wendy Ruona
University of Georgia

Jean Woodall
Oxford Brookes University

Managing Editor

Kelley Chisholm
North Carolina State University

VOLUME 17   WINTER 2006   NUMBER 4

Human Resource Development Quarterly (print ISSN 1044-8004; online ISSN 1532-1096 at www.interscience.wiley.com) is published quarterly by Wiley Subscription Services, Inc., A Wiley Company, at Jossey-Bass, 989 Market Street, San Francisco, CA 94103-1741, and is sponsored by ASTD and the Academy of Human Resource Development.

Copyright © 2006 Wiley Periodicals, Inc., A Wiley Company

Jossey-Bass is a registered trademark of John Wiley & Sons, Inc.

No part of this publication may be reproduced, stored in a retrieval system, or transmitted in any form or by any means, electronic, mechanical, photocopying, recording, scanning, or otherwise, except as permitted under Sections 107 or 108 of the 1976 United States Copyright Act, without either the prior written permission of the Publisher or authorization through payment of the appropriate per-copy fee to the Copyright Clearance Center, 222 Rosewood Drive, Danvers, MA 01923, (978) 750-8400, fax (978) 646-8600. Requests to the Publisher for permission should be addressed to the Permissions Department, c/o John Wiley & Sons, Inc., 111 River Street, Hoboken, NJ 07030, (201) 748-6011, fax (201) 748-6008, www.wiley.com/go/permissions.

MICROFILM copies of issues and articles are available in 16mm and 35mm, as well as microfiche in 105mm, through University Microfilms Inc., 300 North Zeeb Road, Ann Arbor, Michigan 48106-1346.

Human Resource Development Quarterly is indexed in Anbar Abstracts, Business Education Index, Current Index to Journals in Education (ERIC), PsycINFO, Sociological Abstracts, and Up-to-Date Publications.

Human Resource Development Quarterly is published in one volume of four issues a year, appearing in March, June, September, and December. Subscription rates: for institutions and libraries, $279 in the United States, $319 in Canada and Mexico, $353 in the rest of the world; for individuals, $85 in the United States, Canada, and Mexico, and $109 in the rest of the world. To ensure correct and prompt delivery, all orders must give either the name of an individual or an official purchase order number.

SUBSCRIPTION ORDERS should be mailed to Customer Service, Jossey-Bass, 989 Market Street, San Francisco, CA 94103-1741, or phone (888) 378-2537. *Change-of-address* notifications should provide the subscriber's old and new address. *Missing copies* will be replaced if valid claims are received within 90 days from date of mailing.

EDITORIAL CORRESPONDENCE may be sent via e-mail to the Editor, Tim Hatcher, at tim_hatcher@ncsu.edu, or to the Managing Editor, Kelley Chisholm, at hrdq_ced@ncsu.edu.

COVER ART BY WILLI BAUM.

www.josseybass.com

AHRD Officers and Board of Directors

Jerry Gilley
President
Colorado State University

Lane Morris
President-Elect
University of Tennessee

Larry Dooley
Past President
Texas A&M University

Darren Short
VP Membership
Avanade, Inc.

Darlene Russ-Eft
VP Research
Oregon State University

Toby Egan
Texas A&M University

Andrea Ellinger
University of Illinois

Thomas Garavan
University of Limerick

Tim Hatcher
North Carolina State University

Kathryn S. Hoff
Bowling Green State University

Wendy Ruona
University of Georgia

Dani Truty
Northeastern Illinois University

AHRD Ex Officio Board Members

Wendy Ruona
University of Georgia

Tim Hatcher
North Carolina State University

Jean Woodall
Oxford Brookes University

Richard Torraco
University of Nebraska-Lincoln

Thomas Garavan
University of Limerick

Scott Johnson
University of Illinois at Urbana-Champaign

Kathryn S. Hoff
Bowling Green State University

ACKNOWLEDGMENT OF FINANCIAL SUPPORT

The editors and Editorial Board gratefully acknowledge the financial support given to *Human Resource Development Quarterly* by corporations and organizations. This support helps make it possible to maintain the standards of quality required of a scholarly journal.

The following university is acknowledged as a supporter of HRDQ:

NORTH CAROLINA STATE UNIVERSITY
Raleigh, North Carolina

Manuscript Reviewers

As a refereed journal, *Human Resource Development Quarterly* depends on qualified individuals to serve as manuscript reviewers. Reviewers have a unique way of contributing to the HRD field in that they help determine the quality and nature of the research. Reviewers should expect to receive approximately four manuscripts per volume, although the number may vary depending on the type of manuscripts received and the individual reviewer's expertise. Personal feedback is given to reviewers at the conclusion of each volume.

Individuals who wish to be considered as manuscript reviewers should take the following actions:

- Submit a complete curriculum vitae, listing educational background, professional employment, publications and presentations, service to other journals, and any other relevant information.
- Include a statement describing specific areas of HRD expertise, such as cost-benefit analysis, training transfer, or organizational learning.
- Include a statement describing specific areas of research expertise, such as qualitative methods, ANOVA, or multivariate analysis.

The editor reviews these materials on a continuous basis, so individuals should receive immediate notification of their status as a reviewer. Materials should be sent to Managing Editor, *HRDQ*, North Carolina State University, 310 Poe Hall, Campus Box 7801, Raleigh, NC 27695-7801. E-mail address: hrdq_ced@ncsu.edu.

CONTENTS

◪ EDITORIAL

Anyone? Anyone? Anyone?   365
Richard A. Swanson

◪ ARTICLES

Survey Ranking of Job Competencies by Perceived Employee
Importance: Comparing China's Three Regions   371
Jin Xiao

The purpose of this study was to reveal the core job skills that workforces in China deem essential in the context of their workplace in the
current economic transition across China's three regions. Almost
twenty-six thousand employees from 397 randomly sampled firms were
surveyed. The results of the survey showed differences related to occupation and work experience. Five empirically based competencies are
presented.

Comparing the Effects of Determinants of Turnover Intentions
Between Taiwanese and U.S. Hospital Employees   403
Cherng G. Ding, Chieh-Peng Lin

The authors surveyed 179 Taiwanese and 144 U.S. hospital employees
to compare the direct and indirect effects of career satisfaction on
turnover intention through organizational commitment. Managerial
implications are discussed, and suggestions for future research are
offered.

Tuition Reimbursement, Perceived Organizational Support, and
Turnover Intention Among Graduate Business School Students   423
Marshall Pattie, George S. Benson, Yehuda Baruch

Although there are retention benefits associated with tuition reimbursement, it is possible that companies are paying to develop skills
that help employees switch organizations. The authors investigate the
relationships among receiving tuition reimbursement, the job relatedness of the degree, proximity to graduation, and turnover intention.

Participation in Management Training in a Transitioning Context:
A Case of China   443
Jia Wang, Greg G. Wang

This phenomenological study focused on M.B.A. programs in China
during the country's recent transitional period. It explored critical issues
related to participation in HRD interventions. The authors derived three
propositions for future research on HRD learning participation and
drew practical implications as well.

FORUMS

Mega-Trends in the American Workforce   475
Carl E. Van Horn

Why We Fail: How Hubris, Hamartia, and Anagnosis Shape
Organizational Behavior   481
Randal Ford

 REVIEW

Lost Knowledge: Confronting the Threat of an Aging Workforce,
by David W. DeLong   491
REVIEWED BY KATHY LOHR MILLER

Anyone? Anyone? Anyone?

Richard A. Swanson

I love the scene from that old movie, *Ferris Bueller's Day Off* (1986), where the painfully boring economics teacher played by Ben Stein throws out a question to the class and then prods the zombie-like students for an answer: "Anybody? Anybody? Anybody?" Nobody responds, and Stein goes on to answer his own question.

This is not an angry editorial. Rather, it is an expression of bafflement at the weak response to an existing state of affairs and some thoughts about the role HRD can play in engaging people in systems that fundamentally affect their lives.

There are extraordinary and exemplary leaders threaded through the leadership maze of the United States. However, I have never sensed such a leadership void in the United States. While I have experience in other nations, I feel more confident in restricting my comments to the United States. Given today's global economic, technological, and military forces, the consequences of incompetent or unethical leadership can easily result in war, losses of financial savings for thousands of people, and obscene self-serving greed.

My provoking questions are: How do the people we have overseeing so many business, government, and educational organizations get there in the first place? How do they continue to bore and manipulate us with inane logic? And how is it that we continue to respond to these conditions in manners similar to the teenagers in Ben Stein's history class: staring out the windows, goosing each other, and resting our sleeping heads on our desktops? Are these questions relevant to the human resource development profession? "Anyone? Anyone? Anyone?"

Leadership Crisis

There are two underlying aspects to the leadership crisis in the United States: capacity and integrity. Ultimately I believe they are connected.

HUMAN RESOURCE DEVELOPMENT QUARTERLY, vol. 17, no. 4, Winter 2006 © Wiley Periodicals, Inc.
Published online in Wiley InterScience (www.interscience.wiley.com) • DOI: 10.1002/hrdq.1181

Chief executive officers, presidents of nations, and governors of states are mortal humans. It is probably safe to say that most are at least of average intelligence. I regularly tell students in my graduate classes that they and their classmates are as intelligent as the CEOs of major companies.

In my judgment, the complexity of the demands placed on leaders has greatly expanded, while the capacity of the pool of candidates for leadership positions has remained the same. Leaders are facing more demands than the capacity they personally have to handle them. This observation may be why Lucy Kellaway, *Financial Times* columnist, has estimated that 83 percent of chief executive officers fail (Ormerod, 2005). The mechanisms for coping in top-level pressure-cooker jobs include oversimplification, avoidance, new methods, lying and cheating and greed.

Oversimplification. Leaders who do not understand or acknowledge the complexity of a situation are showing sure signs of limited capacity. I once worked with a Fortune 500 CEO who made all his decisions based on a simple economic model. He never had to intellectually or emotionally deal with the people side of business (employees or customers) or the real nature of the business itself. Applied consistently, his simple economic model did keep the company afloat and attractive enough that it was bought out by a competitor for a strategic component. The new owner sold off the unwanted pieces.

Avoidance. In a former faculty position, I worked under a college dean whose simple model appeared to be that things would work themselves out and not to make any decisions unless forced to (so as to avoid conflict). His painful tenure ended up increasing conflict and numerous lost opportunities for excellence.

In both this instance and the preceding one, the leaders did not want to know anything more about the systems they were overseeing. They refused to listen to information from advisers providing information beyond their shrunken, incomplete, and inaccurate views.

New Methods. Intelligently embracing new and innovative methods offers the promise of expanded system capacity. Engaging employees and customers in analysis and decision making through new rational strategies, policies, and work methods moves the human capacity question to the work team rather than the person at the top. A simple example is Kellogg Company's using the Internet for getting and giving customer information (Steinberg, 2006) and the use of structured on-the-job training as advocated by Jacobs (2003) for the purpose of empowering all employees to be trainers of their particular expertise.

Schizophrenic use of new methods can be counterproductive. One wonders what would have happened to Ford Motor Company if it had stuck to CEO Donald Peterson's 1980s commitment to quality? The follow-up Ford CEO, Red Pohling, ditched Ford's commitment to quality for something else.

Lying and Cheating. Children who find themselves in a losing position often try to change the rules in order to win the game. Unlike the relatively even playing field of the playground, adult leaders are often insulated from much of the system they are meant to serve. Unlike the playground, they can be secretive in their decision making. This is why vigilance is required. The late Ken Lay, convicted former CEO of Enron Corporation, oversaw accounting fraud amounting to $1 billion in employee pensions and the loss of five thousand jobs and huge shareholder losses. Even after the collapse of Enron and before his criminal conviction, Lay spent lavishly: $32,000 for a trip to Park City, Utah, and $200,000 for his wife's birthday party (Ken Lay escapes justice with death, 2006). His capacity for changing the rules even led him to the White House. Lay was the top financial supporter of President George W. Bush and had private energy policy meetings with Vice President Richard Cheney. Anyone? Anyone? Anyone?

Greed. It is important to be reminded of the delusionary effect that money and power can have, along with the resulting behaviors of greed and dishonesty. While there are always inspiring exceptions, greed seems to go with the territory.

Ben Stein, economist and media entertainer, recently mused: "When I was a lad, the chief executive of a major public company was paid 30 or 40 times what a line worker was paid. Now the multiple is 180! Why, as we are being killed by foreign competition, do we need to pay our executives so much?" (Stein, 2006, p. BU-3).

Greed on the part of organizational leaders leads to deep distrust. Those working in the organizations and society as a whole cynically view greedy leaders as unethical, uncaring, and unfair. These leaders are suspect when it comes to sharing the gains of the organization. When organizational leaders exhibit extraordinary greed, as did William McGuire, CEO of UnitedHealth Group, employees and stakeholders will likely withhold support and information. William McGuire took $1.6 billion in stock options (beyond his extravagant salary) in just one year (Forelle & Bandler, 2006). At $58,000 a year, a nurse would have had to have worked from 500 B.C. up to the present day to earn the bonus money that McGuire made in one year (Coleman, 2006). Such personal greed at the top of an organization has to have an effect on those throughout the organization and the society in which such greed takes place. In this case, investor negative reaction to this news caused a serious loss in market value for UnitedHealth (Forester, 2006).

"The titans of corporate America are getting as much as they can get away with and hiring lawyers and public relations people if there is a problem" (Stein, 2006, p. BU3). Paralleling this time of leadership greed, economist Paul Ormerod (2005) reports that social mobility has declined since 1970. Social-democratic thinking has historically prized such upward mobility. Stein (2006) asks in his essay on greed if we are simply maintaining an America that is a financial neighborhood, void of a brotherhood and sisterhood. Ken Lay, former CEO of Enron and convicted criminal, died and never spent a day in jail. Anyone? Anyone? Anyone?

HUMAN RESOURCE DEVELOPMENT QUARTERLY • DOI: 10.1002/hrdq

Response from the HRD Profession

These high-level shenanigans may seem beyond the HRD profession. They will be if that is where the profession chooses to be positioned. The alternative is to proudly note that organizations are human-made entities with all the strengths and weaknesses human beings bring to the table. This is the domain of HRD. Other than HRD, there is very little infrastructure in most organizations that upholds the potential and integrity of the people throughout the organization. Clearly, help is needed. Anyone? Anyone? Anyone?

HRD professionals have the privilege in most organizations of getting close to the people and their work and working across functions in ways that are unique. They can hear, see, and know things of which others are unaware. It is this information base, from studying the organization and the people in it, that serves as the basis for proactive wise counsel back to everybody in the organization and especially to its leaders.

Voice of the Stakeholders. HRD professionals should become a responsible conduit for facilitating idea sharing throughout the organization. In touchy situations, HRD professionals should establish mechanisms for soliciting and sharing ideas when the power interests are at odds and disproportionate. And they should have clear decision rules about confidentiality in doing this work.

Humane Response Time. HRD professionals should learn to carry the message to stakeholders at various levels in the organization about the appropriate intensity and timing of their actions. As the country western song about card playing goes, "Know when to hold 'em, fold 'em, and play 'em." My former dean unable to make a timely decision needed to be confronted about the consequences of his nondecisions, the fact that no decisions were decisions, and that his indecisiveness had large negative consequences.

Fairness. HRD should relentlessly advocate a rational range of equity in the distribution of financial and nonfinancial rewards and recognition throughout the organization. Everybody is not equal in terms of their expertise, effort, contributions, and results that are important to the organization. HRD should not be in the business of hosting pity parties. But when CEO William McGuire takes $1.6 billion in stock options in just one year, this is beyond fair. McGuire did not invent this company (he is not Bill Gates of Microsoft); he was an employee. HRD professions could begin open discussions in an organization aimed at establishing policies around fairness.

Conclusion

HRD professionals who agree with me that there is a leadership void in their organizations need to make a fundamental decision to respond or not respond. In helping to make this decision, it is essential to believe that the ethical theory and practice of HRD is important for sustaining the success of any organization. HRD professionals must first be fully convinced of this. They then must convince their organizations of it through word and deed. Finally, they must exhibit the courage to act so as to help make their organization a better place. Anyone? Anyone? Anyone?

RICHARD A. SWANSON
EDITOR

References

Coleman, N. (2006, May 2). McGuire gives himself a clean bill of health. *Minneapolis Star Tribune.*

Forelle, C., & Bandler, J. (2006, March 18). The perfect payday. *Wall Street Journal,* p. A1.

Forester, J. (2006, May 23). UnitedHealth debt outlook lowered. *Pioneer Press,* p. B1.

Jacobs, R. J. (2003). *Structured on-the-job training: Unleashing employee expertise in the workplace.* San Francisco: Berrett-Koehler.

Ken Lay escapes justice with death. (2006, July 6). *San Francisco Chronicle.*

Omerod, P. (2005). *Why most things fail: Evolution, extinction and economics.* New York: Pantheon.

Stein, B. (2006, July 9). A city on a hill, or a looting opportunity. *New York Times,* p. BU-3.

Steinberg, B. (2006, July 10). The marketing maze. *Wall Street Journal,* pp. R1, R4.

Richard A. Swanson is Distinguished Research Professor of Human Resource Development and the Sam Lindsey Chair, College of Business and Technology, University of Texas at Tyler.

ARTICLES

Survey Ranking of Job Competencies by Perceived Employee Importance: Comparing China's Three Regions

Jin Xiao

The acquisition of skills that match job requirements has become an issue in human resource development. A uniform but vague list of desirable skills often provided by policymakers or advocated by scholars is used as a guide in education and training programs in China. Using survey data, this study analyzes the core skills that workforces in China consider to be important in carrying out job routines in different jobs, different industries, and different geographical regions. This study surveyed 25,933 employees from 397 randomly sampled firms of four counties in each of the East, Central, and West regions of China. Twenty kinds of job skills were deduced from interviews conducted in the field. Five categories of skills were identified by the employees: dispositional characteristics, technical know-how skills, job basics, problem solving, and communication. Using a hierarchical model, the analysis is focused on whether employees in different occupations (for example, managerial, professional, salesperson, frontline workers) had different perceptions of required job skills. The results show both differences related to occupation and work experience and similarities in perceived job competencies among industries and across three regions.

Note: This study is part of a research project entitled "Education and Work: The Efficacy of Schooling in Human Resource Development in Three Regions in China," of which Jin Xiao is the principal investigator. The project is partially funded by the Research Grants Council of Hong Kong (CUHK 4379/00H). Xin Liu, now at Fu Dan University, was a research associate for the project in 2002, when working on a Ph.D. at the Chinese University of Hong Kong. I appreciate his help in running the statistical analysis with me. I am grateful to the reviewers and editors for their constructive comments that helped improve this article.

The transition from a planned to a market-oriented economy in China has led to a demand for skills to equip individuals to become competent at their jobs. A new consensus seems to have been reached that technological innovation and success in global competition will rest on a highly educated workforce and their acquisition of skills (Organization for Economic Cooperation and Development, 1992; Brown, Halsey, Lauder, & Wells, 1997). The Chinese government has readily embraced such an economic consensus, and there are calls for education expansion and human resource development (HRD) to improve the competence of the workforce (Hu, 2001; China Ministry of Education, 2002; China Central Committee and the State Council, 1999). The school curriculum has been overhauled to adopt a more Americanized integrated curriculum for teaching and a project approach to learning (China Ministry of Education, 2001). The rise in demand for training and education has signaled a growing need to transform the workplace (Xiao & Tsang, 1999; Benson & Zhu, 2002; Xiao, 2002, 2004).

Educational attainment of the workforce, or the population as a whole, is often used to measure the highest skill qualifications attained. Thus far, the conception of the qualities required to achieve competence at work has been rather vague. Little effort has been made to examine the types of skills that are required of the workforce in a period of change to inform HRD practice and policymaking. The obvious problem is how to measure the skills required in different jobs. This is because skills or competencies required of job holders vary in work context and across jobs. Also, most jobs require a combination of skills to accomplish the job tasks.

Governments and scholars in industrialized countries and in China have endeavored to devise profiles and standards of job competence (Secretary's Commission on Achieving Necessary Skill, 1992; Garrick & McDonald, 1992; Rosenberg, 1976; Li, 2001; China Central Committee and the State Council, 1999).[1] However, more often, it seems that ideas about the kinds of skills or workplace knowledge are regarded as an individual behavioral issue that can be learned or taught in school to develop a world-class workforce (see China Central Committee and the State Council, 1999; Secretary's Commission on Achieving Necessary Skill, 1992). Another issue is whether developed-country defined competencies are readily transferable to Chinese schools and workplaces. Can we determine what skills are needed simply by using a developed country's level of economic development as an indicator? Or is it necessary to ask what we know from the empirical evidence? There is some doubt that skills demanded and skills in use can be deduced from expectations of future productivity (Ashton & Green, 1999). Brown, Green, and Lauder (2001) asserted that skill formation and economic performance are socially constructed and experienced within social institutions. Some scholars have made efforts to measure competencies with empirically derived evidence and criteria (Stasz, 2001; Hamlin, 2004, 2005; Burchell, Elliott, Rubery, & Wilkinson, 1994; Horrell, Rubery, & Burchell, 1994).

There is also a great interest in competencies that are universally applicable versus those that are job specific or culturally specific (Morrison, 2000; Thomas & Inkson, 2005; Smith, 2005). Efforts have been made to determine if management and leadership competencies have generalizability across organizations and national boundaries (Hamlin, 2004, 2005). While a universally applicable model seems necessary to ensure that multinational businesses succeed, empirical studies in Asian-Pacific regions have found cultural-specific difference in views and attitudes toward leadership (Osman-Gani, 2000; Ahmad, 2001). Human capital theory (Becker, 1964; Bowman, 1995) draws a crucial distinction between general and job-specific skills. Because each firm has its own mission, its own on-the-job training is a better way to provide its employees with the specific job skills they will need and socialize them into the firm's culture (Bowman, 1995; Hake, 1999; Xiao, 1999). Nevertheless, in China, research and policymaking still tend to focus on aggregated data of the workforce in terms of educational attainment (China Economics Research Centre, 2003), and there is little understanding of workplace competencies or skills in practice.

China's economic development takes a regional strategy. Reform started in the early 1980s and concentrated resources along the southeast and east coastal areas. Reform started in the central region during the late 1980s and early 1990s, when the concept of the socialist market economy took shape. Finally, at the end of 1990s, the "Go West" strategy pushed western China to catch up. It is assumed that skills required in workplaces in a more market-oriented economy are different from those required in the planned economy.

The purpose of this study was to reveal what job skills employees see as essential in the context of their workplace in the current economic transition across China's three regions. A questionnaire with items deduced from interviews in the workplace was designed to survey a group of employees on a main production line from 397 sampled firms of four counties in each of the east (ER), central (CR), and west (WR) regions of China. A multilevel model is employed to include both individual and firm characteristics in order to examine whether sociocultural factors have an impact on employees' perceptions of what job skills are important.

This study explores whether there exist commonalities in the five worker-perceived job competencies across occupations, industries, and economically different regions in China or whether workers in different jobs and different firms hold different perceptions on the issue. The next section provides the framework to understand competencies in the workplace. It is followed by sections on methods and the results of five empirical-based competencies. The concluding discussion examines the findings and their implications.

Theoretical Framework

Jobs consist of a complex array of tasks, with the characteristics of tasks determined by the nature of the product or service, technology, and job positions. The undertaking of different types of tasks requires of job holders varying combinations of a wide range of attributes, exercised at varying degrees of intensity (Burchell et al., 1994; Stasz, 1996). Employers, employees, and researchers may name skills in very different ways in different contexts. They include abilities to manipulate tools, knowledge of products and the organization, capacities for cultivating social relationships, acceptance of responsibilities, cognitive or mental ability, and abilities to organize and to coordinate. It is difficult to come up with a consensus on competencies that are required to do work well. A review of the literature (Ashton and Green, 1999; Brown et al., 2001; Morrison, 2000) reveals that there are relatively few data that warrant systematic study and careful interpretation of skills across jobs, sectors, and cultures.

Most often, educational attainments of the workforce, proportion of high-wage jobs, and number of professionals are used for symbolic analysis across countries of skills demanded (Aston & Green, 1999; Brown et al., 2001). Another indirect way to gauge skill trends is through survey data of the amount and types of education and training that the workforce received within a specified time frame (Belanger & Tuijnman, 1997; Ziderman & Horn, 1995; Xiao & Tsang, 1999; Xiao, 2002, 2004). These methods do not identify what competencies are most important to be developed in the workforce, only the supply of education and training that are assumed to be available to improve competencies.

Let us review some studies that explore job skills. Table 1 provides three frameworks of job skills identified by different studies. Burchell and his associates (1994) interviewed 23 employers and selected employees in Northampton in the United Kingdom; they then surveyed 246 employees for the period 1986–1987. Their concern was change of job content and deskilling or division of labor in the market. Their study extracted three groups of skills: specific skills to do work well, responsibilities, and discretion over tasks. The latter two groups are work ethics and power- and resource-related attributes. Comparison was made among jobs ranging from manual worker, technical, professionals, and routine clericals to managers. The other study of the same SCELI project (the Social Change and Economic Life Initiative) by Horrell and associates (1994) conducted a survey of one thousand employees in the same locality in Northampton. Their analysis of the perceptions of skill differences in men and women generated a similar three groups of skills but with some differences in skill measures for job content and responsibilities (see Table 1). Their findings show that the perceptions of skills are very much influenced by the status attached to the job. For instance, perceptions of importance to certain skills are discernible by reference to different types of work and the hierarchical structuring of jobs. That is, part-timers were particularly prone to undervalue the skill level of their job (Horrell et al., 1994), and managers placed less importance on the clerical skills of white-collar workers and the physical skills of manual employees.

Stasz (1996) took a sociocultural approach in exploring skills in technical work. Observations and interviews were conducted in seven types of jobs in

Table 1. Comparison of Skill Competencies

Gender and Skills (Horrell, Rubery, & Burchell, 1994)	Division of Labor and Skills (Burchell, Elliott, Rubery, & Wilkinson, 1994)	Workplace Skills in Practice (Stasz, 1996)
1. Skill for doing the job well	**1. Skill**	**1. Problem solving**
Lengthy experience of work	Physical	Quality control
Knowing about the organization	Clerical	Situation assessment
Good people relations at work	Social	Troubleshooting
Good contacts with customers	Organizational	Testing components
A talent for this type of work	**2. Responsibilities**	**2. Teamwork**
Professional, scientific, technical, or business knowledge	Responses	Self-managing teams
	Records and information	Distributing knowledge
2. Responsibilities	People	Independent work/do
Supervision of others	Output/standards	together
Safety or health of others	**3. Discretion**	**3. Dispositions and**
Checking work		**attitudes**
Machines, materials, or goods		Mutual respect
Confidential information		Reliance
Money		Confidence
Maintaining output or service		Prepared to work
Meeting official or professional standards or quality		Know and do your own job
3. Factors in determining how hard one works		Ask for help
Machine/assembly line		Friendliness
Clients/customers		Patience
Supervisor/boss		Don't pass problem off
Fellow workers or colleagues		**4. Communication**
Own discretion		Audience
Pay incentive		(internal versus external)
Reports/appraisals		Purpose
		Style
		Mode

four workplaces: health care, traffic management, transportation, and semi-conductor manufacturing in the United States. Stasz then developed a framework with four groups of competencies in practice.[2] She found that these skills are generic but are used in quite specific ways in each job; moreover, the requirements for each job vary widely. She also found that these skills, although distinguishable in theory, are in practice typically found together. For instance, solving a problem requires a technician to possess technical knowledge of equipment, study wiring diagrams, have experience, communicate with various people, and be able to work in a team.

Management or leadership study has accumulated a number of studies on competencies. Morrison (2000) has reviewed major studies and literature for global leadership models. There are basically two views of effective leadership competencies. One argues for generalizability: that someone who is effective in his or her own culture will be effective in other context. Some major studies do find a large proportion of leadership competencies generalizable or transferable across cultures. Black et al. (1999) focused on personal characteristics of effective global leaders such as inquisitiveness, perspective, character, and savvy. Interviews of 130 HR managers were conducted, and then a survey was conducted throughout North America, Europe, and Asian. Hamlin (2004, 2005) focused his studies on effective management behavior in organizational planning, team leadership, empowerment, staff development, personal management, and communication. Brockbank and Ulrich (2003) surveyed 7,100 respondents from 241 companies across industries and countries, with a focus on global HR management competencies of business knowledge, strategic contribution, HR technology, personal credibility, and HR delivery, a more comprehensive scheme. Although each group of studies claimed that effective leadership is generalizable across cultures, each focused on different dimensions of management and leadership.

The other view sees leadership as context specific, which might involve occupational differences as well as cultural differences. In regard to occupational difference, Blanthorne, Bhamornsiri, and Guinn (2005) provided an interesting survey in response to the debate over soft skills versus technical skills in the accounting business in the United States. The survey covered six skills: technical, communication, interpersonal, administrative, leadership, and practice development. For promotion from junior staff to senior staff, technical, communication, and interpersonal skills are considered most important; from senior staff to manager, technical skills become more important; and from manager to partner, interpersonal, leadership, and communication skills rise significantly. Competencies vary at different career stages. A study of Spanish tourism (Agust & Grau, 2002) was carried out to analyze technical and generic managerial competencies needs. The results showed that technical competency needs (market analysis, computing) were found but not in the general competencies. It is interesting that the study in Spain did not find general competencies as important.

The cross-cultural management literature notes that the most capable managers have been in situations in which they have had little experience; for example, what works in the United States does not always work in China or India. Osman-Gani (2000) conducted a study of expatriate multinational enterprise managers in Singapore from five countries across three continents. The results show different views in ranking training needs. American and German managers ranked human resource, sociocultural, and general management as the three top areas for training. In contrast, Korean expatriates considered accounting, financial, and taxation policies of the host country to be more important and production technology less important. A study in Malaysia, a multiethnic and collectivist society, found that a firm's leadership is sensitive to the values of employees from different ethnic groups, such as Malays, Chinese, and Indians (Ahmad, 2001). Managers need to keep their leadership in line with diversified values and develop an original "recipe" to suit all ethnicities in the workforce.

In economic reform, more and more multinational companies have entered China. However, both human resource management research and practice have been found problematic. Studies in China have been conducted primarily from a Western perspective (Ahlstrom, Foley, Young, & Chan, 2005). Theories are not equally useful in the Chinese cultural and organizational context. It is important to consider the cultural context in anticipating how employees and employers interpret HR strategies. With its long history, China has a unique way of doing business that in several ways is different from other cultures in conducting business (Bjerke, 1999). In addition to *guanxi* (relationships), strategy is often viewed as flexibility, and power is associated with inequality and hierarchy. Although harmony is stressed, there is a lack of trust and open discussion about business management. This group of comparative studies highlights cultural difference and contextual preference in competencies.

In explaining the links of investment in education and training with workers' wages, human capital theory (Becker, 1964; Mincer, 1974) made a crucial distinction between general and firm-specific skills. General skills are those that can be acquired through education and are transferable across firms. Nevertheless, firms develop their own job requirements and organizational culture based on their mission, history, and theory of management (Bowman, 1995). Therefore, the role of skill in generating competitiveness varies by organization (Brown et al., 2001). Morrison (2000) comments that in order to develop a universally applicable model of global leadership competencies, the core should remain the same, but such factors as home company, culture, company affiliation, and hierarchical and functional positions in the organization will have varying degrees of impact on the characteristics that affect leaders.

Taking the workplace as social context, work is regarded as an interaction between the characteristics of the larger work environment, which includes workers, the norms of practice, and specific aspects of the work organization and job tasks (Stasz, 2001). Barrie and Pace (1998) argue that although in complex work contexts, job tasks require vocational or specific skill, they also involve the cognitive abilities of workers to draw on certain skills and resources to accomplish their assignments. Thus, the situational tasks require both job-specific and generic competencies.

The shortcomings of competencies studies are obvious. Most models lack systematic research and careful interpretation. The sample often includes only a particular group of employees, usually managers, and there is little information about other occupations in the same workplace. There are merits in combining qualitative and quantitative methods (Ashton & Green, 1999; Morrison, 2000; Hamlin, 2004), and some studies have used this approach (Black et al., 1999; Hamlin, 2004, 2005; Stasz, 1995; Osman-Gani, 2000, p. 219). It is necessary to make an extra effort to gather empirical evidence for international comparison.

Regional disparities in China are significant. Xiao (2004) finds that the extent of on-the-job training provided to employees corresponds to the sequential order of reform and argues that the pressure of HRD on firms in each region corresponds to the extent of opening up to market in that locality. Studies of productivity and incomes (Liu & Xiao 2006; Li, 2003; Johnston, 1999; Wu, 2004) have shown significant inequality among regions in the same sequential order.

Therefore, China's three regions, which are at different levels of economic development, served as the most appropriate socioeconomic context to test to what extent competencies can be generalizable. This study addresses the following research questions:

1. What consensus do Chinese employees have on job competencies that are necessary to accomplish their typical job tasks?
2. To what extent are these competencies generalizable across jobs and industries?
3. Does China's regional strategy for development differentiate competencies as required in economic development?

Methods

The study used mixed methods. First, in-depth interviews were conducted with managers, technicians, salespersons, and floor workers, both skilled and non-skilled, about the skills they consider necessary to accomplish their routines; observation was carried out to understand the context and process of production (see Xiao, 1999, 2003, 2006).[3] Interviewees were given unstructured questions to explore every daily job task and skill that they used to do work well, as Stasz's study did (1996). Based on a content analysis, twenty major statements of essential skills, with terms most often used by interviewees to interpret their experience of completing tasks, were used to design twenty measure items on a scale, with 0 as not applicable, 1 as not important, 2 as somewhat important, and 3 as very important. A pilot study was conducted to test the questionnaire in different localities of our samples. Selected interviews were conducted again to validate the measure items. Confirming interviews were also conducted during data analysis.

Two questionnaires were distributed in the autumn of 1998 to collect data. The employee questionnaire collected the following information: (1) the employee's demographic information, (2) amount of schooling completed, (3) education and training experience between 1993 and 1998, (4) the employee's characteristics including job position, level of technical proficiency, and changes experienced in the workplace, and (5) the perception of the importance of jobs for accomplishing routines. The firm questionnaire collected information about such firm characteristics as types of ownership, size, industry, and region.

Sampling. A stratified random sampling method was used to select the sample (Table 2). First, the sample was determined in accordance with geographical

Table 2. Distribution of Samples

Region	Province	County	Firm	Number of Employees Surveyed	Average Number of Employees per Firm	Proportion (%)
East	Jiangsu	Wuxi	69	6,787	98	21.4
		Jiangying	18	1,600	89	5.0
	Guangdong	Jiangmen	37	2,999	81	9.4
		Heshan	16	1,175	73	3.7
Central	Hubei	Zhijiang	16	1,350	84	4.3
		Yichang	62	4,955	80	15.6
	Hebei	Cixian	21	1,278	61	4.0
		Handan	57	4,939	87	15.6
West	Yunnan	Luxi	24	936	39	2.9
		Mile	34	1,546	46	4.9
	Shaanxi	Fengxiang	15	1,232	82	3.9
		Baoji	32	2,939	92	9.3
	Total		401	31,736	79	100

and economic disparities indexed by Hu, Wang, and Kang (1995) in the three regions. In the WR, Yunnan and Shaanxi were included as economically backward provinces; they had a respective GDP about 58.8 percent and 61.9 percent of the national mean. In the CR, Hebei and Hubei were included; their respective GDPs were 85.8 percent and 80.8 percent of the national mean. From the ER, Jiangsu and Guangdong were selected; their respective GDPs were 136.7 percent and 170.5 percent of the national mean. The nature of the disparity coincides with the sequential order of economic reform.

In each province, two counties at the intermediate level of industrialization were selected. Within a county, those in the roster of registered firms were first stratified according to ownership type, size, and industry. Then firms were randomly selected. Within each firm, a major production unit or workshop, such as a whole production line, with all of the employees required for its operation, was sampled. The questionnaires were distributed by a member of the research staff in the county who had received training. This person collected the questionnaires after a couple of days. Of the 34,510 questionnaires that were distributed, 31,736 were collected, for a return rate of 92.0 percent. For the analysis of three three-level models, 25,933 individual cases in 397 firms were used after discarding cases containing missing values in any of the variables at all three levels.

Dependent Variables. Data for the twenty measure items collected were subjected subsequently to various techniques of factor analysis (factor analysis, principal component analysis). Extraction (rotation with varimax) was used for principal component analysis to explore five to six factors for meaning while checking against interview notes and postinterviews for interpretation. About five or six groups of skills used commonly in daily routines were identified as a result of the interviews: (1) dispositions/attitudes, (2) job-specific skills or technical know-how, (3) job basics, (4) problem solving at work, and (5) communication. An effort was made to explore the attribute of teamwork, which is often referred to in the Western literature (see Stasz, 1996). Two items—"Discuss problems with peers" and "Collaborate with peers to complete job assignments"— were used. Both clustered with a dispositional measure item, "Know my merits and weaknesses" (see Table 3 and results of measurement analysis in Table 6 in the next section). Interpretation from postinterview sees that collectiveness or a willingness to do things together is regarded as part of the typical Chinese

Table 3. Measurement Items and Factor Analysis (N = 25,933)

	Scale Component	Mean	SD
Scale 1: Dispositional abilities (variance explained)	(21.12)		
Effectively allocate my time at work	0.696	2.57	0.66
Raise accurate questions about problems at work	0.575	2.64	0.61
Initiate suggestions to improve work quality	0.540	2.47	0.75
Know my merits and weaknesses	0.719	2.61	0.64
Discuss problems in work and life with peers	0.680	2.44	0.66
Collaborate with peers to complete job assignments	0.622	2.57	0.64
Understand the relevance of my job to overall production	0.671	2.52	0.69
Scale 2: Specific skills for job tasks (variance explained)	(12.29)		
Have knowledge about process of my job tasks and required skills	0.845	2.78	0.50
Master skills required by the boss for completing job tasks	0.850	2.80	0.48
Be able to complete job tasks independently	0.590	2.81	0.48
Scale 3: Job basics (variance explained)	(11.51)		
Be able to understand the basic theory of production and operation	0.688	2.56	0.73
Be able to calculate statistics for the job tasks	0.732	2.41	0.89
Be able to record my job tasks	0.415	2.57	0.69
Scale 4: Problem-solving skills (variance explained)	(10.35)		
Be able to search technical causes of the problem at work	0.793	2.56	0.80
Be able to read technical materials to solve problems	0.777	2.41	0.89
Initiate learning to master new knowledge and skills about my job	0.319	2.70	0.58
Scale 5: Communication skills (variance explained)	(10.02)		
Be able to write work reports or technical reports	0.607	2.13	1.02
Be able to exchange ideas and communicate with clients	0.847	2.11	1.09
Accurately communicate with subordinates and give assignments	0.691	2.04	1.21
Accurately report work to superiors	0.305	2.50	0.77

worker's attitude and concept of the value of work. Therefore, those two so-called teamwork items stayed with the disposition items. An overall scale with five constructs of competencies was designed and given a label to describe the nature and classification of measure items loaded onto the respective factors. Through this qualitative-quantitative back-and-forth process, five dimensions of the job competencies derived from interviews, observations, and then survey data were identified.

Table 3 shows the results from a factor analysis, with the twenty items divided among five competencies. A test of internal consistency (Cronbach's alpha) was conducted that resulted in each of the following factors: (1) 0.8666 for dispositions, (2) 0.7804 for job-specific technical skills, (3) 0.7407 for basic or workplace-enabling skills, (4) 0.6301 for problem-solving skills, (5) 0.6021 for communication, and (6) an overall estimation of 0.9128 for all the measure items. These five variables of job competencies become dependent variables.

Individual Characteristics. Individual characteristics fall into two groups. The first group consists of cultural and symbolic attributes, referring to the socialization of individuals before they entered the firm. They include age, gender, and education completed. The argument is that such variables lay the basis for personality and culture and, consequently, a person's relationship with societal institutions (Cookson, 1986; Doray & Arrowsmith, 1997). Age has served as a proxy for indicators of movement through the life cycle and educational stratification of different generations. Initial education may have a far-reaching influence on how people perceive their work experience and envision the future. Differences in socialization account for much of the gender difference in educational pathways.

The second group is individual workplace attributes, including job position, rank in job position, change experienced in the workplace, and on-the-job training received. Employees were assigned to different positions. Job position is ranked into nonranked, usually temporary jobs or contracts leading to junior, middle, and senior status on the job ladder. Employees have different work experiences due to their job position in the job hierarchy. This is referred to as the "resource opportunity structure" in a social institution (Cookson, 1986). This can cause perceptions of job skills to vary. Changes in the workplace now take place constantly, and firms, under competitive pressure, are making changes regularly to improve their products or services.[4] Firms in China have made on-the-job training a means of upgrading job competencies (Xiao & Tsang, 1999; Benson & Zhu, 2002; Xiao, 2002, 2003, 2004), which might have caused employees' perceptions about competence to change. It is hypothesized that employees' perceptions would vary if they vary in individual characteristics.

Table 4 presents individual variables for a level 2 analysis. SEX is a dummy variable, with 0 for female and 1 for male. AGE is put into dummies of four groups. EDUCATION is put into six dummies to represent formal schooling by level and type. POSITION is put largely into four groups, referring to the

Table 4. Description of the Variables

Region Employee Cases (N) Variable Names	Definition and Coding	West 5,211	Central 10,050	East 10,672	Total 25,933
SEX	0 = Females	40.3%	41.9%	45.0%	42.8%
	1 = Males	59.7	58.1	55.0	57.2
AGE					
AGE_1	16–25 (0, 1)	26.2	24.1	18.0	22.0
AGE_2	26–35 (0, 1)	38.7	40.9	39.2	39.8
AGE_3	36–45 (0, 1)	23.6	24.5	27.7	25.6
AGE_4	46 and above (0, 1)	11.4	10.5	15.2	12.6
EDUCATION					
ED_PSL	Primary school or less (0, 1)	5.5	1.9	2.6	2.9
ED_LMS	Lower middle school (0, 1)	32.1	27.6	31.5	30.1
ED_UMS	Upper middle school general (0,1)	29.3	26.8	28.0	27.8
ED_VTE	Vocational/technical education (0, 1)	22.5	29.7	23.9	25.9
ED_JC	Junior college (0, 1)	6.3	7.7	6.5	6.9
ED_UN	University or more (0, 1)	4.4	6.2	7.5	6.4
POSITION					
POSITION_1	Managerial/administrative (0, 1)	22.3	29.5	24.7	26.0
POSITION_2	Professional/technical (0, 1)	12.9	14.0	14.1	13.8
POSITION_3	Salesperson (0, 1)	8.9	7.8	6.9	7.6
POSITION_4	Frontline worker (0, 1)	56.0	48.8	54.3	52.6
PROFICIENCY					
RANK_1	No technical rank in position (0, 1)	38.2	33.7	33.5	34.5
RANK_2	Junior technical rank (0, 1)	32.5	32.3	33.9	33.0
RANK_3	Middle technical rank (0, 1)	23.5	27.7	26.8	26.4
RANK_4	Senior technical rank (0, 1)	5.8	6.4	5.9	6.1
CHANGE	0 = No experience of change in the workplace	61.6	56.7	54.0	56.5
	1 = Yes; experienced change in the workplace	38.4	43.3	46.0	43.5
OJT	0 = Never received on-the-job training	47.5	43.4	32.7	39.8
	1 = Received on-the-job training	52.5	56.6	67.3	60.2

employee's job position in 1998. The grouping reflects a hierarchical order on the payroll, which includes managerial and administrative staff, professionals and technicians, and salespersons and frontline workers. PROFICIENCY refers to the ability to perform in one's assigned position as assessed by the firm in 1998. CHANGE refers to whether the employee experienced a major change in the workplace from 1993 to 1998.[5] OJT refers to whether the employee had ever received any on-the-job training between 1993 and 1998. Table 4 shows that about 60 percent of the sampled employees received on-the-job training provided by their firm. (For details of this training, see Xiao, 2004.)

Firm-Level Characteristics. Economic context has a direct impact on firms, which in turn puts pressure on employees to improve competitiveness (Xiao & Tsang, 1999; Benson & Zhu, 2002; Xiao, 2002, 2004). Investment choice in terms of ownership or industry would also indicate a firm's niche in the market and may determine its business strategies. In addition, a regional-progressive strategy is being taken with regard to the development of the Chinese economy. That is, the ER and coastal regions began developing in the early 1980s, followed by the CR in the later 1980s and early 1990s and, finally, the WR was pushed to catch up in the later 1990s.

Table 5 presents three firm variables. REGION is a predictor to detect whether there are any differences in perception of job competencies required across the three regions. OWNERSHIP is used to distinguish the firms' sources of investment. INDUSTRY signifies the products or sector in which a firm is engaged.

Analysis Models. The hierarchical linear model (HLM) program was used to apply a three-level analysis to the data. Conventionally, after factor analysis, a single score is saved from all measure items for each of the constructs extracted from the analysis; there would be only five separate scores for the five constructs. Then separate regression analysis is applied to predict the impact

Table 5. Description of the Firm Variables

Region Firm (N) Variable	Definition and Coding	West 139	Central 104	East 154	Total 397
REGION	Region in China	26.2%	38.8%	35.0%	100.0%
OWNER_1	State owned (0, 1)	36.5	40.9	38.1	38.8
OWNER_2	Collective/cooperative (0, 1)	26.0	13.6	20.1	19.1
OWNER_3	Private/contract (0, 1)	24.0	19.5	12.9	18.4
OWNER_4	Joint stock (0, 1)	6.7	7.8	12.9	9.3
OWNER_5	Joint investment (foreign, Hong Kong, Macau, Taiwan) (0, 1)	6.7	18.2	15.8	14.4
INDUST_1	Manufacturing (0, 1)	43.3	44.8	41.0	43.1
INDUST_2	Construction, mining, geological prospecting (0, 1)	4.8	6.5	5.8	5.8
INDUST_3	Transportation, telecommunications, real estate (0, 1)	11.5	16.2	12.9	13.9
INDUST_4	Commerce, catering services, tourism (0, 1)	15.4	9.7	10.1	11.3
INDUST_5	Textiles, chemical products for daily life (0, 1)	5.8	13.6	18.0	13.1
INDUST_6	Raw agriculture products processing (0, 1)	14.4	5.2	5.0	7.6
INDUST_7	Electronics industry (0, 1)	4.8	3.9	7.2	5.3

on each of the constructs. That loses statistical information about each measure item that makes the latent construct in the factor analysis.

In this study, a measurement model at level 1 is applied to describe the linkage among all the measure items and the latent constructs (five factor scales for the five competencies of referred skills perceived by each employee). The measurement model is a way to arrange the dependent variables so that estimation for the measure items on each of the five factors could be presented at the same time.[6] The other advantage of the level 1 measurement models is to put five constructs into an overall composite index for a consistent comparison. The model estimates the cohesiveness of items to each of their respective competencies. That makes it possible to compare skills for each of the competencies side by side.

As a person is nested in a work unit and a company is located in a certain locality, the contextual variables make an impact on his or her daily life. With HLM (see Raudenbush & Bryk, 2002, for detail), the structural impact could be captured with a consistent analysis in one model. At level 2, individual variables are used to predict if the five competencies are perceived differently due to differences in individual workers across jobs. At the third level, firm-level variables are used to test if perceptions of the five competencies vary across firms and regions. That will help in determining the variance of the latent true scores of the five competencies.

Results

The purpose of this study is to identify job competencies that Chinese workers have perceived as important in the workplace. The analysis seeks to examine the properties of the five measures of job competencies and compare whether there are differences in the perceptions of employees across occupations, industries, and China's three economically different regions. The results are presented in order of estimation.

Measuring Qualities for Job Competencies. The measurement model puts all the items on five latent constructs of job competencies for comparison. The coefficients of items illustrate the linkage or distance to the reference or the core item of each construct, which is the most weighted measure item in factor analysis; a negative or positive coefficient indicates both the direction and distance of an item score from the latent scale's latent core. When the coefficient of an item turns out not to be significant, it means that the item is perceived with no difference from the core item or measuring the same aspect. If a coefficient turns out to be significant, it means that the item measures an important attribute for that latent construct. These reveal linkages of measure items to the latent construct, which a single saved score of all items on a factor does not. (See Table 6.)

Let us first examine SCALE 1 for employees in WR. Item 1, "Know my merits and weaknesses," with the most weighted score in the factor analysis, is used as a reference item and comes up with an overall composite index

Table 6. Measurement Models: Estimation of Fixed Effects, Variance-Covariance Components, and Coefficient Reliability

	West	Central	East
SCALE 1: Dispositional abilities			
Know my merits and weaknesses	396.99 (4.28)***	416.87 (3.67)***	406.70 (2.68)***
Effectively allocate my time at work	-8.46 (1.68)***	-6.54 (1.12)***	-4.71 (1.11)***
Raise accurate questions about problems at work	-0.11 (1.68)	3.30 (1.12)**	4.52 (1.12)***
Initiate suggestions to improve work quality	-24.30 (1.69)***	-16.25 (1.13)***	-20.74 (1.12)***
Discuss problems in work and life with peers	-28.31 (1.68)***	-27.09 (1.12)***	-20.91 (1.11)***
Collaborate with peers to complete job assignments	-4.05 (1.68)*	-6.58 (1.12)***	-5.50 (1.11)***
Understand the relevance of my job with overall production	-14.65 (1.68)***	-14.24 (1.12)***	-12.26 (1.11)***
SCALE 2: Specific skills for job tasks			
Master skills required by the boss for completing job tasks	441.96 (3.86)***	466.15 (2.68)***	453.12 (2.58)***
Have knowledge about process of my job tasks and required skills	-3.39 (1.62)*	-4.10 (1.09)***	-2.42 (1.08)*
Be able to complete job tasks independently	0.12 (1.63)	-2.03 (1.10)#	4.88 (1.09)***
SCALE 3: Job basics			
Be able to calculate statistics for the job tasks	373.49 (4.47)***	382.15 (3.72)***	385.61 (3.04)***
Be able to understand the basic theory of the production/operation	20.01 (1.70)***	15.58 (1.13)***	26.34 (1.12)***
Be able to record my job tasks	15.71 (1.69)***	14.79 (1.13)***	31.47 (1.12)***
SCALE 4: Problem-solving skills			
Be able to read technical materials to solve problems	375.56 (4.73)***	385.38 (4.11)***	382.01 (2.92)***
Be able to search technical causes of the problem at work	21.01 (1.71)***	21.43 (1.14)***	22.92 (1.13)***
Initiate learning to master new knowledge and skills about my job	37.11 (1.70)***	39.01 (1.13)***	45.76 (1.12)***
SCALE 5: Communication skills			
Be able to exchange ideas and communicate with clients	334.74 (6.62)***	339.83 (4.62)***	342.09 (4.02)***
Be able to write work reports or technical reports	-3.04 (1.75)#	5.50 (1.16)***	3.77 (1.15)**
Accurately communicate with subordinates and give assignments	-18.11 (1.76)***	0.30 (1.17)	-12.00 (1.16)***
Accurately report work to superiors	41.80 (1.72)***	53.36 (1.14)***	59.07 (1.14)***

***$p < 0.000$. **$p < 0.001$. *$p < 0.005$. #$p > 0.05$ but marginal.

(396.99 for WR, 416.87 for CR, and 406.70 for ER),[7] the latent construct of dispositional qualities. Among the seven items measuring this construct, item 3, "Raise accurate questions about problems at work," and item 6, "Collaborate with peers to complete job assignments," are closest to the reference item, that is, with the smallest discrepancy (-0.11 and -4.05, respectively) to the overall composite index. These are about some of the personal qualities required to focus two dimensions for accomplishing job tasks. Next are item 2, "Effectively allocate my time at work," and item 7, "Understand the relevance of my job with overall production," with a larger discrepancy (-8.46 and -14.65, respectively) from the overall composite index. These two items are about using one's intangible resources and the conception of relationship of one's own niche in the firm, that is, the ability to conceive abstract concepts. The last tier comes with item 4, "Initiate suggestions to improve work quality," and item 5, "Discuss problems in work and life with peers," with the largest discrepancy (-24.30 and -28.31, respectively) to the overall composite index. These are more specific activities: initiatives in workplace social settings for problem solving.

In the U.K. context, dispositional abilities are not considered in a separate category, but we do see such items as "knowing about the organization" and "a talent for this type of job" listed under "skill for doing the job well" (see Table 1). In Stasz's framework, such attributes as mutual respect, confidence, asking for help, and friendliness and preparation to work, know, and do your own job are grouped together under the category of "dispositions and attitudes," which share some similarities with the qualities reflected in this analysis. The measure items of this study put more emphasis on behavior, while Stasz's emphasizes qualities behind behaviors.

The most consistently agreed-on item of the latent construct of depositions by sampled employees is "know my merits and weaknesses," a traditional Chinese ethic of becoming a decent person, self-meditation, and reflection for self-improvement. When items move from knowing oneself to knowing problems and then to taking action, coefficients tend to be larger, indicating a looser linkage. The Chinese practical philosophy of becoming a capable person or a sage is to know the substance of problems in nature and to know oneself with a good-hearted intention. The purpose is to tune one's conscience and commitment to serve, prove oneself through self-improvement, and act within the family first, then toward the public and state, and, ultimately, build a peaceful world under heaven as advised in the Chinese classic *Da Xu*, the Great Learning.[8] This group of items represents some core conceptions of Chinese behavioral ethics in terms of handling oneself properly with regard to oneself, one's ability, one's work, and one's relationship with others. The employees' perceptions carry the idea through self-knowledge and issues around and serving through self-improvement and working with others, an approach of reaching out from within. These dispositional abilities adhere closely to Chinese tradition.

All of the coefficients for the three regions show similar patterns in the perception of these qualities of dispositions. The first tier of items is close to the composite scores. The second tier follows the pattern, with a somewhat greater divergence from the common scores. The third tier diverges the most. We might conclude that employees are consistent in regarding these dispositional qualities as the most important for becoming a good employee in the workplace.

The next construct of workplace competence is specific skills for job tasks, that is, the technical ability for handling one's assignments. The most commonly agreed-on item is "master required skills for completing job tasks," reflecting the ability to perform satisfactorily as required for one's job position. Employees in WR and CR perceived "Be able to complete job tasks independently" the same as a core item, but employees in ER perceived it as a different aspect of specific skill. Employees in all three regions see "having knowledge about the procedure of my job tasks and job required skill" another distinctive aspect of this group of skills. The coefficients of "having knowledge about the procedure of my job tasks and job-required skills" and "being able to complete job tasks independently" come very close to that of the core item in all three regions. The conclusion is that employees in all three regions perceived specific job skills in a monolithic way, but with three distinctive aspects of mastering technical skills, having knowledge about the work, and ability to perform.

Stasz's study (see Table 1) looks at generic skills. All four groups of competencies are those that enable workers to do the specific tasks of their technical jobs well, so there is not such categorization in her framework. Burchell and his associates (1994) put skills by type for job categories such as physical or clerical, while Horrell and his associates (1994) include several aspects under the label "skill for doing the job well." There are some similarities to the skills described under the competency construct in this study. With regard to skill for doing work well in Horrell's framework, for "knowing about the organization," this analysis puts it in dispositions, as noted above; for "knowledge of work," this analysis put it as specific skill; for professional and scientist knowledge, this study puts it into job basics. Some aspects are good contacts and relations with people at work and customers, which Stasz puts in the categorization of communication.

The third construct is job basics (SCALE 3). The measure items define abilities to apply mathematics and writing skill in work and use their cognitive ability to understand the workplace. It is the ability to use generic literacy in the form of workplace literacy (Norback & Forenand, 1995). Employees in all three regions have a shared perception that these items measure important aspects of the competency of job basics. Stasz (see Table 1) and the other two studies in United Kingdom do not consider this group of abilities in their framework. Perhaps China is at an earlier stage of economic development and therefore job basics are stressed, in contrast to the United Kingdom and the United States, where employees are performing more complex tasks.

The fourth latent construct is problem solving. This construct focused on abilities to solve technical problems, including reading technical materials, searching technical causes, and learning new knowledge and technical skills. Compare these measures with items 3, 4, 5, and 6 on SCALE 1 of dispositional skills. Terms such as *raise, discuss, initiate suggestions,* and *collaborate* all suggest social interaction in problem solving. *Dispositional abilities* in the Chinese sense is a concept containing intermingled aspects of knowing oneself, knowing the work, solving problems together with peers, managing oneself, and putting the problem in relation to the overall picture of the workplace. In contrast, SCALE 4 captures the technical ability to solve problems. This suggests that employees in China largely see problem solving as a technical issue rather than a social or a cultural one, as scholars in the United States have regarded it (Smith, 2005). Stasz's framework of competencies elaborates problem solving into procedures of work or tasks, including quality control, situational assessment, troubleshooting, and testing. Horrell's and Burchell's studies did not consider problem solving a concern.

Finally, the last construction is communication: communication with clients outside the firm, in written form, and with subordinates as well as with superiors. Stasz has identified similar aspects in practice in the U.S. workplace. In this analysis, employees in the CR seem to regard communicating with subordinates as being important as the core item. In the same way, employees in WR see the ability to write reports as important as the core item. The coefficient for the item "Accurately report work to superior" is the most distant from the core item. It may indicate a difference in connotation, because communications with superiors might reflect a hierarchical relationship in the Chinese workplace instead of an orientation toward job tasks (Bjerke, 1999). In both Horrell's and Burchell's studies, supervisors, clients, and fellow workers are listed as factors important in determining how hard one works or discretion over them. It is more of an empowerment consideration than for work information distribution, as in this analysis.

Compared with SCALES 1 and 2, the magnitude of the coefficients of the items on SCALES 3, 4, and 5 diverges further from the respective core item. This shows that employees agree more on latent constructs extracted at the top of the factor analysis.

Employee Differences in the Ranking of Job Competencies. At level 2, the five latent constructs of competencies become outcome variables, and variables of individual characteristics are used to estimate their impact on perceptions of the five competencies. The analysis provides a large amount of statistical information (see the example in the article appendix).[9] To concentrate on a comparison of commonalities of job competencies across job and among the three regions, coefficients of independent variables were estimated for each of the three regions, abbreviated as E, C, and W and representing China's ER, CR, and WR, respectively. Accompanying them are signs of significance ($***p < 0.001$, $**p < .01$, $*p < 0.05$, and, $^\#p > 0.1$ but marginal) and directions of coefficients (negative and positive signs). This provides a clear pattern of perceptions of job competencies (see Table 7).

Table 7. Individual Variables: Fixed Effects

Variable	SCALE 1			SCALE 2			SCALE 3			SCALE 4			SCALE 5		
	East	Central	West	East	Central	West	East	Central	West	East	Central	West	East	Central	West
SEX	-E	C	W	E	-C	-W**	-E***	-C**	-W**	E***	C***	W***	E***	C***	W*
AGE															
16–25	E#	C	W#	E*	C*	-W	-E	-C***	-W	E*	-C#	W**	-E***	-C***	-W
26–35	E	-C	-W	E	C	-W	-E	-C***	-W***	E	-C	W	-E***	-C***	-W*
36–45 (reference)															
46 and above	-E*	-C	W	-E*	-C#	W	-E*	-C	W	-E	-C	-W	E	-C	W
EDUCATION															
PLS (6 years)	-E***	C	-W	-E***	-C	-W#	-E***	-C***	-W#	-E***	-C*	-W	-E***	-C**	W
LMS (9 years)	-E***	C	-W	-E***	-C*	-W	-E#	C	-W	-E***	-C**	-W	-E***	C	-W
UMS (12 years)	-E	C*	-W	-E*	C	-W	E*	C*	W	-E	-C	-W	-E	C	W
VTE (12 years) (reference)															
JC (14 years)	E	C*	W	-E	-C	-W	E	C	-W	E	C	W	E***	C***	W*
UN (16 years +)	-E	C	-W	-E***	-C	W	-E**	-C**	-W	E	C	W	E**	C**	W**
POSITION															
Managerial	E#	C*	W	-E	-C*	W	E	-C	W	-E***	-C***	-W***	E***	C***	W***
Professional/technical (reference)															
Salesperson	-E	C	W	-E*	-C*	-W#	-E	-C**	-W	-E***	-C***	-W**	E**	C#	W*
Frontline workers	-E***	-C*	-W*	-E***	-C***	-W*	-E***	-C***	-W***	-E***	-C**	-W**	-E***	-C***	-W***
PROFICIENCY															
Ranking 1 (reference)															
Ranking 2	-E*	C	-W	-E	C*	W	-E	C*	-W	E	C	-W	-E***	-C	-W**
Ranking 3	E	C*	W	E**	C**	W**	E	C	-W	E#	C*	W*	E*	C**	-W
Ranking 4	E**	C	W*	E***	C	W*	E***	-C	W	E**	C#	W**	E***	C*	W
CHANGE															
Experienced	E***	C***	W#	E*	C#	W***	E**	C*	W*	E***	C	W#	E***	C#	W*
ON-THE-JOB TRAINING															
Received	E***	C***	W***	E***	C***	W*	E***	C*	W***	E***	C***	W***	E***	C***	W**

Note: For the variable EDUCATION, PLS means that one received primary school or less; LMS is lower-middle school which is about nine years of education together with six years of primary school education; UMS is upper-middle school, another three years of general education; VTE is vocational and technical education, parallel to the upper-middle school; JC is junior college of three years after one finished upper-middle school or vocational and technical education; and UN is university education or more.

#$p > 0.1$. *$p < 0.05$. **$p < 0.01$. ***$p < 0.001$.

First, look at the personal characteristics carried into the firm, such as age, gender, and initial education (see the upper part of Table 7). For instance, under SCALE 1, the coefficient (−E) for SEX indicates that although dispositional competency may be perceived as less important by male employees in the ER than by their female counterparts, the difference is not significant. Male employees in the CR and WR (C and W, respectively) see dispositional competency in the same way as their counterparts do. With regard to SCALE 2, the construct for specific skills for job tasks, this was perceived to be significantly less important by male employees in the WR than by their female counterparts. In SCALE 3, the construct for job basics was perceived to be significantly less important by the male employees in all three regions than by their female counterparts. In contrast, the constructs of problem solving and communication, SCALES 4 and 5, respectively, were perceived to be significantly more important by all male employees than by their female counterparts in all three regions. We cannot reject the argument that men and women differ in their perspectives on basic job skills (SCALE 3), problem-solving skills (SCALE 4), and communication skills (SCALE 5). A general interpretation is that female employees consistently consider basic job skills to be important, but that male employees consider problem solving and communication skills to be more important. Nevertheless, it is interesting to note that both males and females in the three regions agree on dispositional skills. There is a different pattern for SCALE 2, with gender having no effect on perceptions of technical skill in the ER and CR but in the WR.

Employees are put into age groups. For SCALE 3 and SCALE 5, it seems that employees younger than the reference group, ages thirty-five to forty-six, in all of the three regions perceive the skills to be less important, but some regard them as significantly less important and others not. Overall, the results do not show any clear patterns among the three regions in perceptions of all five scales.

In educational attainment, the employees fell into six groups. Looking at SCALE 1, we find that employees in the ER with only nine years of education and primary school education or less tend to perceive SCALE 1 as significantly less important compared to the reference group, employees with vocational and technical education (twelve years). Those with an upper middle school education (twelve years) or junior college (fourteen years) or university education (sixteen years) have the same perception as the reference group. There are different patterns of perceptions of SCALE 1 by employees in the CR and WR with regard to their educational background. If we look at employees in the WR, there is no difference in their perceptions of SCALES 1 to 4, disregarding their educational backgrounds. However, for SCALE 5, employees in the WR with a junior college or university education consider it to be significantly more important than the reference group. In short, it seems that there is no clear general pattern of perceptions of competencies, with education as predicting variable for perceptions of job skills.

The lower part of Table 7 presents a comparison of individual characteristics as acquired in the workplace. Look at variable POSITION first. The first discernible pattern is that the frontline workers in three regions all perceive dispositional abilities to be significantly less important compared to the other occupational groups. This group is at the bottom of the job hierarchy in the workplace. They have the least control over their daily tasks and fewer opportunities. It is found this group of workers tends to have the least amount of on-the-job training in China (Xiao, 2004; Xiao & Tsang, 2004). They receive their directives from foremen and then complete those tasks. It was also found in the United Kingdom that lower-skilled employees were rated as having the least demanding job in seven of the nine job categories, except in physical skill and responsibility over resources (Burchell et al, 1994; also see Table 1), and the comparison was made to higher-skilled workers, technicians and lower professionals, higher professionals, clerical workers, and middle managers. In comparison, with regard to nine job content measures, bar physical skill, managers were rated as being the most the demanding.

Let us look at SCALE 1, dispositional abilities. Managerial staff, professionals and technicians, and salespersons in all three regions hold the same view, except managerial staff in the CR, who regard dispositional abilities as being more significant than professionals do. With regard to SCALE 2, salespersons consider specific know-how skill to be significantly less important than do professionals and technicians. Certainly salespersons do not make much use of this category of skills and technical requirements.[10] Professionals and technicians are obviously in charge of assignments, and their operating agenda is full of technical details. For managerial staff, those in the ER and WR place as much importance on know-how as do the professionals and technicians, except for managerial staff in the CR, who consider it less important.

For SCALE 3, on job basics, managerial staff in all three regions and salespersons in the ER and the WR hold the same perception as professionals and technicians, with the exception of salespersons in the CR, who do not. Frontline workers see job basics as less important because they are less likely to be required to make much use of this group of skills (calculating or writing, for example) to complete their job tasks.

Problem solving (SCALE 4) is at the core of skills advocated by government (Li, 2001; China Central Committee and State Council, 1999) to improve productivity. Nevertheless, our study shows interesting results. Compared with the professional and technical staff, none of the occupation groups in all three regions considers problem solving to be important. This is consistent with discussions on measurement analysis that problem solving is more or less a technical task in the Chinese workplace, which first calls for the attention of technicians.[11] In such cases, employees in other job positions do not feel as much pressure to exercise problem-solving skills. Problems in management and organizational analysis are not considered a "problem" or an open discussion.

Communication skills are usually another category of skills regarded as important for workforce competency. The results show another interesting pattern. While professionals and technicians view problem solving as the most important for their routines, they see communication skills as significantly less important than managerial staff and salespersons do. For both managerial staff and salespersons, getting ideas across to others, whether to their staff or to clients, is a large part of their job and makes up most of their activities. It is not surprising that frontline workers give the lowest rating to communication skills.

In short, the perception of job competencies appears to be associated with the nature of the job of each occupation. Managerial staff tend to care more about communication skills and less about the technical details of problem solving. Professional technicians consider technical know-how and problem-solving skills to be important more than other groups do. They also consider job basics to be as important as do managerial staff. Salespersons consider communication to be the most important among the five scales and technical skills as less important. Except frontline workers, all groups regard dispositional abilities as being very important to being a good employee.

The next variable is PROFICIENCY, defined as one's level of performance in a given job position. Employees without technical rank or at the entry level (ranking 1) are used as the reference group. Generally, those in higher ranks, especially at the middle level or above, tend to have a positive perception of all five scales of skills. This may signify that these job competencies that employees acquired enabled them to perform satisfactorily or to have obtained promotions; thus, they felt more positive about these skills.

Both CHANGE and ON-THE-JOB TRAINING signify purpose-driven events in the workplace. The variable CHANGE represents the major changes that the employees experienced during the five-year period (1993–1998). The results clearly indicate that those who have experienced a major change or transformation in the workplace (for example, replacement of technology, production of new products, or promotion) would consistently consider all five scales to be significantly important for accomplishing job tasks, with the exception of one case.[12] The exception is employees in the CR, who did not perceive problem-solving skills as important as compared with those who did not experience any change. It is even more interesting to see that those who received on-the-job training provided by their firm during the five-year period considered all five scales of job competencies to be significantly more important than employees who did not receive any training. The pattern is consistent for all three regions. This may signify that workplace training transforms both employees' competencies and attitudes toward them (Bowman, 1995). In short, the findings show that employees' work experiences have an impact on their perception of job competencies. Those who are at the higher end of the workplace hierarchy, in the middle of a transition, and with more opportunities to be integrated into the firm tend to have a positive perception of the five job competencies.

Firm Differences in the Ranking of Job Competencies. Table 8 captures the impact of firm characteristics on five latent competencies perceived by the employees. We first examine firm ownership. Compared to employees in state-owned firms (the reference group), employees in private firms in the ER consider dispositional skills to be significantly less important than their counterparts in any other type of ownership. Employees in collective firms and corporate firms in the CR consider SCALE 1 to be less important than do employees in state-owned firms. For SCALES 3, 4, and 5, employees in firms of all types of ownership have the same perception. There is no clear pattern among types of ownership for SCALES 1 and 2. It can be concluded that ownership does not have a discernible pattern of impact on the perceptions of employees.

Among seven industries, employees in the commercial and service industries in all three regions viewed communication skills as significantly more important than did employees in manufacturing industry. For SCALE 1, among seven types of industries in all three regions, only four groups out of eighteen show different perceptions from those in the manufacturing sector. For SCALE 2, employees in all industries in three regions have the same perceptions about technical skills. For SCALES 3 and 4, there are a couple of cases in which employees perceived these skills differently from those in the manufacturing industry. Employees in the commercial and service sector view communications as significantly important. Otherwise, being in a firm of different ownership, sector, or size does not lead to differences in perceptions of job competence.[13]

Conclusion

This study revealed an array of competencies perceived by employees as being important for accomplishing routine tasks in the Chinese workplace. This sample included the entire group of employees on one main production line or work group of the sampled firms, from managerial staff, technicians/professionals, and salespersons to frontline workers. Therefore, their perceptions of competencies for carrying out their jobs reflect skills required

Table 8. Firm Variables: Fixed Effects

	SCALE 1			SCALE 2			SCALE 3			SCALE 4			SCALE 5		
	East	Central	West	East	Central	West	East	Central	West	East	Central	West	East	Central	West
OWNERSHIP															
State-owned (reference)															
Collective	-E	-C	W	-E	-C*	-W	-E	-C	W	-E	-C	W	-E	-C	W
Private	-E*	-C	W*	-E	-C	W	-E	-C	W	-E	-C	W	-E	-C	W
Corporate	-E	-C*	W	-E	-C*	-W	-E	-C*	W	-E	-C	W	-E#	-C	W
Foreign	E	-C	W	E	-C	W	E	C	W	E	-C	W	E	-C	-W
INDUSTRY															
Manufacturing (reference)															
Mining/geometers	-E	-C	W	-E	C	W	-E	-C	W*	E	-C	W*	-E	-C*	W**
Transport/ telecommunications	-E*	C*	-W	-E	C	-W	E#	C	-W	-E	C*	W	-E	C*	W
Commercial/service	E	C	-W	E	C	-W	E*	-C	-W	E*	-C*	W	E**	C**	W*
Light industries	E**	-C	-W	E	-C	-W	E*	-C	-W	E**	-C	-W	E**	-C	-W
Agricultural product	E	C	W	-E	-C	W	-E	C	W	E	-C	W	—	-C	W#
Electronics	-E	C#	W	E	-C	W	-E	C	W	-E	C	W	E#	C*	W

#p < 0.1. *p < 0.05. **p < 0.01. ***p < 0.001.

for all types of positions in the same workplace, and this sampling makes the framework comparable across occupations. The results show that employees across China's three regions largely have a consensus on the five groups of competencies identified from their workplace. However, perceptions of job competencies vary across types of occupations. That is, types of job or contents of their work and their workplace experience define much of the perceptions of skills that are necessary to accomplish work. The level of economic development at different stages does not particularly differentiate skills required of the workplace. Neither the type of industry and ownership nor the size of the firm has much impact on employees' perceptions of the five competencies.

The empirically based results of competencies that employees view as essential to accomplish job tasks are different from the government's policy advocates. It is obvious that this array of competencies shares some similarities to Stasz's framework of generic skills of carrying out technical/professional jobs (Stasz, 1996) but more differences from job skill studies in the United Kingdom (Burchell et al., 1994; Horrell et al., 1994). This framework of competencies shares some similarities with Stasz's framework of skills in that both are concerned about skills needed to carry out routine tasks. Both frameworks cover the competencies of dispositions, problem solving, and communication. However, Stasz's framework does not use specific technical skills as a single category of skills. Instead, she looks at how the other four groups of skills help job holders accomplish their technical-oriented tasks. She does not have job basics or workplace literacy as a category either, which this framework of Chinese employees contains. Differences in the purpose of study or interest of the researchers may cause a different focus and different findings. Therefore, comparison is not easy.

In looking more closely at these three studies, one finds differences in measures of job competencies. For instance, the dispositions in the Chinese workplace are more or less like a philosophy or ethics of being a person in the society, while dispositions in the U.S. workplace comprise a group of personal qualities. As Bjerke (1999) has noted, everyone in China is at least half philosopher, and Confucius's teachings on personal ethics have been established as a set of rules for daily life. Stasz did not carry a survey out of her field findings of competencies. It is unfortunate that it is not known how generalizable her work framework would be. Joint efforts are needed for international comparative studies in HRD. The results of this study show fewer similarities to the other two frameworks of skills used to survey employees in the United Kingdom (Burchell et al., 1994; Horrell et al., 1994). These studies are concerned with level of skills and labor division, which might have resulted in different classifications of job contents.

Nevertheless, this study shares some similar findings about perceptions of skills with regard to job hierarchy. Employees at the lower end of the job hierarchy hold the least skill-demanding jobs or tend to regard skills as less important than do other job holders (lower skill in Burchell's and my study and part-time workers in Horrell's study). Similarly, people at the upper end of the job ladder tend to view several groups of skills as significantly important. It could be the way that they are successful in their careers because they have been able to master multiple skills and apply them to work. This study also shows that on-the-job training has a positive and significant impact on perceptions of job skills. This finding supports the theoretical argument that workplace training prepares employees for work with relevant skills and becomes an institution of skill formation (Bowman, 1995; Ziderman & Horn, 1995; Brown et al., 2001; Stasz, 2001) and explains why there is increasing demand for on-the-job training of various types (Xiao & Tsang, 1999; Xiao, 2002, 2004).

The findings of this study provide a case that the workplace is a complex social setting. Although some of the job competencies are generalizable, others are subject to job-specific content or cultural definition. Remember that managerial staff and salespersons consider communication as very important and technicians and professionals regard problem solving as important. Nevertheless, different studies of management competencies have focused on different dimensions: with Black et al. (1999) on personal characteristics, Hamlin (2004) on leadership behavior, and Brockbank and Ulrich (2003) on business strategies and knowledge, for example. Therefore, it is difficult to make comparisons and come up with a comprehensive model. Consider Hamlin's studies (2004, 2005). They compare what managers do and their behavior, but there is little information about the nature of their tasks. As indicated in the literature review here, both leaders (Osman-Gani, 2001) and employees (Ahmad, 2001) from different cultures would do things or expect others to do things in different way. Or the same tasks can be accomplished with different behavior or different approaches for effectiveness. Conceptions of management vary across cultures (see Ahmad, 2001; Bjerke, 1999). It would be helpful if future studies defined job-specific competencies by looking more closely at the nature of job tasks and defining the context first. For instance, getting ideas across to employees is a core part of management, but communication is carried out in very different ways for leaders and managers in different cultures or different people for different purposes. This study shows that communication with superiors is quite a different matter from communication with customers and subordinates. Studies by Bjerke (1999) and Ahlstrom and associates (2005) also indicate that management is not carried out in an explicit or analytical manner in the Chinese culture. This study, consisting of interviews and observations, did not find such terms as

HUMAN RESOURCE DEVELOPMENT QUARTERLY • DOI: 10.1002/hrdq

organizational analysis, open diagnosis or *discussion,* or *collective participation* mentioned.

The workplace is so complex that I conclude that employees' perceptions of job competencies are partially associated with the nature of job tasks and partially associated with cultural norms. With the nature of job tasks as reference, the variation of culture might become discernible. Problem-solving competency signifies such a case. The way of viewing problem solving is very different in China as compared to that in the United States (compare Tables 1 and 6). Chinese workers see problem solving as looking for technical information and knowledge, while Americans look at four procedures or actions. In the United States, carrying out a job task requires a combination of several sets of skills, with different sets of skills important at different career stages (Stasz, 1996; Blanthorne et al., 2005).

Finally, it is worth noting that among the five constructs of job competencies, the dispositional skills and specific skills are extracted at the top. In the Chinese tradition, it is a common teaching that one should be a good person first and then one be able to do a job. This empirical study has revealed that dispositional abilities carry cultural connotations of becoming a responsible social being. Becoming a good person involves "not only one aspect or capacity but multiple aspects"[14] that make a whole person decent. Thus, becoming a capable man requires a set of technical capacities to support oneself and one's family economically. It is the basic requirement for earning one's own livelihood and not becoming a burden to society and, further, to raise one's family and serve the country. These two constructs contain the fundamentals of the Chinese ideology of becoming a decent person.

This research is a starting point for studying job competencies in China's workplaces. The findings show that employees have their own way of looking at job skills. Imposing foreign models or experts' opinions on training and education programs may disrupt the progress of reforms underway. To ensure that the focus of HRD in China is on the most important competencies, it is necessary to conduct systematic research and inform HRD practice with sound and empirically supported information. As this study shows that skills vary mainly across jobs, future studies may stress the nature of different types of occupations and their job content in identifying the skills that help to accomplish job tasks. As more and more multinational companies move into China, a comparative study of jobs across different companies would help to identify the nature of the job content, skills required, and the cultural variations in practice. By joining the international discourse, both research and practice in HRD in China will gradually make steady progress, and the merits of Chinese culture can be shared.

Appendix: Estimation of Fixed Effects, Western Region

Individual Characteristics	SCALE 1	SCALE 2	SCALE 3	SCALE 4	SCALE 5
Intercept	356.04 (9.05)***	419.59 (7.95)***	370.50 (10.10)***	358.73 (10.30)***	293.14 (14.07)***
SEX	−3.26 (2.12)	−4.98 (1.88)**	−7.07 (2.71)**	9.67 (2.63)***	6.28 (3.15)*
AGE					
AGE 1-1	6.07 (3.36)#	−3.88 (2.98)	−3.48 (4.28)	11.20 (4.17)**	−7.15 (5.03)
AGE 1-2	−2.27 (2.78)	−1.64 (2.45)	−9.62 (3.56)***	4.20 (3.46)	−9.30 (4.14)*
AGE 1-3	RF	RF	RF	RF	RF
AGE 1-4	3.86 (3.74)	1.47 (3.32)	2.23 (4.79)	−1.45 (4.65)	7.09 (5.55)
EDUCATION					
Primary	−4.55 (5.72)	−8.92 (5.04)#	−12.32 (7.31)#	−8.10 (7.08)	5.25 (8.55)
Lower middle	−3.35 (3.04)	−2.17 (2.70)	−4.77 (3.87)	−5.74 (3.76)	−6.98 (4.51)
Upper middle	−0.05 (2.95)	2.61 (2.62)	4.76 (3.77)	−4.79 (3.65)	2.94 (4.38)
Vocational	RF	RF	RF	RF	RF
Junior college	1.04 (4.40)	−0.38 (3.93)	−0.70 (5.62)	2.91 (5.44)	14.46 (6.49)*
University	−0.64 (5.23)	4.63 (4.69)	−5.66 (6.67)	0.98 (6.47)	20.39 (7.69)**
OCCUPATION					
Managerial	3.46 (3.53)	0.40 (3.15)	1.80 (4.49)	−18.00 (4.36)***	27.92 (5.21)***
Technical and professional	RF	RF	RF	RF	RF
Sales	3.80 (4.50)	−7.58 (4.49)#	−9.07 (6.39)	−20.60 (6.26)**	18.79 (7.42)**
Frontline workers	−8.30 (3.33)*	−5.91 (2.97)*	−16.33 (4.24)***	−14.32 (4.11)**	−29.59 (4.93)***
RANKING					
Ranking 1	RF	RF	RF	RF	RF
Ranking 2	−3.79 (2.57)	0.88 (2.29)	−3.43 (3.29)	−3.29 (3.19)	−12.16 (3.83)**
Ranking 3	4.61 (2.83)	7.17 (2.51)**	−2.75 (3.62)	7.68 (3.50)*	−2.41 (4.21)
Ranking 4	12.03 (4.77)*	10.76 (4.25)*	2.57 (6.08)	21.07 (5.90)**	9.99 (7.09)
WORKPLACE CHANGES	4.14 (2.26)#	7.01 (2.02)***	6.70 (2.87)*	4.87 (2.79)#	6.57 (3.36)**
On-the-job training	2.11 (0.62)***	1.25 (0.56)*	3.67 (0.79)***	2.57 (0.77)**	3.02 (0.93)**

#$p < 0.1$. *$p < 0.05$. **$p < 0.01$. ***$p < 0.001$. The numbers in parentheses are standard errors. RF = reference group.

Notes

1. The Chinese government's policy paper on the issue lists in the following order the abilities that a school should nurture: the ability to work independently, solve problems, create, work in a team, and self-discipline (Li, 2001; China Central Committee and State Council, 1999). There is little discussion of what these skills consist of. In comparison, the U.S. Labor Department (Secretary's Commission on Achieving Necessary Skill, 1992) provides a comprehensive framework of competencies or abilities to make use of various resources, develop interpersonal skills and work with others, acquire information, understand different systems, and use technology. We select the U.S. framework here for comparison because China has taken the United States as a model for modernization.
2. Other scholars have also tried to identify different types of skills that would improve value-added performance, including the multidimensional skills of decision making, cooperation, and obtaining information. See Rosenberg (1976).
3. Interviews and observations were carried out in several localities in China for cross-checking. Analysis was conducted and published. The interviews and observations describe how work in the workplace is carried out in transition and skills that develop in the workplace (Xiao, 1999, 2003). One article on the preliminary analysis of types of competencies also compares qualities required in the workplace to qualities that teachers develop in their students (Xiao, 2006).
4. Some scholars (Hake, 1999; Winterton & Winterton, 1997) have argued that the removal of traditional elements and the application of new knowledge mean that employees need to acquire new skills to develop their competence.
5. In the survey, employees were asked if they had experienced four kinds of changes: the introduction of new products or services, new equipment, new production technology, and new job positions.
6. For details of methods, see Raudenbush and Bryk (2002) and Raudenbush, Rowan, and Kang (1991). Information about running the model is available from the author.
7. In transforming item scores into standardized scores, 100 is used to amplify the score so that the results are easy to read. See Raudenbush et al. (1991).
8. See Chapter One in *Da Xu,* the Great Learning (http://www.chinapage.com/confucius/confucius.html).
9. The appendix presents an example of estimation for the five scales with level 2 results for the WR only. Statistics with both level 2 and 3 variables for all three regions are available on request.
10. Excerpt from field notes.
11. Excerpt from field notes.
12. The comparison shows that among the three regions, only those in the WR for SCALES 1 and 4 and those in the CR for SCALES 2 and 5 show the impact at a marginal level, $p < 0.1$.
13. The size of a business had no impact at all on employees' perceptions of the five types of job competencies. Therefore, this factor was dropped from the analysis.
14. From field notes.

References

Agust, S., & Grau, R. (2002). Managerial competency needs and training requests: The case of the Spanish tourist industry. *Human Resource Development Quarterly, 13* (1), 31–51.

Ahlstrom, D., Foley, S., Young, M. N., & Chan, E. S. (2005). Human resource strategies in post WTO China. *Thunderbird International Business Review, 47* (4), 263–285.

Ahmad, K. (2001). Corporate leadership and workplace motivation in Malaysia. *International Journal of Commerce and Management, 11* (1), 82–102.

Ashton, D., & Green, F. (1999). *Education, training and global economy.* Cheltenham: Edward Elgar.

Barrie, J., & Pace, W. (1998). Learning of organizational effectiveness: Philosophy of education and human resources development. *Human Resource Development Quarterly, 9* (1), 39–54.

Becker, G. S. (1964). *Human capital.* New York: Columbia University Press.

Belanger, P., & Tuijnman, A. (Eds.). (1997). *New patterns of adult learning: A six-country comparative study.* New York: Pergamon.

Benson, J., & Zhu, Y. (2002). The emerging external labor market and the impact on enterprise's human resource development in China. *Human Resource Development Quarterly, 13* (4), 449–466.

Bjerke, B. (1999). *Business leadership and culture.* Cheltenham, UK: Edward Elgar.

Black, S., Morrison, A., & Gregersen, H. (1999). *Global explorers: The next generation of leaders.* New York: Routledge.

Blanthorne, C., Bhamornsiri, S., & Guinn, R. E. (2005). Are technical skills still important? *CPA Journal, 75* (3), 64–65.

Bowman, M. J. (1995). Training on the job. In A. C. Tuijnman (Ed.), *International encyclopaedia of adult education and training* (2nd ed., pp. 48–53). New York: Pergamon.

Brockbank, W., & Ulrich, D. (2003, May). *The new HR agenda: 2002 Human Resource Competency Study (FRCS): Executive summary.* Ann Arbor: University of Michigan Business School. Retrieved June 11, 2006, from http://webuser.bus.umich.edu/Programs/hrcs/HRCS2002Executive Summary.pdf.

Brown, P., Green, A., & Lauder, H. (2001). *High skills: Globalization, competitiveness, and skill formation.* New York: Oxford University Press.

Brown, P., Halsey, A. H., Lauder, H., & Wells, A. S. (1997). *Education: Culture, economy, society.* New York: Oxford University Press.

Burchell, B., Elliott, J. Rubery, J., & Wilkinson, F. (1994). Management and employee perceptions of skills. In G. Penn, M. Rose, & J. Rubery (Eds.), *Skill and occupational change* (pp. 159–188). New York: Oxford University Press.

Cookson, P. S. (1986). A framework for theory and research on adult education participation. *Adult Education Quarterly, 46,* 130–141.

China Central Committee and the State Council. (1999). *Decision on a full scale education reform and pushing for a nationwide movement for education quality* (Zhonggong zhongyang guowuyuan guanyu shenhua jiaoyu gaige, quanmian tujin suzhi jiaoyu de jueding). Beijing: Ministry of Education. www.moe.edu.cn.edoas/website18/info3314.htm.

China Economics Research Centre. (2003, April 21). *Report on China's urban labor market and employment* (Zhongguo chengshi laodongli shichang he jiuye xianzhuang diaocha baogao). Beijing: Peking University. http://www.usc.cuhk.edu.hk/wkgb.asp.

China Ministry of Education. (2001). *Guideline to reform of basic education curriculum* (Jichu jiaoyu kecheng gaige gangyao). Beijing: Ministry of Education.

China Ministry of Education. (2002). Guide and outline for building up troops of capable professionals across China for the period of 2000–2005 (2000–2005 nian quanguo rencai duiwu jianshe guihua gangyao). *Policy Bulletin of Ministry of Education (Jiaoyubu zhengbao), 7/8,* 293–300.

Doray, P., & Arrowsmith, S. (1997). Patterns of participation in adult education: Cross-national comparison. In P. Belanger & A. Tuijnman (Eds.), *New patterns of adult learning: A six-country comparative study* (pp. 39–75). New York: Pergamon.

Garrick, J., & McDonald, R. (1992). Competence standards for industry trainers: Alternative models. *Journal of European Industrial Training, 16* (7), 16–20.

Hake, B. J. (1999). Lifelong learning in late modernity: The challenges to society, organisations, and individuals. *Adult Education Quarterly, 49* (2), 79–90.

Hamlin, R. G. (2004). In support of universalistic models of managerial and leadership effectiveness: Implications for HRD research and practice. *Human Resource Development Quarterly, 15* (2), 189–215.

Hamlin, R. G. (2005). Toward universalistic models of managerial leader effectiveness: A comparative study of recent British and American derived models of leadership. *Human Resource Development International, 8* (1), 5–25.

Horrell, S., Rubery, J., & Burchell, B. (1994). Gender and skill. In G. Penn, M. Rose, & J. Rubery (Eds.), *Skill and occupational change* (pp. 189–222). New York: Oxford University Press.

Hu, A. G. (2001). *Knowledge and development: A new catch-up strategy in the 21st century* (21 zhishi yu fazhan: shiji xi zhuigan zhanlue). Beijing: Peking University Press.

Hu, A. G., Wang, S. G., & Kang, X. G. (1995). *Report on regional disparities in China* (Zhongguo diqu chayi baogao). Shenyang: Liaoning People's Press.

Johnston, M. F. (1999). Beyond regional analysis: Manufacturing zones, urban employment and spatial inequality in China. *China Quarterly, 157,* 1–21.

Li, H. (2003). Economic transition and returns to education in China. *Economics of Education Review, 22* (3), 317–328.

Li, L. Q. (2001). *Strive for basic education reform, speed up the improvement of education for quality in order to provide capable professionals and intelligence for the socialist construction: Speech at National Basic Education Work Meeting* (Shenhua jichu jiaoyu gaoge, jiakuai suzhi jiaoyu bufa, wei xiandaihua jianshe tigong rencai chubei he zhili zhichi). Beijing: Ministry of Education.

Liu, Z. Y., & Xiao, J. (2006). Human capital accumulation over time and their impact on salary growth in China. *Education Economics, 14* (2), 155–180.

Middleton, J., Ziderman, A., & Adams, A. V. (1993). *Skills for productivity: Vocational education and training in developing countries.* New York: Oxford University Press.

Mincer, J. (1974). *Schooling, experience, and earnings.* New York: Columbia University Press.

Morrison, A. (2000). Developing a global leadership model. *Human Resource Management, 39* (2), 117–131.

Norback, J. S., & Forehand, G. A. (1995). *Job literacy: A framework for categorizing skill and assessing complexity.* Princeton, NJ: Center for Skills Enhancement. (ERIC Document Reproduction Service No. ED 389885)

Organization for Economic Cooperation and Development. (1992). *Technology and the economy: The key relationships.* Paris: Author.

Osman-Gani, A. M. (2000). Developing expatriates for the Asian-Pacific region: A comparative analysis of multinational enterprise managers from five countries across three continents. *Human Resource Development Quarterly, 11* (3), 213–235.

Raudenbush, S. W., & Bryk, A. S. (2002). *Hierarchical linear models: Applications and data analysis methods* (2nd ed.). Thousand Oaks, CA: Sage.

Raudenbush, S. W., Rowan, B., & Kang, S. J. (1991). A multilevel, multivariate model for studying school climate with estimation via the EM algorithm and application to U.S. high-school data. *Journal of Educational Statistics, 16* (4), 295–330.

Rosenberg, N. (1976). *Perspectives on technology.* Cambridge: Cambridge University Press.

Secretary's Commission on Achieving Necessary Skill. (1992). *Learning a living: A blueprint for high performance: A SCANS report for America 2000,* Washington, DC: U.S. Department of Labor.

Smith, E. A. (2005). Communities of competence: New resources in the workplace. *Journal of Workplace Learning, 17* (1/2), 7–23.

Stasz, C. (1996, April). *Workplace skills in practice: Case studies of technical work.* Berkeley, CA: National Center for Research in Vocational Education. (ERIC Document Reproduction Service No. ED 398413)

Stasz, C. (2001). Assessing skills for work: Two perspectives. *Oxford Economics Papers, 3,* 385–405.

Thomas, D. C., & Inkson, K. (2005). People skills for a global workplace. *Consulting to Management, 16,* 5–10.

Winterton, J., & Winterton, R. (1997). Workplace training and enskilling. In S. Walters (Ed.), *Globalisation, adult education and training: Impacts and issues* (pp. 154–164). Hamburg, Germany: UNESCO Institute of Education.

Wu, D. G. (2004). *Reports on disparities in education in China.* Hong Kong: Universities Service Centre, Chinese University of Hong Kong [in Chinese].

Xiao, J. (1999). Alternative learning approaches in an emerging economy: An experience of Shenzhen, China. *Educational Practice and Theory, 21* (1), 27–49.

Xiao, J. (2002). Human capital development in a transforming economy: The experience of Shanghai, China. *Current Politics and Economics of China, 3* (2), 345–391.

Xiao, J. (2003). Redefining adult education in an emerging economy: Complements to development. *International Review of Education, 49* (5), 487–508.

Xiao, J. (2004). *Human capital development in the economic transition: Firms' strategy.* Beijing: Beijing Normal University Press.

Xiao, J. (2006). Classroom teaching and non-farm jobs in Yunnan, China. In G. Postilione (Ed.), *Education, stratification and social change in China.* Armonk, NY: M. E. Sharpe.

Xiao, J., & Tsang, M. C. (1999). Human capital development in an emerging economy: The experience of Shenzhen, China. *China Quarterly, 157,* 72–114.

Xiao, J., & Tsang, M. C. (2004). Determinants of participation and non-participation in job-related education and training in Shenzhen, China. *Human Resource Development Quarterly, 15* (4), 389–420.

Ziderman, A., & Horn, R. (1995). Many paths to skilled employment: A reverse tracer study of seven occupations in Colombia. *Education Economics, 3* (1), 61–79.

Jin Xiao is on the Faculty of Education, Chinese University of Hong Kong, Hong Kong, China.

Comparing the Effects of Determinants of Turnover Intentions Between Taiwanese and U.S. Hospital Employees

Cherng G. Ding, Chieh-Peng Lin

This research assesses how the direct effects of career satisfaction and job satisfaction on turnover intentions and the indirect effects through organizational commitment differ between Taiwanese and U.S. hospital employees. Using data collected from 179 Taiwanese and 144 U.S. hospital employees, the test results find the following differences: the direct effect of job satisfaction on turnover intentions is negative and significant for Taiwanese hospital employees but not for U.S. hospital employees; the indirect effect of job satisfaction on turnover intentions through organizational commitment is stronger for Taiwanese hospital employees than for U.S. hospital employees; and the negative direct effect of career satisfaction on turnover intentions and the indirect effect through organizational commitment are stronger for U.S. hospital employees than for Taiwanese hospital employees. Finally, the managerial implications for human resource development are discussed.

The issues regarding turnover intentions, career satisfaction, and job satisfaction have attracted much more attention in the Western world than in other societies and regions. Since non-Western values and culture are sharply different from those in the West, more research is needed to elucidate the relationships among these constructs in non-Western nations. Cross-cultural (Western versus non-Western) research results regarding turnover intentions may provide quite different implications for human resource development

Note: This work was supported by the National Science Council, Republic of China, under grant NSC 92–2416-H009–023.

(HRD) management given that employees are likely to have strong turnover intentions when they are dissatisfied with their personal development in their job or career. Designing suitable HRD programs that satisfy employees' growth needs toward their job or career should improve their perception of the organization and consequently strengthen their willingness to stay.

Turnover intentions can be defined as a psychological response to specific organizational conditions and fall along a continuum of organizational withdrawal behaviors ranging from daydreaming to quitting (Kraut, 1975). The focus of this research is on the formation of turnover intentions and dealing with how these intentions are influenced by their antecedents. Some previous research studies on predicting turnover intentions using individual difference variables have focused on such demographic characteristics as gender, age, organizational tenure, educational level, and family size (Chen & Francesco, 2000). The results generally display a consistent negative relationship between age and turnover intentions and also between tenure and turnover intentions (Martin, 1979; Parasuraman & Futrell, 1983).

Career satisfaction, job satisfaction, and organizational commitment are regarded as influencing turnover intentions. Turnover intentions are negatively related to job satisfaction and career satisfaction (Abraham, 1999; Cotton & Tuttle, 1986; Igbaria & Greenhaus, 1992; Igbaria & Siegel, 1992a; Michaels & Spector, 1982). Specifically, comparisons of stayers and leavers in various occupations reveal higher job satisfaction for stayers. Increasing worker satisfaction can significantly reduce turnover intentions (Abraham, 1999). At the same time, employees who are satisfied with their careers perceive greater benefits in remaining with their organizations than employees whose careers have been less gratifying (Igbaria & Greenhaus, 1992).

Satisfaction and organizational commitment are distinct attitudes, with satisfaction being an affective response to specific aspects of a job or career, and commitment is an affective response to the organization as a whole (Locke, 1976; Porter, Steers, Mowday, & Boulian, 1974; Williams & Hazar, 1986), but both have been suggested to be positively related (Igbaria & Greenhaus, 1992; Mannheim, Baruch, & Tal, 1997). A higher level of job or career satisfaction enhances organizational commitment. Moreover, organizational commitment negatively influences turnover intentions (Davy, Kinicki, & Scheck, 1991; Michaels & Spector, 1982; Williams & Hazer, 1986). Employees who are highly committed to their organization are less likely to leave than employees who are relatively uncommitted. Williams and Hazer (1986) reviewed several turnover models and concluded with an empirical analysis that both job satisfaction and organizational commitment are important antecedents of turnover intentions, and organizational commitment plays a mediating role between job satisfaction and turnover intentions (Lin & Ma, 2004; Lin & Chen, 2004).

Plenty of research concerning turnover intentions has been conducted on U.S. organizations and samples, including employees in military organizations (Bluedorn, 1979), employees in mental health centers (Michaels & Spector,

1982), accountants (Arnold & Feldman, 1982), and high-tech personnel (Igbaria & Siegel, 1992b). Chinese society, including the three major "mini dragons"—Taiwan, Hong Kong, and Singapore—constitutes the largest foreign direct investment absorption territory in the world (Luo, 1997). Therefore, from management's viewpoint, it is of interest to see if and how the formation of turnover intentions is different from that in the United States. Although some preliminary work has been done (Yousef, 1998), the role of culture as a moderator has been rarely explored from a HRD perspective by offering strategies for management. Since employees in hospitals are mostly doctors and nurses, with high training costs, understanding how their turnover intentions are influenced by their antecedents is important for hospital supervisors.

Different cultures may possess different causal relationships, and therefore different management approaches may be required. Since Taiwan and the United States represent two important but different cultures, they are used as the target nations in this study. The purpose of the research is to examine the role of national cultures (Taiwan versus the United States) as a moderator on the formation of turnover intentions in hospitals. Is the influence of satisfaction (or organizational commitment) on turnover intentions stronger or weaker for hospital employees in Taiwan than for those in the United States? Is the influence of satisfaction on organizational commitment stronger or weaker for hospital employees in Taiwan? How does the formation process differ between Taiwan and the United States? Based on cross-cultural empirical results, managerial implications will be discussed.

Research Model and Development of Hypotheses

This study's research model is shown as Figure 1. In the model, turnover intentions are influenced directly by organizational commitment, job satisfaction, and career satisfaction, while job satisfaction and career satisfaction are also influenced by turnover intentions indirectly through the mediation of organizational commitment. Each of the relationships is moderated by national culture (Taiwan versus the U.S.), as marked by H1 through H5. National values and cultures significantly influence business development and performance of subsidiaries (Hofstede, Neuijen, Ohayv, & Sanders, 1990). Furthermore, cultural differences (values) may lead workers to support organizational goals without question (Near, 1989), and they may also cause management to accept a mission that emphasizes people (Pascale & Athos, 1981).

For thousands of years, Chinese values and cultures have affected the values of collectivism and homogeneity in the conduct of social life and business (Barnum, Philip, Reynolds, Shauf, & Thompson, 2001; Nahavandi & Aranda, 1994; Pornpitakpan, 2000). For instance, Confucius in the sixth century B.C. provided a code on the ties between an individual to his or her family and society based on each person's respective roles and positions in the environment. A consequence of such a collectivistic culture is *guanxi,* or interpersonal connections (Barnum et al., 2001; Hwang, 1987; Morris, Leung, Ames, & Lickel, 1999;

Figure 1. Research Model

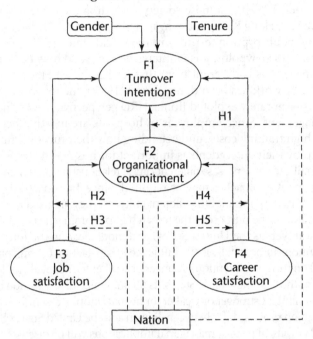

Tsui & Farh, 1997), which is considered one of the critical interpersonal relationship values in Chinese society (Kao, 1993; Osland, 1989) and, until recently, a vital ingredient for the success of East Asian economies (Montagu-Pollock, 1991).

Guanxi (a form of collectivist culture) is used here to explain the differences toward job issues across the two nations, because home country cultures are believed to affect employees' job perceptions and organizational structures (Wong & Birnbaum-More, 1994). It has been found that different cultures (individualist versus collectivist) may moderate the links between job satisfaction and other factors such as social support and sales performance (Lin, Chang, & Chu, 2003). Following previous research (Lin et al., 2003), this study examines job issues by considering national culture as a critical moderator from the perspective of guanxi, which may well reflect the differences among nations (Buttery & Leung, 1998; Chen & Francesco, 2000; Pornpitakpan, 2000; Tsang, 1998).

In Chinese society, organizational behavior revolves around guanxi. Because of the influence of traditional Chinese collectivist beliefs that emphasize guanxi, employees' organizational commitment in Taiwanese organizations is expected to be highly connected with loyalty to the organization, resulting in lower turnover intentions. Research done on guanxi in Chinese society has confirmed the importance of it in the employment setting (Buttery & Leung, 1998; Chen & Francesco, 2000; Tsang, 1998; Xin & Pearce, 1996); in the

Western world, such a variable as *guanxi* has been ignored thus far, suggesting that this difference helps explain the divergence across Western and non-Western cultures (Chen & Francesco, 2000; Hofstede, 1980; Pornpitakpan, 2000; Tsang, 1998; Xin & Pearce, 1996).

Chinese *guanxi* is considered the important social interactions within the network organization (Su & Littlefield, 2001). That is, the attitudes and perceptions of an individual employee about his or her job are likely influenced by his or her *guanxi* in the organization. In addition, *guanxi* represents pre-existing relationships of superior and subordinate in the same workplace, involving a hierarchically structured network of relationships embedded with mutual obligations through a self-conscious manipulation of face, *renqing* (favor), and related symbols (Wong & Tam, 2000; Yang, 1988). Thus, studies about Chinese business organizations have found that people who have good *guanxi* with or who are loyal to the top boss have a better chance of promotion in the organization (Cheng, 1995a, 1995b). Indeed, Chinese businessmen often defend their own social network by bonding the members inside *quanxi* (Wong & Tam, 2000). In other words, good *guanxi* in Chinese society implies that employees should be loyal to the boss, who is regarded as the representative and symbol of the organization (Chen & Francesco, 2000), resulting in stronger intentions to stay with the organization. However, this phenomenon may not be so salient in a society like the United States, indicating that relationships between turnover intentions and their antecedents may be moderated by culture.

Collectivist values among Chinese employees also suggest particular views, including a preference for more personal ties to supervisors (Chen & Francesco, 2000), an acceptance of more paternalistic treatment, and a propensity for a more affective relationship to an organization. These factors may result in greater employee commitment to the firm and fewer intentions to leave than in other cultures, suggesting that the relationships between the organization and its antecedents may be moderated by culture. Furthermore, *guanxi* is highly related to job satisfaction, especially in Chinese society, since better *guanxi* yields significantly higher reciprocal exchanges of favors than in Western countries, bringing with them pleasure in the job and satisfaction with it. In contrast to the Chinese culture, American culture is thought to be more individualist and heterogeneous, and it focuses on different values (Hofstede, 1980; Nahavandi & Aranda, 1994; Near, 1989; Pornpitakpan, 2000). The relationship between U.S. employees' work attitudes and organizational commitment is likely to be less obvious (Near, 1989). Career satisfaction reflects more of an individualist color; it is highly related to the degree to which the individual's own success criteria are believed to have been met (Gattiker & Larwood, 1988).

In summary, this study considers national culture as the critical moderator reflecting significant differences across two nations, because it is consistent with many earlier works and seems more likely than other variables highlighted in international research to be related to the two types of societies—Chinese and the United States. The simple discussions given above may underlie the following research hypotheses:

HYPOTHESIS 1 (H1): *The influence of organizational commitment on turnover intentions for hospital employees is moderated by culture (Taiwan versus the United States).*

HYPOTHESIS 2 (H2): *The influence of job satisfaction on turnover intentions for hospital employees is moderated by culture (Taiwan versus the United States).*

HYPOTHESIS 3 (H3): *The influence of job satisfaction on organizational commitment for hospital employees is moderated by culture (Taiwan versus the United States).*

HYPOTHESIS 4 (H4): *The influence of career satisfaction on turnover intentions for hospital employees is moderated by culture (Taiwan versus the United States).*

HYPOTHESIS 5 (H5): *The influence of career satisfaction on organizational commitment for hospital employees is moderated by culture (Taiwan versus the United States).*

Method

Participants. This study obtained cross-sectional data from employees of a large hospital in Taiwan and one in the United States. Both hospitals are located in large cities. Using a sample within a single organization can reduce the influence of subcultures in other organizations on the hypothesized relationships to be tested (Herndon, Fraedrich, & Yeh, 2001). The employees in the hospitals include both doctors and nurses, given that they are the majority in a hospital and play a critical role on human resource development (HRD) in a medical system (Table 1). The hospital selected from Taiwan, a large, private hospital in

Table 1. Characteristics of the Employees in the Sample

Characteristic	Taiwan (n = 179)	United States (n = 144)
Gender		
Male	48 (27%)	54 (38%)
Female	131 (73%)	90 (62%)
Age		
Under twenty	38 (21%)	27 (19%)
Twenty to thirty	64 (36%)	63 (44%)
Thirty-one to forty	39 (22%)	31 (22%)
Forty-one to fifty	23 (13%)	13 (9%)
Over fifty	15 (8%)	10 (6%)
Tenure		
Five years or less	53 (30%)	51 (35%)
Six to ten years	76 (42%)	65 (45%)
Eleven years or over	50 (28%)	28 (20%)
Position		
Doctor	45 (25%)	33 (23%)
Nurse	134 (75%)	111 (77%)

Taipei City, contains approximately twenty-five hundred employees and more than a thousand beds. The hospital selected from the United States, also a large, private one, is in Nashville, Tennessee; it contains approximately twenty-eight hundred employees and more than six hundred beds. The hospitals selected were willing to cooperate with this research. Each represents a typical hospital in its region. With help from an employee in the sample hospital in the United States and from several employees in the sample hospital in Taiwan for data collection, 200 questionnaires were distributed to each of the hospitals; there were 179 usable returned questionnaires in Taiwan and 144 in the United States.

Measures. Three steps were employed to determine items for measuring the constructs. First, the items were taken from the literature and appropriately adapted. Second, the items were pretested through face-to-face interviews with ten hospital employees in Taiwan. They were asked to point out items they thought were confusing or irrelevant. Finally, a back-translation, recommended by Reynolds, Diamantopoulos, and Schlegelmilch (1993), was used in composing a Chinese version of the questionnaire. That is, some important tips proposed by Reynolds et al. (1993) for back-translation were taken into serious consideration to translate the Chinese-language version of the questionnaire into English. The Chinese-language version was then compared word for word to the English version. A high degree of correspondence between the two questionnaires assured us that the translation process did not introduce artificial biases in our Chinese-language questionnaire. The utilization of the back-translation procedure was a consideration for limiting translation biases. The process achieved the content validity of the questionnaire.

We used a five-point Likert-type scale with anchors of "strongly disagree" (1) and "strongly agree" (5).

Turnover Intentions. Employees responded to three items designed to assess their intentions to leave the organization. These three items were used by Landau and Hammer (1986). The example items included, "I am actively looking for a job outside the hospital," and "As soon as I can find a better job, I'll leave this hospital."

Organizational Commitment (OC). A nine-item measure developed by Porter et al. (1974) was adopted to measure affective OC. Six items were used according to the factor loadings of the test results of principal components analysis by Wayne, Shore, and Liden (1997). The example items included, "I am willing to put in a general deal of effort beyond that normally expected in order to help my hospital be successful," and "I really care about the fate of my hospital."

Career Satisfaction. Career satisfaction was measured by five items developed by Greenhaus, Parasuraman, and Wormley (1990). The example items included, "I am satisfied with the success I have achieved in my career," and "I am satisfied with the progress I have made toward meeting my overall career goal."

Job Satisfaction. Four items drawn from Churchill, Ford, and Walker (1974) were used to measure job satisfaction. The example items included, "My work is satisfying," and "My job is often dull and monotonous."

Data Analysis. Following data collection, SEM (structural equation modeling) was applied to conduct data analysis. SEM is a multivariate statistical technique used to confirm the causal relations among latent variables. This study followed a two-step procedure proposed by Anderson and Gerbing (1988): developing an effective measurement model with confirmatory factor analysis and then analyzing the structural model. Both SAS and AMOS were adopted as the tools for analyzing the data for reconfirmation.

Testing of the Measurement Model. Through repeated filtering, the indicators retained in both the Taiwan and U.S. models were identical for comparisons across groups. Every construct in the final measurement models was measured using at least two indicator variables. The overall goodness-of-fit indexes shown in Table 2 (chi square/df smaller than 2.0; CFI, GFI, NFI, and NNFI all greater than 0.9 except AGFI slightly smaller than 0.9) indicated that the fits of the models were satisfactory (Bentler & Bonett, 1980; Bentler, 1989).

Reliability. In confirmatory factor analysis, reliability reflects the internal consistency of the indicators measuring a given factor. As shown in Table 3, reliabilities for all constructs exceeded 0.70 for both the Taiwan and U.S. models, satisfying the general requirement of reliability for research instruments (Hatcher, 1994).

Convergent Validity. Convergent validity is achieved if different indicators used to measure the same construct obtain strongly correlated scores. In SEM, convergent validity is assessed by reviewing the *t*-tests for the factor loadings (Hatcher, 1994). Here, for both models, all factor loadings for indicators measuring the same construct were statistically significant, showing that all indicators effectively measured their corresponding construct (Anderson & Gerbing, 1988) and support convergent validity.

Table 2. Goodness-of-Fit Indexes for the Final Measurement Model

Nation	χ^2	df	p-value	NFI	NNFI	CFI	GFI	AGFI	RMR
Taiwan	63.20	38	0.006	.95	.97	.98	.94	.90	0.05
United States	57.36	38	0.023	.95	.97	.98	.93	.88	0.03

Table 3. Reliabilities (Cronbach's Alpha) for the Constructs

Construct	Number of Indicators	Taiwan	United States
Turnover intentions (F1)	3	0.92	0.85
Organizational commitment (F2)	3	0.78	0.91
Job satisfaction (F3)	3	0.91	0.92
Career satisfaction (F4)	2	0.89	0.74

Discriminant Validity. Discriminant validity is achieved if the correlations among different constructs, measured with their respective indicators, are relatively weak. The chi-square difference test can be used to assess the discriminant validity of two constructs by calculating the difference in the chi-square statistics for the constrained and unconstrained measurement models (Hatcher, 1994). The constrained model is identical to the unconstrained model, in which all constructs are allowed to covary, except that the correlation between the two constructs of interest is fixed at 1. Discriminant validity is demonstrated if the chi-square difference (with 1 df) is significant, meaning that the model in which the two constructs are viewed as distinct (but correlated) factors is superior. Since we needed to test the discriminant validity for every pair of five constructs, we controlled the experiment-wise error rate (the overall significance level). By using the Bonferroni method under the overall 0.01 level, the critical value of the chi-square test is $\chi^2(1, 0.01/10) = 10.83$. Since the chi-square difference statistics for every two constructs all exceeded 10.83 for both the U.S. and Taiwanese groups (see Table 4), discriminant validity was successfully achieved.

Control Variables. To avoid making improper inferences, gender was included as a control variable since previous researchers have found that work-related attitudes such as job satisfaction and work values differ between male and female employees (Cheung & Scherling, 1999). Tenure was also used as a control variable (a categorical variable) in this study, because it is somewhat negatively related to turnover intentions in the literature. Consequently, both gender and tenure were used as critical control variables using the application of dummy variables in this study to reduce experimental errors. Controlling these demographic variables prevents this cross-cultural study from being influenced or moderated by employees' personal characteristics.

Testing for the Moderating Effect. This study used Singh's analytical strategy (1995) to examine the existence of the moderating effect on the structural

Table 4. Chi-Square Difference Tests for Examining Discriminant Validity

Construct Pair	Taiwan (Unconstrained $\chi^2(38) = 63.20$)		United States (Unconstrained $\chi^2(38) = 57.36$)	
	Constrained $\chi^2(39)$	χ^2 Difference	Constrained $\chi^2(39)$	χ^2 Difference
(F1, F2)	175.91	112.71***	183.11	125.75***
(F1, F3)	390.89	327.69***	271.98	214.62***
(F1, F4)	255.89	192.69***	155.34	97.98***
(F2, F3)	147.05	83.85***	320.16	262.80***
(F2, F4)	220.18	156.98***	79.23	21.87***
(F3, F4)	260.60	197.40***	105.55	48.19***

***Significant at the 0.01 overall significance level by using the Bonferroni method.

model. First, an unconstrained model is estimated, in which path coefficients are allowed to vary across the cross-group data sets. Next, a fully constrained model is estimated by requiring that all path coefficients are constrained to be equal for cross-group data sets. The fully constrained model is thus based on the notion of cross-group variance in model relationships. Comparing the goodness-of-fit statistics for the unconstrained and fully constrained models using a chi-square difference test yielded evidence to examine our hypotheses. The chi-square statistics for the unconstrained and constrained models were 171.83 (df = 124) and 211.81 (df = 129), respectively. Their difference was 39.98, with five degrees of freedom. The significant difference (at the 1 percent level) indicated that moderating effects existed. The chi-square difference test was used again to test for the moderating effects of individual paths, as displayed in Figure 1. However, the chi-square statistics for the unconstrained and the partially constrained models are compared here. "Partially constrained" means that only the target path coefficients are set to be equal for cross-group data sets.

Results

The test results in Tables 5 and 6 indicate that the influence of organizational commitment on turnover intentions was similar for both the U.S. and Taiwanese groups (H1 was not supported). The influences of job satisfaction on turnover intentions and organizational commitment were stronger for the Taiwanese group than for the U.S. group (H2 and H3 were supported). The influences of career satisfaction on turnover intentions and organizational commitment were both stronger for the U.S. group than for Taiwanese group (H4 and H5 were supported).

Table 5. Hypothesis Results

Hypothesis	Unconstrained Model	Constrained Model	χ^2 Difference	Conclusion
H1	$\chi^2 = 171.83$ (df = 124)	$\chi^2 = 174.02$ (df = 125)	2.19 (df = 1)	Not Supported
H2	$\chi^2 = 171.83$ (df = 124)	$\chi^2 = 175.56$ (df = 125)	3.73* (df = 1)	Supported
H3	$\chi^2 = 171.83$ (df = 124)	$\chi^2 = 176.22$ (df = 125)	4.39** (df = 1)	Supported
H4	$\chi^2 = 171.83$ (df = 124)	$\chi^2 = 174.91$ (df = 125)	3.08* (df = 1)	Supported
H5	$\chi^2 = 171.83$ (df = 124)	$\chi^2 = 204.81$ (df = 125)	32.98*** (df = 1)	Supported

Gender was included here as a control variable.

*Significant at the 0.10 significance level. **Significant at the 0.05 significance level. ***Significant at the 0.01 significance level.

Table 6. Path Coefficients and *t* Value

Path	Taiwan		United States		Taiwan vs. United States
	Standardized Coefficient	t Value	Standardized Coefficient	t Value	
F2 → F1	−0.37***	−3.11	−0.31**	−2.17	|T| = |U|
F3 → F1	−0.23**	−2.27	0.03	0.35	|T| > |U|
F3 → F2	0.66***	6.51	0.14*	1.75	T > U
F4 → F1	−0.13*	−1.69	−0.39**	−2.42	|T| < |U|
F4 → F2	0.19**	2.53	0.67***	6.06	T < U

*Significant at the 0.10 significance level. **Significant at the 0.05 significance level. ***Significant at the 0.01 significance level.

The unexpected testing result for H1 is interesting and deserves more discussion in future studies. A possible explanation for the results could be that the path is not culturally specific, or other Chinese cultural characteristics such as integration (which concerns integrative stability) or Confucian work dynamism (which concerns the Confucian work ethic) (Chinese Culture Connection, 1986) could be the factors neutralizing the influence of *guanxi* in the unsupported path.

Discussion and Managerial Implications. Albeit previous literature has suggested that both career satisfaction and job satisfaction may be influenced in large part by various factors such as leadership style (Lok & Crawford, 2004), work experiences (Burke, 2001), and social support (Lin et al., 2003), this study examines career satisfaction and job satisfaction from a different perspective. The empirical results of the study indicate that two work-related attitudes—career satisfaction and job satisfaction—have the most significant effects on turnover intentions among hospital professionals, and organizational commitment plays a mediating role in the model. Restated, the findings imply that an investment in developing staff satisfaction toward job and career may benefit hospitals substantially due to enhanced organizational commitment and reduced turnover intentions.

The findings of this study point to the importance of a formal career development program for employees due to the significant influence of career satisfaction on organizational commitment and turnover intentions. Such a program may be promoted as a system designed by management to help employees with their future plans both inside and outside the organization. Hence, HRD supervisors may monitor the level of staff attitudes on an ongoing basis and try to learn which factors contribute to the development of positive work attitudes. Periodic surveys of staff attitudes would help supervisors gauge current work attitudes and trace changes in work attitudes over time. The administration of periodic surveys can be accompanied by factors thought to influence job and career satisfaction (such as the promotion system, the reward system, and on-the-job training) so that potential areas for improvement in the working environment can be identified. HRD practices that emphasize individual perceptions of work and promote an employee-friendly environment in the organization may modify negative reactions toward their job and organization.

HRD management who approach this task with an attitude of "whatever works in U.S. hospitals will surely work in hospitals in a Chinese society" may be very much mistaken (Herndon et al., 2001). No matter what efforts HRD management takes to reduce turnover intentions, the effects of these efforts remain subject to the influence of different cultures. Practically, knowing how *guanxi* affects job-related attitudes based on the findings of this study guides management in taking proper actions to improve employees' turnover intention, and such findings also provide an additional support for the research by Wong, Ngo, and Wong (2003).

The differences across culture found in this study suggest that managers who understand such cultural differences are likely to initiate development activities designed to improve employee retention (Tansky & Cohen, 2001). For example, a career development policy that is simultaneously applied to employees in both Taiwan and the United States may be inappropriate due to cultural differences. This viewpoint is also supported by previous research reporting that organizational commitment was significantly correlated with satisfaction with career development in a hospital setting (Tansky & Cohen, 2001). Likely employee development activities for management may include mentoring, communicating, counseling, listening, problem solving, and inspiring employees to develop new skills based on cultural differences (Kram, 1988; Tansky & Cohen, 2001). HRD activities will not work well if differences across culture are not considered.

Although the relationships among proposed constructs of this study have been extensively discussed across different industries in previous studies, the important effects of *guanxi* based on a moderating perspective have not been previously explored. The concept of *guanxi* is key when comparing Western culture to Eastern culture, where relationships have provided the foundations for business activity for thousands of years (Ambler & Styles, 2000). Following this rationale, this study reveals that four out of five paths are significantly moderated by culture, indicating that the implications on the four paths are critical for supervisors to manage cross-national investment in healthy industries. It is important to point out the implications and recommendations for Taiwan's supervisors (based on H2 and H3) and for U.S. professionals (based on H4 and H5), given the test results of this study.

For Taiwan's supervisors, the stronger influence of job satisfaction on organizational commitment and turnover intentions for Taiwanese professionals than for U.S. ones (H2 and H3) indicates that Taiwanese professionals react more sensitively to organizational commitment and turnover intentions than U.S. ones in terms of the impact of job satisfaction. In other words, the difference between Taiwanese and U.S. professionals is a catalyst to influence the relationships among job satisfaction, organizational commitment, and turnover intentions. It is reasonable that the importance of *guanxi* in Chinese society generally brings more pleasure for employees in a workplace and thus reduces psychological intentions to quit, given that well-established *guanxi* can help employees address many job difficulties effectively in a Chinese society. In addition to addressing the sources of disaffection and performing job reviews periodically, supervisors may plan more tasks based on teamwork. Given that *guanxi* is often referred to as social capital (Luo, 1997), working as a team not only reduces the risk of mistakes caused by individual ignorance, but also increases individual social capital through team members' interdependency and interaction.

The findings offer additional support for the argument of Bailey, Chen, and Dou (1997) that Chinese culture fosters an allocentric conception of self that discourages employees from showing initiative or perceiving that their job environment provides individual-oriented feedback. For example, sponsorship for employee get-togethers can be provided to establish quality *guanxi*. In this way, turnover intentions may drop dramatically as job satisfaction increases through close interdependency and allocentric conception.

For U.S. supervisors, the stronger influence of career satisfaction on organizational commitment and turnover intentions for U.S. professionals than for Taiwanese ones (H4 and H5) implies that U.S. professionals are more sensitive to individual achievement and advancement, given that *networking* (similarly to *guanxi*) in the Western management literature is the term more associated with commercial-based relations (Luo, 1997) and from an individual perspective. As soon as staff members perceive limited opportunities for career advancement, HRD management should develop creative developmental approaches—for example, job rotation or promotion opportunities. By evaluating staff for motivational needs and matching those patterns with the potential need fulfillment of workers' career and job, the organization may be able to establish a dual career track system for hospital professionals, where a managerial track is established that parallels a technical track in position and salary. For those who wish to enter management, the dual career track solution can be provided with hospital management practices so as to help them successfully switch to this area.

For those who are interested in staying in a technical area, the dual career track solution can offer advanced medical study opportunities to attract those who wish to stay at their hospital. Career track counseling by professional counselors should include an investigation of an employee's need profile to make sure this person is heading for a career that is likely to satisfy his or her needs for career development. Supervisors are also encouraged to provide hospital professionals with flexible alternatives to vertical job mobility. Accordingly, the findings here offer additional support for the argument of Bailey et al. (1997) that Western culture fosters an independent, idiocentric conception of self that encourages employees to prefer success feedback, show initiative, and perceive that the feedback is provided in the job environment. Therefore, opportunities may be provided to allow employees to set individual job standards so as to boost their sense of personal achievement and to receive regular feedback from the organization explaining how their company can help them advance in their career. In this way, turnover intentions will drop dramatically.

In summary, organizations need to regularly assess differences across cultures if they want to survive in today's rapidly changing environment. Good HRD policies may help facilitate nonstop learning and reduce unnecessary turnover in the long run. Globalization means that HRD management must take global perspectives to deal with HRD issues regarding job and career development that differ across cultures. As professionals in Taiwanese hospitals are motivated by HRD activities different from those in U.S. hospitals (Bartlett, 2001; Low, 1998; Tansky & Cohen, 2001), the practice of recruiting, training, developing, and motivating those professionals should also be different. Such practice has been alluded to by previous research (Yeh, 1991). As hospitals become more heterogeneous as a result of multinational staffs, hospital supervisors will need a better understanding of differences across cultures (Saeed, 1999). Understanding these differences not only offers help in understanding hospital staff professionals but also reduces uncertainties and national cultural conflicts in the long run.

Limitations and Future Research. This research suffers from some limitations that relate to data collection and interpretation of results. The first limitation is related to the fact that a single sample in each country with small sample sizes was used. Studies based on several hospitals with large samples may support stronger inferences. For examples, samples drawn from two hospitals in the same country with different organizational cultures and systems might reflect somewhat different strengths for the model paths of this study.

The second limitation is the possibility of common method bias in this study. This study used a single questionnaire to measure all constructs, which may inflate the strength of the relationships among these constructs. Another threat to validity is the use of only one hospital in each country in this study. However, sampling employees simultaneously from several organizations may create additional problems. For example, Churchill and Peter (1984) conducted a meta-analysis of 116 sales force studies and found that pooling samples from several organizations can attenuate relationships among constructs because of organizational idiosyncrasies. Future researchers can take note of these shortcomings in planning their research work.

The third limitation is that the sponsors of sample hospitals are not examined here. For example, some hospitals in the United States and Taiwan are private and have religious affiliations. Thus, it is important to acknowledge that variables such as turnover intentions and job satisfaction may change in hospitals with different kinds of sponsorships.

Finally, given that both national cultures are encountering dramatic economic and social changes, it is expected that some characteristics of culture will differ significantly a few years from now. Therefore, longitudinal analysis could be performed to develop a complementary understanding of the influence of cultural change on turnover intentions. Further research can also make an improvement on this study by collecting more data from more diverse populations. For example, personal ties to supervisors, paternalism, and the organization may be surveyed so that further analyses can be performed to provide more general insights.

Appendixes: Correlation Matrices

Correlation Matrix for Taiwanese Data

Indicator	1	2	3	4	5	6	7	8	9	10	11	12	13	14	15	16	17	18
Mean	1.97	2.21	2.09	3.70	3.79	3.58	3.42	3.77	3.66	3.05	2.88	3.76	3.29	3.76	3.37	3.74	3.35	2.56
Standard deviation	0.82	0.97	0.87	0.85	0.83	0.82	0.95	0.73	0.92	1.12	1.12	0.93	1.14	0.84	1.10	0.85	1.06	1.03
1	1.00	0.77	0.81	-0.41	-0.50	-0.20	-0.38	-0.48	-0.57	-0.40	-0.37	-0.50	-0.39	-0.60	-0.14	-0.59	-0.21	-0.22
2		1.00	0.82	-0.42	-0.51	-0.26	-0.45	-0.51	-0.58	-0.42	-0.43	-0.55	-0.40	-0.57	-0.09	-0.57	-0.13	-0.29
3			1.00	-0.39	-0.46	-0.18	-0.40	-0.45	-0.53	-0.37	-0.34	-0.50	-0.41	-0.57	-0.12	-0.55	-0.17	-0.21
4				1.00	0.47	0.47	0.67	0.43	0.54	0.49	0.46	0.39	0.52	0.56	0.13	0.61	0.18	0.35
5					1.00	0.43	0.45	0.54	0.61	0.36	0.40	0.46	0.34	0.77	0.25	0.75	0.26	0.37
6						1.00	0.48	0.38	0.37	0.37	0.43	0.23	0.37	0.46	0.00	0.51	0.03	0.38
7							1.00	0.43	0.55	0.50	0.53	0.34	0.55	0.54	0.11	0.53	0.12	0.53
8								1.00	0.57	0.29	0.36	0.44	0.31	0.55	0.19	0.58	0.19	0.23
9									1.00	0.34	0.36	0.52	0.35	0.62	0.23	0.63	0.23	0.25
10										1.00	0.87	0.39	0.77	0.46	-0.09	0.47	-0.01	0.62
11											1.00	0.39	0.68	0.47	-0.04	0.48	-0.01	0.70
12												1.00	0.44	0.50	0.27	0.55	0.29	0.26
13													1.00	0.46	0.03	0.54	0.10	0.59
14														1.00	0.26	0.46	0.32	0.36
15															1.00	0.24	0.82	0.02
16																1.00	0.26	0.36
17																	1.00	0.05
18																		1.00

Correlation Matrix for U.S. Data

Indicator	1	2	3	4	5	6	7	8	9	10	11	12	13	14	15	16	17	18
Mean	2.08	2.28	2.60	3.70	3.71	3.60	3.66	3.65	3.60	2.68	2.53	3.63	2.81	3.72	3.63	3.44	3.71	2.36
Standard deviation	0.76	0.86	0.98	0.80	0.92	0.87	0.86	0.76	0.80	0.97	0.95	0.84	1.02	0.76	0.88	0.81	0.82	0.96
1	1.00	0.69	0.59	-0.37	-0.38	-0.52	-0.36	-0.42	-0.45	-0.15	-0.23	-0.38	-0.15	-0.37	-0.39	-0.36	-0.38	-0.20
2		1.00	0.71	-0.43	-0.43	-0.47	-0.44	-0.55	-0.59	-0.22	-0.29	-0.41	-0.23	-0.32	-0.44	-0.46	-0.33	-0.30
3			1.00	-0.34	-0.34	-0.43	-0.42	-0.47	-0.48	-0.24	-0.24	-0.39	-0.29	-0.23	-0.41	-0.41	-0.34	-0.29
4				1.00	0.72	0.79	0.76	0.61	0.56	0.37	0.36	0.44	0.30	0.51	0.48	0.55	0.53	0.36
5					1.00	0.72	0.62	0.55	0.54	0.47	0.50	0.47	0.36	0.42	0.52	0.49	0.51	0.37
6						1.00	0.72	0.60	0.60	0.35	0.39	0.48	0.28	0.52	0.54	0.59	0.49	0.37
7							1.00	0.80	0.75	0.37	0.39	0.40	0.31	0.54	0.51	0.52	0.44	0.40
8								1.00	0.68	0.27	0.33	0.44	0.26	0.49	0.51	0.49	0.40	0.29
9									1.00	0.20	0.28	0.37	0.16	0.43	0.45	0.53	0.35	0.32
10										1.00	0.84	0.29	0.85	0.27	0.28	0.34	0.33	0.62
11											1.00	0.35	0.72	0.28	0.37	0.35	0.34	0.70
12												1.00	0.27	0.29	0.64	0.43	0.51	0.28
13													1.00	0.15	0.26	0.29	0.31	0.55
14														1.00	0.42	0.52	0.29	0.21
15															1.00	0.48	0.58	0.30
16																1.00	0.44	0.36
17																	1.00	0.29
18																		1.00

References

Abraham, R. (1999). The impact of emotional dissonance on organizational commitment and intention to turnover. *Journal of Psychology, 133,* 441–455.

Ambler, T., & Styles, C. (2000). The future of relational research in international marketing: Constructs and conduits. *International Marketing Review, 17* (6), 492–508.

Anderson, J. C., & Gerbing, D. W. (1988). Structural equation modeling in practice: A review and recommended two-step approach. *Psychological Bulletin, 103,* 411–423.

Arnold, H., & Feldman, D. C. (1982). A multivariate analysis of the determinants of job turnover. *Journal of Applied Psychology, 67,* 350–360.

Bailey, J. R., Chen, C. C., & Dou, S. G. (1997). Conceptions of self and performance-related feedback in the U.S., Japan and China. *Journal of International Business Studies, 28,* 605–625.

Barnum, C. M., Philip, K., Reynolds, A., Shauf, M. S., & Thompson, T. M. (2001). Globalizing technical communication: A field report from China. *Technical Communication, 48,* 397–420.

Bartlett, K. R. (2001). The relationship between training and organizational commitment: A study in the health care field. *Human Resource Development Quarterly, 12,* 335–352.

Bentler, P. M. (1989). *EQS structural equations program manual.* Los Angeles: BMDP Statistical Software.

Bentler, P. M., & Bonett, D. G. (1980). Significance tests and goodness-of-fit in the analysis of covariance structures. *Psychological Bulletin, 88,* 588-606.

Bluedorn, A. C. (1979). Structure, environment, and satisfaction: Toward a causal model of turnover from military organizations. *Journal of Military and Political Sociology, 7,* 181–207.

Burke, R. J. (2001). Managerial women's career experiences, satisfaction and well-being: A five country study. *Cross Cultural Management, 8,* 117–133.

Buttery, E. A., & Leung, T.K.P. (1998). The difference between Chinese and Western negotiations. *European Journal of Marketing, 32,* 374–389.

Chen, Z. X., & Francesco, A. M. (2000). Employee demography, organizational commitment, and turnover intentions in China: Do cultural differences matter? *Human Relations, 53,* 869–887.

Cheng, B. S. (1995a). *Chaxugeju* (differential mode of association) and Chinese organizational behavior. *Indigenous Psychological Research in Chinese Society, 3,* 142–219.

Cheng, B. S. (1995b). *Chinese CEOs' employee categorization and managerial behavior.* Paper presented at the International Association of Applied Psychology, 1995 Symposium on Indigenous Behavior in Effective Management and Organizations, Guangzhou, PRC.

Cheung, C. K., & Scherling, S. A. (1999). Job satisfaction, work values, and sex differences in Taiwan's organizations. *Journal of Psychology, 133,* 563–575.

Chinese Culture Connection. (1986). Chinese value and the search for culture-free dimensions of culture. *Journal of Cross-Cultural Psychology, 18,* 43–64.

Churchill, G. A., Ford, N. M., & Walker, O. C. (1974). Measuring the job satisfaction of industrial salesmen. *Journal of Marketing Research, 11,* 254–260.

Churchill, G. A., & Peter, J. P. (1984). Research design effects on the reliability of rating scales: A meta-analysis. *Journal of Marketing Research, 21,* 360–375.

Cotton, J. L., & Tuttle, J. M. (1986). Employee turnover: A meta-analysis and review with implications for research. *Academy of Management Review, 11,* 55–70.

Davy, J. A., Kinicki, A. J., & Scheck, C. L. (1991). Developing and testing a model of survivor responses to layoffs. *Journal of Vocational Behavior, 38,* 302–317.

Gattiker, U. E., & Larwood, L. (1988). Predictors for managers' career mobility, success, and satisfaction. *Human Relations, 41,* 569–591.

Greenhaus, J. H., Parasuraman, S., & Wormley, W. M. (1990). Effects of race on organizational experiences, job performance evaluations, and career outcomes. *Academy of Management Journal, 33,* 64–86.

Hatcher, L. (1994). *A step-by-step approach to using the SAS system for factor analysis and structural equation modeling.* Cary, NC: SAS Institute.

Herndon, Jr., N. C., Fraedrich, J. P., & Yeh, Q. J. (2001). An investigation of moral values and the ethical content of the corporate culture: Taiwanese versus U.S. sales people. *Journal of Business Ethics, 30,* 73–85.

Hofstede, G. (1980). Motivation, leadership and organization: Do American theories apply abroad? *Organizational Dynamics, 8,* 42–63.

Hofstede, G., Neuijen, B., Ohayv, D. D., & Sanders, G. (1990). Measuring organizational cultures. *Administrative Science Quarterly, 35,* 286–316.

Hwang, E. R. (1987). Face and favor: The Chinese power game. *American Journal of Sociology, 92,* 35–41.

Igbaria, M., & Greenhaus, J. H. (1992). The career advancement prospects of managers and professionals: Are MIS employees unique? *Decision Sciences, 23,* 478–499.

Igbaria, M., & Siegel, S. R. (1992a). An examination of the antecedents of turnover propensity of engineers: An integrated model. *Journal of Engineering and Technology Management, 9,* 101–126.

Igbaria, M., & Siegel, S. R. (1992b). The reasons for turnover of information systems personnel. *Information and Management, 23,* 321–330.

Kao, J. (1993). The worldwide web of Chinese business. *Harvard Business Review, 53,* 24–36.

Kram, K. (1988). *Mentoring at work* (2nd ed.). Lanham, MD: University Press of America.

Kraut, A. I. (1975). Predicting turnover of employees from measured job attitudes. *Organizational Behavior and Human Performance, 13,* 233–243.

Landau, J., & Hammer, T. H. (1986). Clerical employees' perceptions of intraorganizational career opportunities. *Academy of Management Journal, 29,* 385–404.

Lin, C. P., Chang, S. S., & Chu, C. S. (2003). A causal model of job satisfaction under two different cultures. *Asia Pacific Management Review, 8,* 71–98.

Lin, C. P., & Chen, M. F. (2004). Career commitment as a moderator of the relationships among procedural justice, perceived organizational support, organizational commitment, and turnover intentions. *Asia Pacific Management Review, 9,* 519–538.

Lin, C. P., & Ma, H. C. (2004). Effects of leader-member exchange, job satisfaction, and organizational commitment on diagnosing employee job performance using career stage as a moderator. *Asia Pacific Management Review, 9,* 79–99.

Low, L. (1998). Human resource development in the Asia–Pacific. *Asian-Pacific Economic Literature, 12,* 27–40.

Locke, E. (1976). The nature and causes of job satisfaction. In M. D. Dunnetter (Ed.), *Handbook of industrial and organizational psychology* (pp. 1297–1349). Skokie, IL: Rand McNally.

Lok, P., & Crawford, J. (2004). The effect of organizational culture and leadership style on job satisfaction and organizational commitment: A cross-national comparison. *Journal of Management Development, 23,* 321–338.

Luo, Y. (1997). Guanxi: Principles, philosophies, and implications. *Human Systems Management, 16,* 43–51.

Mannheim, B., Baruch, Y., & Tal, J. (1997). Alternative models for antecedents and outcomes of work centrality and job satisfaction of high-tech personnel. *Human Relations, 50,* 1537–1562.

Martin, T. N. (1979). A contextual model of employee turnover intentions. *Academy of Management Journal, 22,* 313–324.

Michaels, C. E., & Spector, P. E. (1982). Causes of employee turnover: A test of the Mobley, Griffeth, Hand, and Meglino model. *Journal of Applied Psychology, 67,* 53–59.

Montagu-Pollock, M. (1991). All the right connections. *Asian Business, 27,* 20–24.

Morris, M. W., Leung, K., Ames, D., & Lickel, B. (1999). Views from inside and outside: Integrating emic and etic insights about culture and justice judgment. *Academy of Management Review, 24,* 781–796.

Nahavandi, A., & Aranda, E. (1994). Restructuring teams for the re-engineered organization. *Academy of Management Executive, 8,* 58–68.

Near, J. P. (1989). Organizational commitment among Japanese and U.S. workers. *Organization Studies, 10,* 281–300.

Osland, G. E. (1989). Doing business in China: A framework for cross-cultural understanding. *Marketing Intelligence and Planning, 8,* 4–14.

Parasuraman, A., & Futrell, C. M. (1983). Demographics, job satisfaction, and propensity to leave of industrial salesmen. *Journal of Business Research, 11,* 33–48.

Pascale, R. T., & Athos, A. G. (1981). *The art of Japanese management.* New York: Simon and Schuster.

Pornpitakpan, C. (2000). Trade in Thailand: A three-way cultural comparison. *Business Horizons, 43,* 61–70.

Porter, L. W., Steers, R. M., Mowday, R. T., & Boulian, P. V. (1974). Organizational commitment, job satisfaction, and turnover among psychiatric technicians. *Journal of Applied Psychology, 59,* 603–609.

Reynolds, N., Diamantopoulos, A., & Schlegelmilch, B. B. (1993). Pretesting in questionnaire design: A review of the literature and suggestions for further research. *Journal of the Market Research Society, 35,* 171–182.

Saeed, K.S.B. (1999). How physician executives and clinicians perceive ethical issues in Saudi Arabian hospitals. *Journal of Business Ethics, 25,* 51–56.

Singh, J. (1995). Measurement issues in cross-national research. *Journal of International Business Studies, 26,* 597–619.

Su, C., & Littlefield, J. E. (2001). Entering *guanxi*: A business ethical dilemma in Mainland China? *Journal of Business Ethics, 33,* 199–210.

Tansky, J. W., & Cohen, D. J. (2001). The relationship between organizational support, employee development, and organizational commitment: An empirical study. *Human Resource Development Quarterly, 12,* 285–300.

Tsang, E.W.K. (1998). Can *guanxi* be a source of sustained competitive advantage for doing business in China? *Academy of Management Executive, 12,* 64–73.

Tsui, A. S., & Farh, J. L. (1997). Where *guanxi* matters: Relational demography and *guanxi* in the Chinese context. *Work and Occupations, 24,* 56–79.

Wayne, S. J., Shore, L. M., & Liden, R. C. (1997). Perceived organizational support and leader-member exchange: A social exchange perspective. *Academy of Management Journal, 40,* 82–111.

Williams, L. J., & Hazer, J. T. (1986). Antecedents and consequences of satisfaction and commitment in turnover models: A reanalysis using latent variable structural equation methods. *Journal of Applied Psychology, 71,* 219–231.

Wong, G.Y.Y., & Birnbaum-More, P. H. (1994). Culture, context and structure: A test on Hong Kong banks. *Organization Studies, 15,* 99–123.

Wong, Y. H., & Tam, J.L.M. (2000). Mapping relationships in China: *Guanxi* dynamic approach. *Journal of Business and Industrial Marketing, 15,* 57–70.

Wong, Y. T., Ngo, H. Y., & Wong, C. S. (2003). Antecedents and outcomes of employees' trust in Chinese joint ventures. *Asia Pacific Journal of Management, 20,* 481–499.

Xin, K. R., & Pearce, J. L. (1996). *Guanxi*: Connections as substitutes for formal institutional support. *Academy of Management Journal, 39,* 1641–1658.

Yang, M. M. (1988). The modernity of power in the Chinese socialist order. *Cultural Anthropology, 3,* 408–427.

Yeh, R. S. (1991). Management practices of Taiwanese firms: As compared to those of American and Japanese subsidiaries in Taiwan. *Asia Pacific Journal of Management, 8,* 1–14.

Yousef, D. A. (1998). Satisfaction with job security as a predictor of organizational commitment and job performance in a multicultural environment. *International Journal of Manpower, 19,* 184–189.

Cherng G. Ding is a professor in the Institute of Business and Management, National Chiao Tung University, Taiwan.

Chieh-Peng Lin is an assistant professor in the Department of Business Administration, Vanung University, Taiwan.

Tuition Reimbursement, Perceived Organizational Support, and Turnover Intention Among Graduate Business School Students

Marshall Pattie, George S. Benson, Yehuda Baruch

Recent research has shown that while tuition reimbursement is generally associated with employee retention, employees may be more inclined to switch jobs when they earn graduate degrees. This article investigates the relationship between employees currently receiving tuition reimbursement and intention to leave the organization. Analysis of survey data from 322 employed graduate students shows that receiving tuition reimbursement is positively related to perceived organizational support, which reduces turnover intention. However, employees working toward degrees unrelated to their current jobs express greater intention to leave the organization, which increases as they near graduation.

Tuition reimbursement is a popular benefit in which employers pay all or part of an employee's tuition for college education. Employer-provided assistance for education expenses can be provided through grants, scholarships, or reimbursements. Surveys of both students and organizations in the United States indicate that educational assistance and tuition reimbursement programs are widespread. A national survey found that 67 percent of Society for Human Resource Management (SHRM) members report having at least one education benefit program (SHRM, 2004). And a National Center for Educational Statistics survey in 1996 found that among students who identified themselves as working, 25 percent of undergraduates and 42 percent of graduate students

received some form of employer aid. The extensive use of tuition reimbursement as a human resource development (HRD) tool in the United States suggests that it is a good test of the effects of employer-paid training and development on turnover.

Organization expenditures on tuition reimbursement follow the prevailing notion that employee development helps in retaining quality employees (ASTD, 1999). However, since employers are paying for the employees to have an opportunity to earn university degrees that are marketable to other firms, it is possible that they are paying to develop skills that help employees switch organizations. Cappelli (2004) investigated this question using a nationally representative survey and found that establishments with tuition reimbursement programs actually have lower turnover rates on average than those without some form of educational assistance. He concluded that there were retention benefits for tuition reimbursement, particularly when the employees are enrolled in the program. In a study of workers within a single organization, Benson, Finegold, and Mohrman (2004) found that the likelihood of turnover decreases while employees are in school but increases after employees earn graduate degrees.

The purpose of this study is to investigate the relationships between receiving tuition reimbursement, the job relatedness of the degree, the proximity to graduation, and turnover intention. Understanding the impact of tuition reimbursement programs on turnover intention is important HRD research because these significant investments in employees provide more marketable skills than traditional HRD such as classroom training or formal on-the-job training (Benson, 2006). Tuition reimbursement programs also develop a greater depth and breadth of skills than typical HRD programs that last a number of days (Swanson, 2001). In terms of time commitment, even two-year degrees can take significantly longer when employees are working full time. Employees enrolled in a degree program receive training in numerous related and unrelated classes as opposed to most organization-provided training, which typically deals with a single topic directly related to employees' jobs. In financial terms, tuition and other related expenses cost organizations thousands of dollars (Cappelli, 2004). Furthermore, tuition reimbursement is a large and growing aspect of HRD that until recently has been largely ignored in the literature (Benson et al., 2004; Cappelli, 2004). After reviewing the literature on employee development and turnover, we develop and test four hypotheses using data from 322 employed business school graduate students.

Literature Review and Hypotheses

While the estimates of spending on tuition reimbursement in the United States range up to $10 billion annually (Meisler, 2004), only a handful of recent studies have examined whether these investments are meeting their stated goals in employee relations and retention (Benson et al., 2004; Cappelli, 2004). This research details two competing theories of the ways by which these programs are thought to affect employee turnover. On one hand, the HRD literature generally views employee development as a benefit that leads to perceptions of organizational support and retention (Bartlett, 2001; Birdi, Allen, & Warr, 1997; Gaertner & Nolen, 1989; Meyer & Smith, 2000; Noe, Wilk, Mullen, & Wanek, 1997; Nordhaug, 1989; Tansky & Cohen, 2001; Tsui, Pearce, Porter, & Tripoli, 1997). On the other hand, human capital theory focuses on the new skills and credentials gained through education and predicts that employees are more likely to leave the organization when they graduate (Krueger & Rouse, 1998; Loewenstein & Spletzer, 1999; Lynch, 1991). More likely, tuition reimbursement generates perceptions of organizational support and marketable skills through college degrees simultaneously. We review each of these mechanisms separately and use the literature on employee turnover to examine how each of these is likely to contribute to employees' decisions to remain with a firm when they participate in tuition reimbursement.

Although there is wide and varied literature on turnover, the different theoretical perspectives generally agree that employees' attitudes about their jobs and employers interact with perceived alternatives to influence an individual's decision to leave (Griffeth, Steel, Allen, & Bryan, 2005). Turnover theory for many years has primarily focused on job satisfaction and ease of movement considerations as the two main factors predicting turnover (Bluedorn, 1982; Hom & Kinicki, 2001; March & Simon, 1958; Mobley, 1977; Mobley, Griffeth, Hand, & Meglino, 1979; Steers & Mowday, 1981). More recent turnover theory views turnover as a process that takes place over time as a function of how embedded a person is in his or her current job (Lee, Mitchell, Wise, & Fireman, 1996; Lee, Mitchell, Sablynksi, Burton, & Holtom, 2004; Mitchell, Holtom, Lee, Sablynski, & Erez, 2001). Both of these turnover perspectives can accommodate the possibility that participating in tuition reimbursement might influence employee attitudes toward the firm and potential job alternatives at the same time.

Conventional turnover theory and the newer "unfolding" model of turnover both include job dissatisfaction as an important driver of job search and eventual turnover (Hom & Kinicki, 2001; Lee, Mitchell, Holton, McDaniel, & Hill, 1999). This relationship is well documented and has been the foundation for a number of studies that have linked various human resource practices to intention to leave the organization through job attitudes (Huselid, 1995; Vandenberg, Richardson & Eastman, 1999). But rather than acting on job satisfaction directly, this research suggests that perceived organizational support (POS) mediates the impact of many different types of HR practices, including development on job satisfaction and turnover intention (Allen, Shore, & Griffeth, 2003; Meyer & Smith, 2000). After reviewing the literature that focuses on the relationship between employee development and attitudes, we develop two hypotheses that predict that participation in tuition reimbursement is negatively related to intention to switch jobs through perceived organizational support.

Tuition reimbursement is also likely related to turnover intention through the skills and credentials gained with a graduate degree. In addition to job satisfaction, all turnover models include the evaluation of job alternatives for employees. Employees with greater human capital, including education and experience, are thought to have greater access to job alternatives (Kirschenbaum & Mano-Negrin, 1999; Loewenstein & Spletzer, 1999; Veum, 1999). While dissatisfaction may lead employees to seek out and evaluate other jobs, the opportunities they find are determined by their skills and experience matched to the labor market (Trevor, 2001). Conventional turnover theory predicts that a graduate degree earned through tuition reimbursement has a positive impact on turnover intention by increasing job alternatives or ease of movement independent of any impact that the tuition reimbursement has on employee attitudes or the desirability of leaving the firm.

Within the "unfolding" model of turnover, however, the skills gained through graduate study are also likely to affect the employees' fit, or perceived compatibility, with their current jobs (Lee et al., 1999; Mitchell et al., 2001). Among other things, employees' goals and plans for the future should match the knowledge and skill demands of their jobs (Mitchell et al., 2001). This suggests that employee retention depends in part on the match between the skills developed through a graduate program and the skills needed for employees' jobs. When job-related graduate studies help keep employees current in their skills, earning the degree may serve to increase fit with the demands of the job and therefore retention (Lee & Maurer, 1997). But if employees pursue a degree unrelated to their current job, a decrease in fit, combined with the marketability of a graduate degree, is likely to increase turnover intention (Lee et al., 1999). In the next section, we review HRD literature that focuses on offering employees new skills and credentials and develop two hypotheses that predict turnover intention.

Tuition Reimbursement and Turnover Intention

Theories of employee development generally assume that employees who participate will respond with positive attitudes toward the organization (Noe et al., 1997). One important way that employees respond to practices such as employee development is through POS, the perception that employees hold about the level of commitment from their organizations (Eisenberger, Huntington, Hutchison, & Sowa, 1986). POS can also be seen as aid from the organization to help employees complete their job effectively (George, Reed, Ballard, Colin, & Fielding, 1993). POS is thought to be based on a social exchange in which employees respond with POS to commitments and benefits from their organizations (Eisenberger, Fasolo, & Davis-LaMastro, 1990; Eisenberger, Cummings, Armelo, & Lynch, 1997).

Nordhaug (1989) showed that workers perceive the provision of training to be a benefit offered by their employers along with pay and other fringe benefits. A number of studies have specifically found that organization-financed employee development is positively related to POS (Bartlett, 2001; Galunic & Anderson, 2000; Meyer & Smith, 2000). For example, Tansky and Cohen (2001) found training and development positively related to POS among a sample of nurses. Birdi et al. (1997) found a similar result among autoworkers. A meta-analysis shows that training is an antecedent of POS, with a correlation of .21 (Rhoades & Eisenberger, 2002). Tuition reimbursement is a widespread, voluntary benefit that signals a willingness to invest in employees and should therefore be positively related to POS among employees who participate:

HYPOTHESIS 1: *Receiving tuition reimbursement is positively related to POS.*

Organization expenditures on tuition reimbursement are often cited as benefits to increase employee skills, foster positive attitudes toward the organization, and facilitate retention (ASTD, 1999; Cappelli, 2001). The impact of tuition reimbursement on retention is particularly important to understand as organizations need to retain trained employees to realize a return on this investment in new skills and college degrees. This study uses employee turnover intention to examine the relationship between tuition reimbursement and employee retention. Turnover intention is based on the general behavioral model that ascertains that attitudes, values, and norms are antecedents to intentions, inclinations, and tendencies, which in turn generate actions (Fishbein & Ajzen, 1975; Ajzen & Fishbein, 1980). Evidence including meta-analyses suggests a positive but moderate association between turnover intention and actual turnover (Griffeth & Hom, 1988; Griffeth, Hom, & Gaertner, 2000; Hom & Griffeth, 1995).

Research on turnover intention has identified a great number of personal, job, and work environment antecedents (Bluedorn, 1982; Lee et al., 1999; Mobley, 1977; Mobley et al., 1979; Steers & Mowday, 1981; Hom & Griffeth, 1991). An important set of predictors of turnover intention in these models are employee attitudes, including POS. Research has consistently shown a negative relationship between POS and turnover intentions and actual turnover (Allen et al., 1999; Guzzo, Noonan, & Elron, 1994; Rhoades & Eisenberger, 2002; Wayne, Shore, & Liden, 1997). In addition, Allen et al. (2003) show that HR practices such as employee development often work through POS to effect turnover. Based on this, we predict that POS mediates a relationship between tuition reimbursement and influences turnover intention:

HYPOTHESIS 2: *POS mediates a negative relationship between tuition reimbursement and turnover intention.*

Job Relatedness of Skills

While participation in a tuition reimbursement program works to decrease turnover intention through POS, human capital theory suggests the skills and credentials earned through a graduate degree play an independent role in employee turnover decisions. Employees who earn graduate degrees develop general skills useful across a wide range of organizations, which increases the likelihood that they will change jobs (Becker, 1965; Krueger & Rouse, 1998; Lynch, 1991; Loewenstein & Spletzer, 1999; Mincer, 1988). Moreover, Benson et al. (2004) found that employees were more likely to switch jobs once they had completed a graduate degree through tuition reimbursement unless they received a promotion. One reason is that graduate degrees are strongly related to earnings and career opportunities (Griffeth et al., 2005). Both conventional turnover theory and the "unfolding" model of turnover suggest that attractive job alternatives can contribute to turnover intention. For example, education is often used in studies of turnover to control for job opportunities (Trevor, 2001). Taken together, this suggests that earning a graduate degree through tuition reimbursement should have a positive impact on turnover intention by increasing job opportunities for employees.

The attractiveness of alternative jobs, however, depends on the person's current job for comparison. Human capital theory suggests that individuals decide whether to stay with an organization based in part on whether their jobs provide the best fit and returns on their skills (Bishop, 1997; Liu, 1986). From a human capital perspective, employees are likely to seek employment that is a better match to their newly acquired skills (Pergamit & Veum, 1999). Research has consistently shown that individuals whose schooling was related to their occupation reported a significantly larger increase in salary when compared to those whose schooling was unrelated to their current occupation (Eck, 1993; Gullason, 1999). This suggests that whether the skills developed through graduate study are related to an employee's current job should play a role in turnover intention. Employees who earn degrees unrelated to their current jobs should therefore express greater intention to switch jobs as they seek a job to better match their new skills (Lee & Maurer, 1997). Assuming that students desire to work in the fields they have chosen for graduate study, the attractiveness of other jobs will increase if they provide a greater perceived match to the skills gained:

HYPOTHESIS 3: *Employees who are earning degrees unrelated to their current jobs will report higher turnover intention than employees earning degrees related to their current jobs.*

While earning graduate degrees unrelated to their current jobs is likely to increase intention to leave for a better job, research has shown that the utility of graduate study for career advancement accrues on graduation (Acemoglu & Pischke, 1998, 1999). Graduation is important because of the influence it has over the marketability of new skills gained through graduate classes. Research into the relationship between education and wages finds that earning a degree is different from attending classes, because earning a degree signals competence to potential employers (Acemoglu & Pischke, 1998, 1999; Spence, 1973; Spilerman & Lunde, 1991). While education increases employees' skills and

Figure 1. Summary of Hypotheses

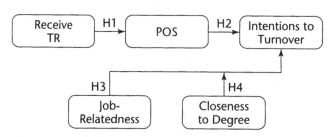

future earning potential (Mincer, 1988), the wage effects of education are more closely tied to completing a degree than simply staying in school. Therefore, employees who understand the importance of graduation as a signal to potential employers are more likely to wait until they earn their degrees before seeking out a new job. Accordingly, we should expect that turnover intention among employees earning degrees unrelated to their current jobs should increase as they near graduation:

HYPOTHESIS 4: *Hours of course work completed will moderate the relationship between job relatedness and turnover intention such that employees who are further along in their studies and are obtaining non-job-related degrees will report higher turnover intention.*

Figure 1 summaries the four hypotheses.

Methods

Sample. All 928 master's degree candidates studying business in a large southwestern university were asked to participate in an online survey. E-mails from the dean's office were sent to each subject with a link to the survey asking a number of questions about their graduate studies, current employment, work attitudes, and participation in tuition reimbursement. To encourage responses, five hundred-dollar rewards were offered to randomly selected study participants. Two follow-up reminders were sent to nonrespondents in weekly intervals. A total of 534 surveys were completed, and 75 of the e-mails were returned undeliverable. After incomplete surveys were eliminated, the final sample size was 473 usable surveys, representing a healthy 51 percent response rate (Baruch, 1999).

This sample is appropriate for studying tuition reimbursement because of the number of employed students (79 percent) who were receiving tuition reimbursement (39 percent). While in many cases using student samples is considered a convenience sample, for our investigation of tuition reimbursement, the sample was ideal. First, participants of tuition reimbursement programs are students. Second, our student sample represents 111 different tuition reimbursement programs. The organizations represented in the sample range from Fortune 500 and large multinational companies to regional and small, local organizations. The diversity of tuition reimbursement programs and participants represented suggests that the sample can be generalized to other large metropolitan areas in the United States. This study examines only the 322 respondents who were working either full or part time. The employed respondents were 52 percent female and 37 percent minority and on average were thirty-one years old. One-fifth of the respondents were international students. Slightly more than half (55 percent) of the respondents were studying for the M.B.A., and the remainder were in a variety of master's programs, including health care administration (17 percent), accounting (7 percent), and marketing (6 percent).

Measures. All of the measures below were obtained from the survey participants, with the exception of the number of hours the student had completed in the master's program. This variable was acquired from an archival data set provided by the dean's office.

Turnover Intention. A single-item was used to measure turnover intention: "What are the chances that you are going to quit your job in the next 12 months?" This item is similar to ones used in previous research (Davy, Kinicki, & Scheck, 1997; Hom, Griffeth, & Sellaro, 1994). The respondents answered by giving the percentage likeliness that they would leave their organization. Their answers were normally distributed, with 20 percent responding that there was zero chance that they would leave their organization within twelve months and 8 percent responding that there was a 100 percent chance they would leave their organization within twelve months.

Perceived Organizational Support. To assess employees' perceived organizational support, we selected five items from Eisenberger et al.'s survey (1986) of perceived organizational support (SPOS). Because of the length of the SPOS (thirty-six items), it is common for researchers to shorten the scale (Eisenberger et al., 1997). In most cases, three to eight items from the original POS scale are used (Eisenberger, Stinglhamber, Vandenberghe, Sucharski, & Rhoades, 2002). We used the same items that have been used in other studies that shortened the scale (Eisenberger et al., 2002). Items included "Help is available from our organization when I have a problem" and "My organization is willing to help me if I need a special favor." Cronbach's alpha for the shortened POS was .89.

Receiving Tuition Reimbursement. Participation in tuition reimbursement is measured as a (1/0) dummy variable. Employed students were asked (yes or no) whether they currently received tuition reimbursement. Of the employed respondents, 49 percent were receiving some form of tuition reimbursement.

Hours Completed in Master's Program. The hours that each student had completed were matched from university records. Students had completed from zero to sixty-six graduate-level hours. The average student had completed almost eighteen hours of course work.

Salary. Participants were asked to indicate their current salary on eleven check boxes that ranged from "below $20,000" to "above $110,000." In between were $10,000 increments such as "$20,000 to $29,000." For use in the regressions, this response was converted to a continuous variable by taking the midpoint of each category (for example, $25,000, $35,000) for each employed respondent. The 23 percent of respondents in the lowest category were coded as $15,000, and the 3 percent of respondents in the highest category were coded as $115,000. After recoding, the mean salary was $50,680.

Tenure. Participants gave their length of employment at their current organization in years and months. Tenure ranged from less than a month to more than 27 years, with an average of 3.4 years. Tenure has been shown to play a significant role in predicting participation in voluntary development activities (Griffith et al., 2000; Noe & Wilk, 1993) and is typically used as a control in POS research (Eisenberger et al., 2002; Rhoades & Eisenberger, 2002).

Full-Time or Part-Time Employment. Participants provided the average number of hours they worked each week. This continuous variable was converted into a dichotomous variable, with employees working fewer than thirty-five hours considered as part-time employees, whereas employees working more than thirty-five hours were considered full time. Previous literature has found that employment status can affect POS levels (Gakovic & Tetrick, 2003) and turnover intention levels (Thorsteinson, 2003). Furthermore, very few part-time employees received tuition reimbursement. In our sample, only 8 percent of part-time employees received tuition reimbursement compared to 58 percent of the full-time employees.

Job Relatedness. We developed a four-item scale for the study to measure the degree to which the course of graduate study is related to the student's current job: "The degree I am working on is related to my current job," "The skills gained from my degree will not improve my performance of my current job," "The degree I am acquiring at [name of school] is not related to my current job," and "Knowledge gained from a degree will improve my performance in my current job." Items were reversed so that the scale ranged from 1 (degree is unrelated to the employees' current job) to 5 (degree is related to the employees' current job). Cronbach's alpha for job relatedness was .84. To ensure that the items used to measure job relatedness and POS separated into two clear factors, exploratory factor analysis and varimax rotation were employed. Correlations between the independent measures do not suggest the presence of multicollinearity in the models.

Analyses. All four hypotheses were tested using hierarchical ordinary least squares regression controlling for salary level, full-time or part-time employment, and years of tenure. Hypothesis 1 was tested by regressing POS on the set of control variables in step 1 and adding tuition reimbursement in step 2. Hypothesis 2 proposes that POS mediates a relationship between tuition reimbursement and turnover intention and was tested using Baron and Kenny's methodology (1986). Following evidence of a relationship between tuition reimbursement and POS from testing hypothesis 1, a regression predicting turnover intention was run with control variables in step 1 and tuition reimbursement added in step 2. In step 3, POS was used to predict turnover intention without tuition reimbursement. Finally, POS and tuition reimbursement were used together in step 4 to predict turnover intention.

Hypothesis 3 predicts that employees studying for degrees unrelated to their current jobs will express greater turnover intention and was tested in a series of regressions predicting turnover intention and beginning with controls in step 1. Because the relationship between the job relatedness of the degree and turnover intention is thought to be independent of the relationship that tuition benefits have on employee attitudes, POS was also entered as a control variable in step 1. In step 2, the job relatedness of the degree was entered. Hypothesis 4 predicts an interaction between job relatedness and hours of graduate study completed and was tested by entering the control variables along with POS in step 1. Job relatedness of the degree and hours of graduate study completed were then entered in step 2 and interaction between job relatedness and hours completed in step 3.

Results

Descriptive statistics and correlations are presented in Table 1. Regression results are presented in Tables 2 through 5. The results of the first set of regressions in Table 2 support hypothesis 1 that employed students who receive tuition reimbursement report higher POS than employed students who do not receive tuition reimbursement. Following the control variables entered in step 1, receiving tuition reimbursement was entered in step 2 and significantly predicted POS ($\beta = .17, p < .01$). Receiving tuition reimbursement explained an additional 3.1 percent ($p < .01$) of the variance in POS.

Regression results testing hypothesis 2 are reported in Table 3. Hypothesis 2 predicts that POS mediates a negative relationship between participation in tuition reimbursement and intention to switch jobs in the next twelve months. Following a model with control variables only in step 1, a negative relationship between the receiving tuition reimbursement and intention to turnover is shown in step 2 ($\beta = -.14, p < .05$). This regression was significant ($F = 12.45, p < .001$), with 13.5 percent variance explained. Step 3 shows a significant negative relationship between POS and turnover intention ($\beta = -.39, p < .001$). In step 4, receiving tuition reimbursement and POS

Table 1. Descriptive Statistics and Correlations

	Mean	S.D.	N	1	2	3	4	5	6	7	8
Turnover intention	38.51	38.19	322	1.00							
Closeness to degree	17.86	14.90	322	0.18	1.00						
Job relatedness	-2.34	1.05	322	0.38	-0.12	1.00					
Perceived organizational support	3.43	0.87	322	-0.37	-0.08	-0.31	1.00				
Receiving tuition reimbursement	0.49	0.50	322	-0.26	0.05	-0.25	0.13	1.00			
Salary level[a]	50.70	22.40	322	-0.31	0.17	-0.23	0.03	0.32	1.00		
Full time or part time	0.82	0.39	322	-0.28	0.12	-0.19	-0.08	0.38	0.46	1.00	
Tenure (years)	3.35	3.97	322	-0.10	0.17	-0.01	-0.08	0.05	0.31	0.17	1.00

Note: Values greater than .116 are significant at $p < .05$. Values greater than .164 are significant at $p < .001$.

[a]000s

Table 2. Regression Results for Perceived Organizational Support

| | Hypothesis 1: POS | | | |
| | Step 1 | | Step 2 | |
	Beta	t	Beta	t
Salary level	0.11	1.76[+]	0.08	1.23
Full time or part time	−0.11	−1.80[+]	−0.16	−2.52**
Tenure (years)	−0.10	−1.70[+]	−0.09	−1.56
Receiving tenure reimbursement			0.17	2.76**
R^2		.020		0.043
R^2 change				0.023**
F		2.23[+]		3.61**
N		323		323

[+]$p < .10$. *$p < .05$. **$p < .01$. ***$p < .001$.

were entered together to predict turnover intention. This regression was significant ($F = 23.74$, $p < .001$), with 26 percent total variance explained. Tuition reimbursement was no longer significant, while POS remained significant ($\beta = -.38$, $p < .001$). Following Barron and Kenny (1986), this pattern of regression results, along with the positive relationship between receiving tuition reimbursement and POS in Table 2, supports hypothesis 2 that POS mediates a negative relationship between tuition reimbursement and turnover intention.

Table 4 reports regression results testing hypothesis 3 that employed students pursuing degrees related to their current jobs will express lower turnover intention than students pursuing degrees unrelated to their current jobs. Control variables including POS were entered in step 1. Job relatedness was entered into the model in step 2 and was significant ($\beta = .22$, $p < .001$). Job relatedness explained an additional 4 percent ($p < .001$) of variance in turnover intention, and hypothesis 3 was supported.

Table 5 details the test of hypothesis 4 that employees who pursue degrees unrelated to their current jobs will express greater turnover intention the closer they are to graduation. Control variables were entered in step 1 followed by the job relatedness of the degree and the number of graduate hours completed entered in step 2. In step 2, both the job relatedness ($\beta = .25$, $p < .001$) and the number of graduate hours completed ($\beta = .25$, $p < .001$) were significant. These results indicate that employed students in general express greater turnover intention as they complete more credit hours and move closer to finishing their degree. In step 3, the interaction between the job relatedness of the degree and the hours of graduate study completed was significant ($\beta = .30$, $p < .05$). Hypothesis 4 was supported.

HUMAN RESOURCE DEVELOPMENT QUARTERLY • DOI: 10.1002/hrdq

Table 3. Regression Results for Perceived Organizational Support as a Mediator

	Step 1		Step 2		Step 3		Step 4	
			Hypothesis 2: Turnover Intention					
	Beta	t	Beta	t	Beta	t	Beta	t
Salary level	−0.22	−3.63***	−0.19	−3.14**	−0.18	−3.17**	−0.16	−2.88**
Full time or part time	−0.18	−3.13**	−0.14	−2.34*	−0.23	−4.21***	−0.20	−3.61***
Tenure (years)	0.01	0.16	0.01	0.02	−0.03	−0.58	−0.03	−0.65
Receiving tuition reimbursement			−0.14	−2.43*			−0.08	−1.44
POS					−0.39	−8.03***	−0.38	−7.73***
R^2 (adjusted R^2)	0.120		0.135		0.267		0.272	
R^2 change			0.016*				0.153***	
F	14.41***		12.45***		29.06***		23.74***	
N	323		323		323		323	

$^+p < .10.$ $^*p < .05.$ $^{**}p < .01.$ $^{***}p < .001.$

Table 4. Regression Results for Job Relatedness

| | Hypothesis 3: Turnover Intention | | | |
| | Step 1 | | Step 2 | |
	Beta	t	Beta	t
Salary level	−0.18	−3.20**	−0.14	−2.60**
Full time or part time	−0.23	−4.17***	−0.20	−3.64***
Tenure (years)	−0.03	−0.60	−0.04	−0.82
POS	−0.39	−7.99***	−0.32	−6.38***
Degree unrelated to current job			0.22	4.20***
R^2 (adjusted R^2)		0.267 (0.257)		0.305 (0.294)
R^2 change		0.15***		0.04***
F		28.92***		27.87***
N		322		322

$^+p < .10.$ $^*p < .05.$ $^{**}p < .01.$ $^{***}p < .001.$

Discussion

The widespread use of tuition reimbursement as an educational benefit has become an issue of concern over the past several years due primarily to the large expense and popularity of these programs. This study is relevant to HRD researchers and practitioners as tuition reimbursement provides an interesting theoretical test of how employees react to employer-financed development since tuition reimbursement is a significant benefit for employees that also provides them with transferable skills and credentials. A number of studies show that employees who participate in company-provided development activities in general report increased POS and intention to remain with their organizations (Meyer & Smith, 2000; Tanksy & Cohen, 2001). The results of this study extend these findings to participation in tuition reimbursement programs. Hypotheses 1 and 2 were supported, showing that receiving tuition reimbursement has a positive relationship with POS, which mediates a negative relationship with turnover intention. This fits with recent research showing that employees are less likely to switch jobs while they are in school and receiving tuition reimbursement (Cappelli, 2004). However, this study also shows that graduate study through tuition reimbursement has an additional impact on turnover intention that depends on how the new skills gained are related to the employee's current job. Hypotheses 3 and 4 were supported, showing that employees who earn degrees unrelated to their current jobs report greater turnover intention and that turnover intention increases as employees move closer to graduation.

Table 5. Regression Analysis for Hours of Graduate Study Completed as a Moderator

Hypothesis 4: Turnover Intention

	Step 1		Step 2		Step 3	
	Beta	t	Beta	t	Beta	t
Salary level	−0.18	−3.19**	−0.17	−3.13**	−0.16	−3.02**
Full time or part time	−0.23	−4.14***	−0.20	−3.8***	−0.21	−4.04***
Tenure (years)	−0.03	−0.63	−0.07	−1.51	−0.07	−1.41
POS	−0.39	−7.93***	−0.29	−6.01***	−0.28	−5.90***
Degree unrelated to current job			0.25	4.99***	0.12	1.69+
Hours of study completed			0.25	5.40***	−0.02	3.75***
Job relatedness ×hours completed					0.30	−2.50*
R^2 (adjusted R^2)	0.265 (0.256)		0.363 (0.350)		0.375 (0.361)	
R^2 change	0.146***		0.098***		0.012**	
F	28.58***		29.87***		26.92***	
N	321		321		321	

+$p < .10$. *$p < .05$. **$p < .01$. ***$p < .001$.

This provides additional understanding to previous research that shows employees are more likely to switch jobs when they earn a graduate degree through tuition reimbursement (Benson et al., 2004).

This detailed examination of employee participation in tuition reimbursement also provides an illustration of the ways in which employee development affects turnover more generally. These results imply that competing theories concerning both employee development and turnover have merit and should be considered together. Organizations that provide tuition reimbursement are paying to provide employees with skills and college degrees that they perceive as a benefit and react positively with perceptions of organizational support. While this perceived support encourages employees to remain with their firms, a graduate degree also provides them with skills and marketable credentials. When employees pursue graduate business studies through tuition reimbursement that are unrelated to their current jobs, earning a degree increases their turnover intention even after controlling for the positive impact that receiving tuition reimbursement has on POS. These results indicate that tuition reimbursement acts on turnover intention in at least two ways. Future research should examine whether the same is true for other forms of development that provide general skills to employees.

Limitations. While this study provides a relatively clean test of the hypotheses, several limitations should be noted. Most important, it suffers from the typical problems associated with a one-time questionnaire study. Conducting a longitudinal study and collecting data to examine how attitudes toward the organization and turnover intention change over time would provide better understanding of the influence of tuition reimbursement. In addition, this study relies on turnover intention rather than actual turnover data. Although actual turnover would be preferable, intentions to quit have been demonstrated as a valid antecedent of actual turnover and are commonly used as a surrogate variable to quitting behavior (see Hom & Griffeth, 1991; Hom et al., 1992; Hom & Griffeth, 1995; Hom & Kinicki, 2001; Lee & Mowaday, 1987; Lee et al., 1999; Lee & Mitchell, 1994). Furthermore, there is inherent weakness when using a single-item dependent variable such as turnover intention. Finally, this study also includes only graduate business students from a single university in the United States. Repeating the study with different students (for example, in engineering or the arts) and in other institutions in other countries would indicate whether our findings are indeed robust or limited to a population similar to the one tested in this study.

Implications. Organizations often face dilemmas when recruiting employees who have valuable skills and developing workforces with a flexible skill base (Garavan, 1991). Providing the opportunity for employees to obtain degrees through tuition reimbursement helps ensure continual skill development and a workforce with adaptable skills but is inherently risky. Tuition reimbursement is expensive, and organizations must retain program participants in order to realize a return on these investments in employees. This study demonstrates that tuition reimbursement can be used successfully to develop and retain employees. However, the risk of employee turnover is increased significantly if employees choose to pursue degrees unrelated to their current jobs. These results begin to provide some guidance for HRD practitioners on how to refine tuition reimbursement programs and increase general human capital. Our findings support previous assumptions that providing HRD for employees promotes positive feelings toward the organization, which decrease intentions to leave the organization. However, this study also suggests that HRD should be strategically implemented to encourage and fund graduate study that is related to employees' jobs or place employees in jobs that allow them to use the skills they gain through tuition reimbursement.

Employees who perceive a match between their current jobs and their graduate degrees are likely to see better career and growth opportunities as crucial when compared to those who feel they need to change jobs to apply their new skills. Furthermore, our results show that the closer an employee comes to completing the degree, the more urgent HRD practitioners should become in ensuring alignment between the new skills and the employee's job. One possible way to handle employees who will soon earn graduate degrees unrelated to their current jobs is to reassign or promote them on graduation. This suggests that tuition reimbursement programs can be highly effective retention tools when matched with career systems that recognize employees when they develop new skills.

References

Acemoglu, D., & Pischke, J. S. (1998). Why do firms train? Theory and evidence. *Quarterly Journal of Economics, 113,* 79–119.

Acemoglu, D., & Pischke, J. S. (1999). Beyond Becker: Training in imperfect labour markets. *Economic Journal, 109,* F112-F142.

Ajzen I., & Fishbein, M. (1980). *Understanding attitudes and predicting social behavior.* Upper Saddle River, NJ: Prentice Hall.

Allen, D. G., Shore, L. M., & Griffeth, R. W. (2003). The role of perceived organizational support and supportive human resource practices in the turnover process. *Journal of Management, 29,* 99–119.

American Society for Training and Development. (1999). *Recruiting and retaining employees: Using training and education in the war for talent.* Alexandria, VA: Author.

Baron, R. M., & Kenny, D. A. (1986). The moderator-mediator variable distinction in social psychological research: Conceptual, strategic, and statistical considerations. *Journal of Personality and Social Psychology, 51,* 1173–1182.

Bartlett, K. (2001). The relationship between training and organizational commitment: A study in the health care field. *Human Resource Development Quarterly, 12,* 335–353.

Baruch, Y. (1999). Response rate in academic studies: A comparative analysis. *Human Relations, 52,* 421–438.

Becker, G. (1965). *Human capital.* Chicago: University of Chicago Press.

Benson, G. (2006). Employee development, commitment and intention to turnover: A test of "employability" policies in action. *Human Resource Management Journal, 16* (2), 173–192.

Benson, G. S., Finegold, D., & Mohrman, S. A. (2004). You paid for the skills, now keep them: Tuition reimbursement and voluntary turnover. *Academy of Management Journal, 47,* 315–331.

Birdi, K., Allan, C., & Warr, P. (1997). Correlates and perceived outcomes of four types of development activity. *Journal of Applied Psychology, 82,* 845–857.

Bishop, J. H. (1997). What we know about employer-provided training: A review of the literature. *Research in Labor Economics, 16,* 19–87.

Bluedorn, A. (1982). A unified model of turnover from organizations. *Human Relations, 35,* 135–153.

Cappelli, P. (2001). The National Employer Survey: Employer data on employment practices. *Industrial Relations, 40,* 635–648.

Cappelli, P. (2004). Why do employers pay for college? *Journal of Econometrics, 121,* 213–241.

Davy, J., Kinicki, A., & Scheck, C. (1997). A test of job security's direct and mediated effects of withdrawal cognitions. *Journal of Organizational Behavior, 18,* 323–349.

Eck, A. (1993). Job-related education and training: Their impact on earnings. *Monthly Labor Review, 116,* 21–37.

Eisenberger, R., Cummings, J., Armelo, S., & Lynch, P. (1997). Perceived organizational support, discretionary treatment, and job satisfaction. *Journal of Applied Psychology, 86,* 812–820.

Eisenberger, R., Fasolo P., & Davis-LaMastro, V. (1990). Perceived organizational support and employee diligence, commitment, and innovation. *Journal of Applied Psychology, 75,* 51–59.

Eisenberger, R., Huntington, R., Hutchison, S., & Sowa, D. (1986). Perceived organizational support. *Journal of Applied Psychology, 71,* 500–507.

Eisenberger, R., Stinglhamber, F., Vandenberghe, C., Sucharski, I. L., & Rhoades, L. (2002). Perceived supervisor support: Contributions to perceived organizational support. *Journal of Applied Psychology, 87,* 565–573.

Fishbein, M., & Ajzen, I. (1975). *Belief, attitude, intention, and behavior: An introduction to theory and research.* Reading, MA: Addison-Wesley.

Gaertner, K., & Nollen, S. (1989). Career experience, perceptions of employment practices, and psychological commitment to the organization. *Human Relations, 42,* 975–991.

Gakovic, A., & Tetrick, L. E. (2003). Perceived organizational support and work status: A comparison of part-time and full-time employees attending university classes. *Journal of Organizational Behavior, 24,* 649–666.

Galunic, D., & Anderson, E. (2000). From security to mobility: Generalized investments in human capital and agent commitment. *Organizational Science, 11,* 1–20.

Garavan, T. N. (1991). Strategic human resource development. *Journal of European Industrial Training, 15,* 17–30.

George, J. M., Reed, T. F., Ballard, K. A., Colin, J., & Fielding, J. (1993). Contact with AIDS patients as a source of work-related distress: Effects of organizational and social support. *Academy of Management Journal, 36,* 157–172.

Griffeth, R., & Hom, P. (1988). A comparison of different conceptualizations of perceived alternatives in turnover research. *Journal of Organizational Behavior, 9,* 103–111.

Griffeth, R., Hom, P., & Gaertner, K. (2000). A meta-analysis of antecedents and correlates of employee turnover: Update, moderator tests, and research implications for the next millennium. *Journal of Management, 26,* 463–488.

Griffeth, R. W., Steel, R. P., Allen, D. G., & Bryan, N. (2005). The development of a multidimensional measure of job market cognitions: The employment opportunity index (EOI). *Journal of Applied Psychology, 90,* 335–349.

Gullason, E. T. (1999). The stability pattern of sheepskin effects and its implications for the human capital theory-screening hypothesis debate. *Eastern Economic Journal, 25,* 141–149.

Guzzo, R. A., Noonan, K. A., & Elron, E. (1994). Expatriate managers and the psychological contract. *Journal of Applied Psychology, 79,* 617–626.

Hom, P., Caranikas-Walker, F., Prussia, G., & Griffeth, R. (1992). A meta-analytical structural equations analysis of a model of employee turnover. *Journal of Applied Psychology, 77,* 890–909.

Hom, P. W., & Griffeth, R. (1991). A structural equations modeling test of a turnover theory: Cross-sectional and longitudinal analysis. *Journal of Applied Psychology, 76,* 350–366.

Hom, P. W., & Griffeth, R. (1995). *Employee turnover.* Cincinnati, OH: South-Western.

Hom, P., Griffeth, R., & Sellaro, L. (1994). The validity of Mobley's (1977) model of employee turnover. *Organizational Behavior and Human Performance, 34,* 141–174.

Hom, P. W., & Kinicki, A. J. (2001). Toward a greater understanding of how dissatisfaction drives employee turnover. *Academy of Management Journal, 44,* 975–987.

Huselid, M. A. (1995). Impact of human resource management practices on turnover, productivity, and corporate financial performance. *Academy of Management Journal, 38,* 635–672.

Kirschenbaum, A., & Mano-Negrin, R. (1999). Underlying labor market dimensions of "opportunities": The case of employee turnover. *Human Relations, 52,* 1233–1255.

Krueger, A., & Rouse, C. (1998). The effects of workplace education on earnings, turnover, and job performance. *Journal of Labor Economics, 16,* 61–94.

Lee, T. W., & Maurer, S. D. (1997). The retention of knowledge workers with the unfolding model of voluntary turnover. *Human Resource Management Review, 7,* 247–275.

Lee, T. W., & Mitchell, T. R. (1994). An alternative approach: The unfolding model of voluntary employee turnover. *Academy of Management Review, 19,* 51–89.

Lee, T. W., Mitchell, T. R., Holton, B. C., McDaniel, L. S., & Hill, J. W. (1999). The unfolding model of voluntary turnover: A replication and extension. *Academy of Management Journal, 42,* 450–462.

Lee, T. W., Mitchell, T. R., Sablynski, C. J., Burton, J. P., & Holtom, B. C. (2004). The effects of job embeddedness on organizational citizenship, job performance, vocational absences, and voluntary turnover. *Academy of Management Journal, 47,* 711–722.

Lee, T. W., Mitchell, T. R., Wise, L., & Fireman, S. (1996). An unfolding model of voluntary employee turnover. *Academy of Management Journal, 39,* 5–36.

Liu, P. W. (1986). Human capital, job matching and earnings growth between jobs: An empirical analysis. *Applied Economics, 18,* 1135–1147.

Loewenstein, M., & Spletzer, J. (1999). General and specific training: Evidence and implications. *Journal of Human Resources, 34,* 710–733.

Lynch, L. (1991). The role of off-the-job vs. on-the-job training for the mobility of women workers. *American Economic Review, 81,* 299–312.

March, J. G., & Simon, H. A. (1958). *Organizations.* Hoboken, NJ: Wiley.

Meisler, A. (2004). A matter of degrees. *Workforce Management, 83,* 32–38

Meyer, J. P., & Smith, C. (2000). HRM practices and organizational commitment: Test of a mediation model. *Canadian Journal of Administrative Sciences, 17,* 319–331.

Mincer, J. (1988). *Job Training, wage growth, and labor turnover.* NBER working paper no. 2690. Cambridge, MA: National Bureau of Economic Research.

Mitchell, T. R., Holtom, B. C., Lee, T. W., Sablynski, C. J., & Erez, M. (2001). Why people stay: Using job embeddedness to predict voluntary turnover. *Academy of Management Journal, 44,* 1102–1121.

Mobley, W. H. (1977). Intermediate linkages in the relationship between job satisfaction and employee turnover. *Journal of Applied Psychology, 62,* 237–240.

Mobley, W., Griffeth, R., Hand, H., & Meglino, B. (1979). Review and conceptual analysis of the employee turnover process. *Psychological Bulletin, 86,* 493–522.

National Center for Educational Statistics. (1996). *Employer aid for postsecondary education.* Washington, DC: U.S. Department of Education.

Noe, R., & Wilk, S. (1993). Investigation of the factors that influence employees' participation in development activities. *Journal of Applied Psychology, 78,* 291–302.

Noe, R., Wilk, S., Mullen, E., & Wanek, J. (1997). Employee development: Issues in construct definition and investigation of antecedents. In J. Ford (Ed.), *Improving training effectiveness in work organizations* (pp. 153–189). Mahwah, NJ: Erlbaum.

Nordhaug, O. (1989). Reward functions of personnel training. *Human Relations, 42,* 373–388.

Pergamit, M., & Veum, J. (1999). What is a promotion? *Industrial and Labor Relations Review, 52,* 581–601.

Rhoades, L., & Eisenberger, R. (2002). Perceived organizational support: A review of the literature. *Journal of Applied Psychology, 87,* 698–714.

Society for Human Resource Management. *2004 benefits.* Alexandria, VA: Author.

Spence, M. (1973). Job market signaling. *Quarterly Journal of Economics, 90,* 225–243.

Spilerman, S., & Lunde, T. (1991). Features of educational attainment and promotion prospects. *American Journal of Sociology, 97,* 689–720.

Steers, R., & Mowday, R. (1981). Employee turnover and post-decision justification. In L. L. Cummings & B. M. Staw (Eds.), *Research in organizational behavior* (pp. 235–272). Greenwich, CT: JAI Press.

Swanson, R. A. (2001). *Assessing the financial benefits of human resource development.* Cambridge, MA: Perseus.

Tansky, J., & Cohen, D. (2001). The relationship between organizational support, employee development, and organizational commitment: An empirical study. *Human Resource Development Quarterly, 12,* 285–300.

Thorsteinson, T. J. (2003). Job attitudes of part-time vs. full-time workers: A meta-analytic review. *Journal of Occupational and Organizational Psychology, 76,* 151–178.

Trevor, C. (2001). Interactions among actual ease-of-movement determinants and job satisfaction in prediction of voluntary turnover. *Academy of Management Journal, 44,* 621–638.

Tsui, A., Pearce, J., Porter, L., & Tripoli, A. (1997). Alternative approaches to the employee-organization relationship: Does investment in employees pay off? *Academy of Management Journal, 40,* 1089–1121.

Vandenberg, R. J., Richardson, H. A., & Eastman, L. J. (1999). The impact of high involvement work processes on organizational effectiveness. *Group and Organization Management, 24,* 300–339.

Veum, J. R. (1999). Training, wages, and the human capital model. *Southern Economic Journal, 65,* 526–538.

Wayne, S. J., Shore, L. M., & Liden, R. C. (1997). Perceived organizational support and leader-member exchange: A social exchange perspective. *Academy of Management Journal, 40,* 82–111.

Marshall Pattie is a doctoral candidate in the Department of Management, College of Business Administration, University of Texas at Arlington.

George S. Benson is an assistant professor in the Department of Management, College of Business Administration, University of Texas at Arlington.

Yehuda Baruch is a professor in the School of Management, University of East Anglia, Norwich, England.

Participation in Management Training in a Transitioning Context: A Case of China

Jia Wang, Greg G. Wang

This phenomenological study explores critical issues related to participation in human resource development (HRD) interventions. Specifically focusing on master of business administration (M.B.A.) training programs in China, we conducted in-depth individual interviews with twelve middle-level managers to understand their perceptions and experience of this academic program during the country's recent transitional period. The findings suggest that HRD participation in a specific transitioning cultural context may present features that have not been explored by previous learning participation studies in either HRD or adult education. In the light of the transitioning nature of the Chinese cultural context, we derived three propositions for future research on HRD learning participation. Practical implications for learning participation are also drawn based on the results of the study.

Learning participation is a multidimensional decision process involving program selection, engagement, and completion of a learning activity by a given employee in organizational settings (Wang & Wang, 2004). Employee participation in learning interventions has significant implications for organizational management as well as theory building in human resource development (HRD). To be effective and achieve their intended organizational outcomes, HRD learning interventions depend on employees' full participation and engagement.

Note: We express our appreciation to four anonymous reviewers and the editors, Tim Hatcher and Tonette Rocco, for their helpful comments and critiques during two rounds of reviews. An earlier version of this article was presented at the 2005 Academy of HRD International Research Conference at Estes Park, Colorado.

However, unlike its counterpart in adult education research, employee participation in HRD interventions has received limited attention from researchers except a few empirical studies in management and industry and organization (I/O) psychology literature (Hicks & Klimoski, 1987; Maurer & Tarulli, 1994; Noe & Wilk, 1993). As a result, there is only sparse literature to help us understand why employees participate in HRD interventions and what their experience feels like and means to them.

This study explores learning participation from a management development (MD) perspective for two reasons. First, MD is a core component of HRD (Brewster, 2004). In fact, continuing radical environmental and organizational changes have precipitated a search for a more strategic and integrated model of developing individuals who lead and manage organizations (Garavan, Barnicle, & O'Suilleabhain, 1999). Within this changing context, MD is viewed as a major driver and facilitator of change and adaptation (Beddowes, 1994; Storey, 1989a, 1989b) and the key to organizational renewal (McClelland, 1994). Second, while the importance of MD to organizational effectiveness and success is increasingly recognized (Brewster, 2004; Mabey, 2004; Peteraf, 1993; Wright, Dunford, & Snell, 2001; Youndt, Scott, Dean, & Lepak, 1996), considerable debate exists among academics and practitioners on the value and impact of MD interventions, as reported by a number of empirical studies (Luoma, 2005; Meldrum & Atkinson, 1998; Winterton & Winterton, 1997).

Problem: The Case of China

This study is situated in the context of the People's Republic of China. China presents a unique case for study because MD, as a newly emerged phenomenon, is not only positioned in complex historical, economic, organizational, and cultural contexts but is operating with a backdrop of ongoing turbulence, major transformations, and dramatic change. The past two decades have witnessed China's transition in every aspect of society. Such transitions have had a fundamental impact on Chinese managers. China's economic and enterprise reforms, for example, have caused millions of China's bureaucratic administrators to become strategic decision makers instead (Branine, 1996). In fact, their managerial knowledge is increasingly inadequate and obsolete in this situation (Newell, 1999). In addition, China's global development initiatives (for example, its open door policies and membership in the World Trade Organization) have exposed Chinese managers to tougher global competition and higher international standards of performance and competencies (Wang & Wang, 2006). In the light of these profound changes, how to attract and develop high-quality managers has become not only a pressing issue among domestic organizations (Li, 2003; Wang, 2002), but also a constant and relentless pursuit by many multinational corporations (MNCs) operating in the country (Boston Consulting & Wharton School, 2004). The paucity of management resources is now widely recognized as a major obstacle to China's further development (Bu & Mitchell, 1992; Frazer, 1999; Newell, 1999; Wang, 1999, 2002).

In response to the enormous demand for competent managers, management education and development have been given top priority and have gained increasing prominence among Chinese universities, government agencies, and industrial organizations. Among various MD initiatives, the M.B.A. education/training has been actively promoted by the central government and widely adopted by organizations as a key intervention for developing high-quality managers in China (Branine, 2005; Cheng, 2000; Shi, 2000; Wang & Wang, 2006). The focus of this study is to explore managers' experiences of participating in M.B.A. programs.

Because management development was not emphasized until the early 1980s (Newell, 1999; Wright, Szeto, & Cheng, 2002), much of the current knowledge base for China M.B.A. programs has been imported from the West (Newell, 1999; Shi, 2000). Given that, there is a strong sense that China's M.B.A. programs are not meeting the needs and expectations of both Chinese managers and organizational environments in spite of the extensive demand for this type of intervention. The literature has regularly reported problems associated with both domestic and imported M.B.A. programs (Frazer, 1999; Johnstone, 1997; Lau & Roffey, 2002; Newell, 1999; Shi, 2000; Zhang, Yang, & Zhang, 2002; Fan, 1998). Nevertheless, M.B.A. training programs perhaps remain the most popular choice of Chinese managers who want to upgrade their managerial competencies (Cheng, 2000). Due to the relatively short history and emerging nature of China's M.B.A. training, as well as the paucity of research in these areas (Frazer, 1999; Lau & Roffey, 2002), we have only limited knowledge about China and the M.B.A.: its nature, value, impact, and challenges. Without a better understanding, it will be difficult to fully understand why managers continue to favor this type of training in spite of the numerous problems that have been reported. It will also be unlikely that international HRD professionals will be able to select and design effective MD interventions to prepare Chinese managers for the transitional period.

Purpose and Significance

Given the emerging nature and continuing popularity of the M.B.A. as a core HRD intervention for developing managers in China's transitioning context, our goal for this study was to capture and describe how middle managers experience their participation in M.B.A. training—in other words, how they perceive the experience, describe it, feel about it, judge it, remember it, make sense of it, and talk about it with others. We focused on middle managers because they have traditionally received much less attention as subjects of analysis compared to senior managers, even in Western management research (Livian & Burgoyne, 1997). The primary research question was, What is the essence of middle managers' experience of participating in an M.B.A. training program in China? Two subquestions were formulated to explore and investigate this phenomenon:

- What makes middle managers decide to participate in an M.B.A. training program in China in its transition?
- How do middle managers perceive and describe their experience of participating in an M.B.A. training program in the transitional context?

Answers to these research questions are important. First, given the importance of China in the global economy and high-impact changes occurring at all levels, the country offers a solid ground for conducting research on emerging HRD-related phenomena. In fact, China is a case in which HRD professionals have to interact with dynamic transitional environments characterized by revitalizing, ongoing large-scale changes and a high level of ambiguity and uncertainty. This context has presented tremendous challenges for HRD practitioners in developing quality managers (Branine, 2005). The findings from this study may both shed light on crucial aspects of HRD learning participation in general and allow HRD professionals to get a better grasp of the unique and complicated issues facing Chinese middle managers in particular. With greater knowledge, HRD professionals may be better positioned to design and implement management development programs that are suitable and applicable to the Chinese organizational context and thus more likely to have a positive impact on managers and organizations.

Second, unlike most previous studies on adult learning participation that have primarily adopted quantitative approaches (Livingston, 1999; O'Connell, 1999; Sargant, 2000; Wang & Wang, 2004), this study used the phenomenological methodology to acquire an emic perspective (Merriam, 2001). The rich data collected, even on a small scale, can promote a more comprehensive understanding of human experiences, the central phenomenon under investigation. The deeper insights generated from the study may also lay the foundation on which new theory can be derived, thus contributing to HRD theory building. Furthermore, given the limited research on Chinese management development and HRD, this study may add much-needed additional knowledge to the existing literature. Finally, with a focus on a developing transitional country, the findings may also serve as a reference point for HRD professionals who work in other countries experiencing similar socioeconomic transitions.

Theoretical Perspectives

This section discusses theoretical perspectives guiding the study. The literature on adult and HRD learning participation provides a general framework for understanding why managers participate in learning and development activities. Studies on management education and training offer insight into unique issues facing management training and development in China and the specific national context this study is grounded in.

Research on Adult Learning Participation. Adult learning participation theories are linked to motivation theories (Wang & Wang, 2004). The study on motivation for participation was initiated by Houle (1961), who defined three categories of learning motivation: goal oriented, activity oriented, and learning oriented. This typology was refined by others, including Sheffield (1964), Burgess (1971), Boshier (1971), and Morstein and Smart (1974). Collectively and progressively, Houle's adult learning motivation typology was expanded to include six motivators: social relationships, external expectations, social welfare, professional advancement, escape and stimulation, and cognitive interest.

Along with learning motivational research, a number of models were developed to explain adult participation in learning activities. For example, Miller (1967) combined the motivational needs hierarchy of Maslow (1954) with the force-field theory of Lewin (1947) and identified positive and negative forces influencing adult learners' participation based on socioeconomic status. Similarly, Boshier (1973) built a congruence model to explain participation in terms of the interaction between personal and social factors. Later, Rubenson (1977) proposed an expectancy-valence model to address the socialization and structural dimensions of adult learners. Other models were also constructed to address different dimensions relevant to participation, such as Darkenwald and Merriam's psychosocial interaction model (1982), Henry and Basile's decision model (1994), and Cross's chain-of-response model (1981). Wang and Wang (2004) provided a more detailed review on studies related to adult learning participation.

Although these concepts and models need further testing, they point to a major issue for adult learning participation: most adults are motivated by intrinsic factors for learning participation rather than extrinsic ones. In fact, one of the purposes of adult learning participation research was to identify the interaction among intrinsic motivating variables influencing participation and assist public policymakers in designing national, local, or community-based adult education programs and policies (Merriam & Caffarella, 1999).

HRD-Related Research on Learning Participation. Unlike adult education research, which has seen a number of theories and models developed, research on learning participation in HRD interventions is sparse despite several independent empirical investigations (Wang & Wang, 2004). In fact, the issue of learning participation in HRD interventions was not addressed much in the literature until the late 1980s.

Perhaps the first relevant empirical study was conducted by Hicks and Klimoski in 1987. The study examined the relationship between employees' degree of choice when selecting a learning program and the learning outcome. Using a similar experimental design, Baldwin, Magjuka, and Lother (1991) investigated the effects of trainee choice of participation on subsequent motivation and learning. They highlighted the provision of choice as a motivation strategy in training contexts. Noe and Wilk (1993) explored factors influencing employees' participation in learning programs, including self-efficacy and work environment perceptions on development activities as mediated by learning attitudes and perceptions of development needs. They observed that motivation to learn was an important attitudinal variable that had a significant and positive influence on different outcomes related to learning activities. Maurer and Tarulli (1994) also examined the relationship between interest and participation in voluntary learning activities and three groups of constructs among nonmanagement employees: perceived environment, perceived incentive and outcome, and person variables. The study revealed that individual characteristics such as job involvement, self-efficacy, beliefs about the need for skill development, and career insight accounted for the most variance in learning participation.

Most recently, Wang and Wang (2004) conducted a comprehensive review on learning participation in HRD and other related fields, including adult education, management, and industry and organization psychology. Analyzing findings of the research deductively, the study proposed a holistic framework that integrates key factors affecting individual participation in HRD learning activities. Specifically, three clusters of factors were identified: individual, learning process, and organization. These clusters are mediated by environmental factors. For the individual cluster, nine elements were found to influence participation: motivation, self-efficacy, organization membership, personal characteristics, learning style, perceived learning benefits, perceived benefits, learning technology orientation, and individual cultural orientation. In addition, Wang and Wang (2004) posited six factors critical in determining learners' motivation and persistence during the learning process: needs assessment, learning subject, instructional design, delivery platforms, instructor, and technology-based learning environment. Regarding the organization cluster, issues such as organization context, organization policies and regulations, and work content are highlighted. Macroenvironmental factors such as economic conditions and uncontrollable external factors are also included in the framework, although their impact on learning has been noted to vary depending on specific situations.

The review of the literature revealed that research on learning participation in adult education and HRD has been conducted on isolated and separate fronts, although these two fields are claimed to be closely related (Yang, 2004). The lack of interconnectedness may be partially explained by the differences in learning participation identified by Wang and Wang (2004): origin of the decision, degree of environmental influences, motivational sources, and investment sources. Furthermore, most adult learning participation studies have been conducted in developed countries such as the United Kingdom (Sargant, 2000), Canada (Livingstone, 1999), and member countries of the Organization for Economic Cooperation and Development in comparison to Australia and the U.S. (O'Connell, 1999). There are very few similar efforts for developing countries, especially those in a transitional economic context. For studies on adult learning participation focusing on developing countries, studies are confined to adult basic education (Muiru & Mukuria, 2005), adult English as a Second Language programs (Skilton-Sylvester, 2002), or literacy training (Cutz & Chandler, 2000). Findings of these studies can hardly assist HRD professionals in operating effectively in these countries, providing no implications on HRD learning participation.

Management Training and Development in China. The prosperity of management development closely follows the rise and fall of the national economy (Wang, He, & Yu, 2003). In a transitioning economy like China, management training and development has been a roller-coaster ride of rise, fall, and rise again (Wang et al., 2003). Due to the serious shortfall of highly skilled management personnel (Bu & Mitchell, 1992; Child, 1994), management education and training have been given top priority and have been widely adopted by the central government and organizations as a core strategy for enhancing organizational and individual effectiveness (Branine, 1996, 2005; Wang, 1999). This is evidenced by efforts to develop related national policies, establish professional management systems, promote management training, and collaborate with Western countries (Wang & Wang, 2006).

Management training in China has taken various forms. Frazer (1999) identified five frequently employed formats: in-house training, regional training centers, local outsourced training, overseas work-study programs, and local university M.B.A. programs. Wang (1999) reported four means: on-the-job technical training programs, formal school-based programs (for example, academic programs in economics and management), M.B.A. programs, and on-the-job training. In terms of developing local managers in foreign companies in China, Zhao (2005) found that both formal and informal training had been provided.

Formal M.B.A. programs have been booming since the 1990s and have become perhaps the most popular avenue for developing managerial capacities (Branine, 2005; Cheng, 2000). However, the quality of the M.B.A. programs offered by Chinese universities has remained a subject of debate. Given its Western roots, particularly the United States, the China M.B.A. has faced the challenge of skills development in the global context and adaptation of Western materials to Chinese organizations. Researchers have raised serious concerns about problems that may be caused by different instructional approaches to management training between China and the West, as well as different cultural and historical roots (Boisot & Fiol, 1987; Wang et al., 2003). This has raised another concern about the relevance of the M.B.A. qualification in China. Chinese enterprises, particularly those in the state-owned enterprise (SOE) sector, tend to resist employing M.B.A. graduates who are predisposed to change long-established management practices. Nonetheless, "M.B.A. fever" (Rosen, 2004) has shown little sign of abating in China.

Method

In this study, our goal was to capture and describe how middle managers perceive, describe, and make sense of their experience with the M.B.A. program they participated in. This purpose, along with the emerging nature and continuing popularity of M.B.A. programs in China, makes phenomenology an appropriate approach to adopt. Through phenomenological inquiry, we sought to understand "the very nature of a phenomenon" (Van Manen, 1990, p. 10), learning participation, and reveal more fully "the essences and meanings of human experience" (Moustakas, 1994, p. 105) as perceived by the subjects (van der Mescht, 1999): Chinese middle managers.

Researchers' Assumptions. Two basic assumptions were embedded in this study. First, our review of the literature led us to believe that China's M.B.A. programs are facing a serious dilemma. On one hand, M.B.A. training has been actively promoted and widely used as one of the most popular interventions for developing quality managers in China. In fact, there is little sign to show the abating of "M.B.A. fever" among Chinese managers. On the other hand, numerous problems have found to be associated with China's M.B.A. programs, such as cultural discrepancy (Fan, 1998; Lau & Roffey, 2002; Newell, 1999), causing serious concern about the effectiveness of and further investment in this type of study (Cheng, 2000). Our interest in studying the M.B.A. participation phenomenon stemmed from this dilemma.

Second, as researchers, we feel that it is imperative to explain our own experiences and background that made us both insiders and outsiders of the study because these positions may have been inadvertently interjected into the findings. Both of us received formal M.B.A. and HRD training from Western programs. These educational experiences have shaped who we are and what we believe. Hence, although we may share the common vocabulary of M.B.A. with the participants, we are likely to embrace different perspectives. Our prior understanding of China M.B.A. programs is largely built on the review of literature and conversation in informal settings during this and other research trips to China, although the second author had some experience with China M.B.A. graduates when working as an HRD expatriate at a multinational corporation's China operations. In addition, both of us have been living outside China for over ten years and have worked primarily in a Western setting; therefore, the assumptions we hold about China M.B.A. programs and organizations may not accurately reflect the reality. In that sense, we became outsiders and may not have captured the full meaning of managers' perceptions and experience through our own interpretation, even though we share the same language with the participants.

Highly aware of our own backgrounds, we made a conscious effort during the research process to bracket (Moustakas, 1994) our preconceived notions about M.B.A. participation in China. In order to arrive at an unprejudiced description of the essence of the topic under study, we constantly reflected on our own presuppositions and critically analyzed them against the participants' experiences. Furthermore, we approached the participants without asking leading questions, suspended our own judgment, and remained as open and receptive as possible to new understanding and discovery.

Participant Selection. We selected the research site based on convenience sampling (Patton, 2002). We identified a major university located in southwestern China through a personal contact, who served as the M.B.A. program director when the study was initiated. Nationally reputed, the university is one of the first providers of formal M.B.A. training programs in China. The fact that one of us comes from this region also ensured easy access to the university and convenience in approaching the participants.

For participant recruitment, we used criterion sampling (Patton, 2002). First, participants must have successfully completed a formal M.B.A. training program. By going through the program, the participants had fully experienced it so that they could better articulate their thoughts (Colaizzi, 1978). Second, participants must have received the M.B.A. within the past five years, which would allow sufficient time for them to complete the program and reflect on the experience (Cheng, 2000). Third, participants must be middle managers since this group has traditionally received much less attention as subjects of analysis compared to senior managers (Livian & Burgoyne, 1997), and it is also a monumental task for China to bring millions of managers up to speed in a very short period (Wang & Wang, 2006). At the same time, participants must be working in domestic organizations that had gone through transformation from being state owned to representing mixed ownership. This criterion put participants in the background of the transitioning context we were particularly interested in.

The resulting participant pool consisted of twelve middle managers (five females and seven males) between ages thirty-five and fifty-five. They represented five domestic enterprises and six functions: human resource management, business development, asset management, finance and accounting, operations management, and public relations. All twelve had completed the M.B.A. program at least a year ago when they participated in this study.

We interviewed the twelve managers following recommendations in the literature (Creswell, 1998; Guest, Bunce, & Johnson, 2006). Recruitment was primarily through our contact, the M.B.A. program director, and completed prior to the first author's seven-week research trip to China. Once the program director identified a potential candidate, she sent the person a cover letter that we had prepared in Chinese explaining the study in detail and the requirements for participating in it. If the participant agreed, we approached him or her with an initial e-mail. A formal informed-consent letter in Chinese was then presented to the participant for subsequent data collection. Prior to the interview, the researcher reviewed the consent form with each participant to ensure he or she fully understood the nature of the study, expectations of participation, and his or her rights as a participant. The interview proceeded after the consent form was signed. For confidentiality, all identifying data were removed, and each participant was assigned a number (1–12) in the original data transcripts and the report of the findings.

Data Collection. We collected data primarily through "in-depth, phenomenologically based interviewing" (Seidman, 1991, p. 9), a method deemed most effective in allowing researchers to enter into a person's perspective and uncover his or her thoughts and feelings (Patton, 2002). All interviews were conducted face-to-face in the individual manager's office by the first author and were audiotaped. There were two rounds with each participant. The first lasted between sixty and ninety minutes, followed by a second round of follow-up interviews, lasting thirty-five to forty-five minutes, to clarify issues and probe for further questions. Since none of the managers felt comfortable speaking English, all interviews were in Mandarin Chinese, the native language shared by the twelve participants and the researchers.

To make the best use of the limited time available for each interview and obtain "more systematic and comprehensive" information from different participants (Patton, 2002, p. 343), we developed an interview guide. It consisted of four broad, semistructured, open-ended questions around two subject areas: (1) experiences that led managers to choose to participate in M.B.A. training in the first place and (2) the meaning of participation as perceived by the individual managers. Each interview began with two questions: "Tell me what made you consider M.B.A. training in the first place." "How would you describe the M.B.A. program you experienced? In other words, what was this experience like?" Answers to these questions helped us gain the participants' perspective of the phenomenon in the broad sense. Then the managers were asked to "describe a situation or think about a time when you were able to effectively engage in learning and what that experience meant to you," and to "tell me a time when it was difficult to participate in learning and how did you feel about it." These two topics were developed to generate deeper insight into the experience itself. We followed the semistructured and open-ended interviewing format while covering a list of research topics; we also remained flexible and receptive to participants' emergent responses (Kvale, 1996).

Data Analysis. To analyze the interview data, we used the constant comparative method developed by Glaser and Strauss (1967). The analysis was performed in three phases:

• Phase One. We transcribed the audiotaped interviews verbatim in Chinese. For convenience in coding, we merged two rounds of interviews with each participant into one document. The transcripts were organized in table format with two columns: one for transcripts and one for our notes. We read the interview data several times for better understanding and additional sorting. We then identified meaningful segments of data (a phrase, sentence, and paragraph) for initial categorizing and coding. Whenever possible, we coded these phrases or sentences using emic codes (Strauss, 1987) or codes taken verbatim from the transcripts. We highlighted key quotes, examples, and stories that were particularly demonstrative or representative of emerging themes. The column for notes was used to synthesize what the participants were saying and record our initial interpretations, hunches, and reflections. At this stage, we reviewed six sets of interview data. Both single-case and cross-case in-depth analyses were conducted with these sets of data, resulting in the development of twelve initial coding categories, such as reasons for participation, perceived value of M.B.A. programs, challenges the managers experienced during learning, significant learning experiences, significant learning transfer experienced, and perceived learning impact.

• Phase Two. The second stage of data analysis involved analyzing and coding the remaining six interviews. As each was coded, the twelve coding categories identified earlier were redefined and reduced to six categories. A synthesis of the participants' description, based on single-case analysis, was developed in the form of a summary sheet for each interview analyzed. These summary sheets were sent to participants for their feedback. In addition, six summary tables were created to demonstrate cross-case analysis, each centering on one major coding category defined up to this stage.

• Phase Three. We analyzed the single-case summary sheets based on the feedback received from participants, and adjusted, reconceptualized, and further refined the codes into three major categories that we considered best captured the meanings of the participants' experiences. Presented in the following sections were major themes clustered into three broad categories: decisional context, formulated meanings of learning participation, and learning beyond participation.

It is worth noting that we performed the data analysis separately from each other. In other words, each of us initially reviewed and coded the transcripts simultaneously but independently. Then we met and compared out analysis results. We discussed each code and theme identified. When we differed, we discussed and negotiated until we reached common agreement. For example, we had different views regarding whether the impact of the learning experience should be considered part of participation. After discussions, we reached a mutual understanding that the learning impact, although beyond participation in a time-series view, influenced how the participants had viewed their experience as a whole. Therefore, we agreed that findings in this area should be reported.

Equally important to note is that we conducted all of the analysis in Chinese to avoid losing any meaning in translation. The summary sheets and tables were developed in Chinese so that participants could read them and provide feedback. While writing in English, we translated, from Chinese into English, only the major themes and direct quotes we chose to present in this article. As researchers, we both felt comfortable conducting the study bilingually for several reasons. First, as native Chinese speakers, we both have studied and worked in English-speaking countries for a minimum of ten years and therefore have good command of English. Second, with our M.B.A. and economics backgrounds, we were familiar with the content being studied. Third, we had prior research experience in both Chinese and English and had also published our research in both languages. Although we consider ourselves competent in conducting studies bilingually, we nevertheless invited a bilingual university faculty member who is also an expatriate to check the accuracy of our translation. The multiple strategies we used sought to strengthen the credibility of the findings.

Findings

The constant comparative analysis elicited multiple themes that answered the primary research question and the two subquestions. These themes were clustered into two broad coding categories: decisional context and formulated meanings of learning participation. The former provides an understanding of the broad context in which the participation decision was made; the latter presents deeper insights into the meaning of participation as perceived, described, and interpreted by the twelve managers interviewed. We also present in this section some unexpected findings, which we define broadly as "learning beyond participation." Although seemingly irrelevant due to its focus on the learning impact, this experience was articulated as being significant in that it shaped and influenced the way the managers perceived and made sense of their overall participation experience. Therefore, although it was not part of the original research agenda, we report it as an integral component of the participation experiences. The coding categories and major themes are depicted in Table 1 and reported in detail with direct quotes and illustrative examples.

Decisional Context. Because learning participation starts with program selection (Wang & Wang, 2004), we asked the twelve managers to describe their reason for choosing an M.B.A. program. Various issues were revealed and informed us of the context in which a participation decision was made. Among them, five themes were prominent. We discuss them in order of importance: (1) environmental changes, (2) a need to develop management competency, (3) perceptions of the M.B.A., (4) commitment to work, and (5) cultural orientation.

Environmental Change. The rapidly changing environments in China were reported by all the managers to be the first and most significant driving force for pursuing an M.B.A. The managers articulated change from two aspects: economic reforms and increased competition. Manager 8 put it this way: "China has changed so much during the past twenty years. Look at the free market system, shareholding enterprises, joint ventures, just to name a few. How much do we know about them?" Building on this view, Manager 1 emphasized, "The rapid development of Chinese society has made it essential for me to keep enriching and improving myself with new knowledge in order to meet the

Table 1. Summary of Major Findings

Coding Category	Major Themes
Decisional context	Environmental change Need for developing management competency Perceptions of M.B.A. Commitment to work Cultural orientation
Formulated meanings of learning participation	Overall participation experience: • valuable, • beneficial, • rewarding, and • significant Learning is meaningful when • linked to real life and • related to day-to-day practice Learning is challenging when • out of touch with Chinese context and • delivered by unqualified instructors
Learning beyond participation	Impact on individuals Impact on organizations: • shared knowledge • improved communication

demand for high quality managers." Manager 2 reverberated further, "Under the new market economy, we are facing more new challenges than ever. I found it no longer enough to lead a division solely based on personal experiences and intuition. I must recharge myself with updated information."

Another aspect of change was described as increased competition brought about by China's global development effort and intensified globalization. In fact, competition was highlighted by more than half of the managers as a critical issue influencing their participation decisions. Manager 3 commented, "China's open door policies exposed all of us to the global community; we are no longer a closed society." Manager 8 articulated a reason for his participation decision: "Back several years ago when I was a government official, I didn't even think about competition. Now I have to compete not only against my Chinese counterparts, but also Western managers who work in China such as in joint ventures. To me, this is a huge change and challenge."

Need for Developing Management Competency. Within the broader changing context, the twelve managers shared a serious concern about not being able to meet new management requirements. These managers recognized that their existing management knowledge and skills appeared to be outdated or inadequate under China's new economic and enterprise systems. Therefore, filling knowledge gaps and skill discrepancies became a top priority for them to stay competitive in their organization. According to these managers, the need for building management competency was prompted directly by the environmental change. Manager 2 shared his experience in this regard: "I worked as an administrator in one of the largest state-owned TV plants for seven years, but I wasn't happy there, so I quit my job and joined my current company. Since then I have been exposed to both opportunities and challenges. While I feel excited, I am also concerned because I realize that the knowledge I acquired from the university ten years ago is no longer adequate in my current management position. That's really scary."

Manager 11 echoed, "I used to work for the government as an official; now I'm a manager in a shareholding enterprise. These are very different roles. It took me a long time just to figure out how to become a real manager and what a typical manager does on a daily basis. Learning has become a must, not a matter of choice."

Perceptions of M.B.A. The managers' choice of an M.B.A. over other types of MD interventions available was manifested through their perceptions of the M.B.A. program itself. Specifically, the participants highlighted the popularity of the degree, the training, and perceived values associated with M.B.A. programs.

First, as a majority of the managers indicated, the fact that the M.B.A. was being so actively marketed by the central government contributed to the increasing popularity of this type of training. This point was best demonstrated by Manager 1: "M.B.A. has been so popular in our country that it has almost become a required credential or qualification for those seeking a managerial position." Indeed, the prominence of the degree, although not explicated by the managers as the top reason for their pursuing it, proved to have a significant influence on their decision-making process.

Second, the managers offered their views of the M.B.A. with reference to other types of managerial programs in China. They distinguished the M.B.A. as (1) focusing strongly on application, (2) providing systematic and comprehensive management knowledge, (3) adopting untraditional approaches to teaching and learning, and (4) having a Western origin. According to these managers, it was the combination of these unique characteristics that led them to choose this path.

Finally, several managers pointed out the values they perceived to be associated with the M.B.A. degree. Three aspects stood out: higher social status, increased career opportunities, and opportunity for social networks. Although hardly illustrating it as a motivator for their participation, three of the managers underscored the higher social status related to the M.B.A. degree as perceived by the general public. Manager 4's remark was the most straightforward: "An M.B.A. sounds impressive; it impresses people. The title sounds like, 'smart businessperson.' I think lots of people see that, especially people who are not formally educated. I think they are very impressed by formal education, M.B.A., Ph.D. or anything that you put an initial on . . . just makes you a little untouchable."

Another benefit of M.B.A. was referred to by the managers as increased career development opportunities. Manager 4 made an interesting point: "I would be a schoolteacher if I had to. But I was hoping that a four-year undergraduate business degree would open doors, and it did. So I figured if a four-year degree opened as many doors as it did, then another two-year M.B.A. degree would open more doors."

The managers also indicated that participating in an M.B.A. program was likely to create the opportunity for social networks. Being part of a business community where relationship, or *guanxi,* means almost everything (Wright et al., 2002), half of the managers in the study described the M.B.A. as a great way for them to get acquainted with other professionals who were perceived as valuable resources. Manager 1 made a claim that "relationship (*guanxi*) is the first productive resource." Therefore, it was not surprising that quite a few managers interviewed chose to participate in M.B.A. education with an expectation of building a professional *guanxi* network: "Most people in the M.B.A. program are from business and industry. We share the same language and similar experiences so that we can help one another academically and professionally. To me, they are the most valuable assets," said Manager 4. Manager 6 said that she is "a wife, mother, and a career woman. My life is basically split between office and home. I have little time for socialization and networks. Taking M.B.A. courses provided me a perfect opportunity to make new friends, particularly with other professional managers."

Commitment to Work. Apart from the strong desire for personal development, the managers also exhibited a high level of work commitment. For instance, Manager 3 described himself this way: "I am a self-motivated person. Whatever job I do, I always try to do it well, no matter whether I like it or not." Similarly, Manager 7 stated, "My boss can count on me for everything. I am a person with a strong sense of responsibility not only for the tasks delegated to me, but also for the company I work for." Manager 8 simply said, "One thing I have learned throughout the years is you either do it well or not do it at all." Indeed, these managers suggested that it was this commitment and work attitude that had driven them to learn how to provide the best performance at work.

Cultural Orientation. Cultural orientation was apparent at both individual and organizational levels. Individually, some managers made remarks that were reflective of a typical Chinese cultural orientation, commonly known as *da-nan-zi-zhu-yi,* meaning, paternalistic ways of thinking and behaving. Manager 1 explained his situation with a big laugh: "My wife had already gotten a master's degree at that time, and I had only a bachelor's degree. As husband, how can I lag behind her? I know this sounds like a joke, but it's true!" Manager 5 supported this view by stating that his wife's pursuit of an M.B.A. degree had made him feel insecure as the head of the family. Although this orientation was not representative of all the managers interviewed, it holds much truth in Chinese culture, in which men are often expected to do more professionally than women.

At the organizational level, three managers defined their organizational culture as learning oriented. All three worked for a large shareholding company that claimed that its vision was to become a learning organization.

Therefore, the company invested heavily in training each year and was sponsoring these three managers for their M.B.A. Other managers reported somewhat similar situations in their organizations. For instance, in the organization where Managers 11 and 12 worked, a series of training policies was formulated and implemented to encourage employees to engage in various learning activities. According to the twelve managers, the five shareholding enterprises they represented were all learning oriented to various degrees.

Formulated Meanings of Learning Participation. When asked to describe a situation or think about a time when they were able to effectively engage in learning and explain what that experience meant to them, the managers reported thirty-five critical incidents that had occurred during their M.B.A. studies and after returning to the workplace. Three themes captured the essence of learning experiences during their study for the M.B.A. degree.

First, the overall learning experience was rewarding and significant. It appeared to be a consensus among the managers that M.B.A. learning was "valuable," "beneficial," "rewarding," or "significant." This point was articulated by the manager in reference to specific benefits or rewards they received through learning participation. The following narratives shed light on how such an experience had benefited the individual managers in terms of the overall management competency:

> M.B.A. has totally changed my way of thinking. Unlike in the past, I am now in a better position to provide solutions to organizational problems in a more systematic, rational, and effective manner. [Manager 1]

> The two-year M.B.A. study has greatly enhanced my overall competency as manager. It has not only equipped me with knowledge and techniques required for modern organization management, but more important, it has developed my ability to think strategically and solve problems systematically. It opened my mind and broadened my vision. It fostered holistic thinking and team spirit. It also taught me how to learn and communicate more effectively. [Manager 4]

> M.B.A. is like human system reengineering. It has changed my career direction and life focus, consciously and unconsciously. I personally view M.B.A. as mind training, just like yoga or Zen. It can take me to a higher level by constantly challenging me intellectually and spiritually. [Manager 6]

> M.B.A. has significantly improved my overall managerial capacity such as in problem solving, strategic thinking, and team working. It has been a very eye-opening and thought-provoking experience. [Manager 7]

In addition to increased management capacity, the rewarding experience of learning was also articulated by several managers from the professional networking perspective. For example, Manager 12 said, "Through the M.B.A. program, I made friends with my teachers and peers. They are valuable sources of social networks and professional connections. Through periodic communication and information exchange, we have identified ample opportunities for personal and professional development."

Another significant experience indicated by a few managers was gained through the development of team spirit. An interesting point came from Manager 3 when commenting on teamwork in the Chinese culture in general: "You would think we Chinese are natural team players, given the influence of Confucian values. Yet we aren't! As a manager of public relations, I feel obliged to foster a safe and comfortable team working environment for all employees. I learned how to do so from the M.B.A. program."

Second, learning became meaningful and applicable when it was directly linked to day-to-day practice. All of the managers noted that their learning related to accounting and finance had proved effective, for they could apply it immediately in their daily practice. Half of the managers interviewed indicated that they had had little or no prior knowledge of accounting or finance, yet they felt comfortable and capable of handling related issues by the end of the program. Manager 5 confirmed, "I am now in a position of making financial decisions that I was unable to do a couple of years ago."

The managers also reported other projects that they were engaged in as part of the M.B.A. training, such as providing consulting services to local organizations, developing marketing plans, and competing at national management forums. They described such learning activities as "bridging the gap between theory and practice" (Manager 1), "facilitating learning" (Manager 3), and "helping see the immediate application of knowledge" (Manager 12). This finding also indicates that actively participating in the learning process may create better learning outcomes.

Third, learning became challenging and difficult when the content was out of touch with the Chinese context and delivered by unqualified instructors. Although many accounts of positive experiences were described, the managers also suggested that there were times when learning became challenging. In addition to expressing their frustration and discomfort, they also mentioned the causes of such challenges, which they frequently referred to as barriers.

One barrier was a lack of Chinese orientation. The majority of managers acknowledged that the learning materials were "too Western oriented." Specifically, they commented that most of the case studies included in their M.B.A. program not only were "outdated" but also "had no direct connections to our world" (Manager 5). In effect, these managers attributed their difficulty in incorporating some of their new learning into daily operations to the apparent disconnection between the Western-based instructional materials and the reality of Chinese organizations. Manager 3 associated this situation with a Chinese expression: "looking at flowers in the fog" (*wu-li-kan-hua*).

A related issue that managers reported was the challenge caused by the way some of the courses were delivered. Manager 3 offered a specific example: "Some courses I took, for example, Organizational Behavior, are fairly new to us. The book we used was directly translated from the Western textbooks, and this course was taught primarily in English. This had caused much difficulty because most of the participants are caders (that is, Chinese administrators appointed by the government due to their military or political background) and managers of state-owned enterprises. They can barely understand English, not to mention participating in class discussion or raising questions."

Finally, all of the managers noted as another barrier to effective learning that most of their M.B.A. instructors had had little or no practical experience in business and industry. This point was articulated by Manager 2: "Most of my instructors have been university professors for years. They are good scholars, but they are not good businesspersons." Manager 8 confirmed: "Some teachers only have theoretical knowledge of management, so they tend to be very theory focused in teaching."

Learning Beyond Participation. Findings under this category were not on the original research agenda. However, we found during interviews that the managers apparently had a much broader definition of the concept of participation than we did for this study. By spending substantial time during interviews and follow-up reflecting on how the newly acquired M.B.A. knowledge had helped them at work and their organization, the managers conveyed a clear message that learning did not stop at the end of the M.B.A. program. In fact, they reported their continuing engagement in learning by finding ways to apply their new knowledge at work. This learning experience, often referred to as learning transfer in the literature, was perceived by the managers as "having much more meaning" than experience with "learning in the moment" and was the ultimate goal for their participation. Since the participants described their extended participation experiences primarily with reference to the learning impact, the findings we present next are centered on this theme.

Impact on the Individual. It was clear that their M.B.A. learning had a positive influence on the managers when they returned to the workplace. Most were using their newly acquired knowledge, such as cost accounting, in daily operations. Other frequently mentioned benefits were teamwork and problem-solving skills. Manager 6 used his mug for a vivid illustration: "I always held the mug handle with my right hand out of habit. When doing so, I see only certain aspects of the mug. Now I can see multiple sides of it because I constantly change the way I hold it. That's what I have learned from the M.B.A." Manager 11 concurred: "My M.B.A. taught me how to think differently. Now I can easily come up with many different solutions when I run into a problem." Other managers reported similar experiences.

Nevertheless, few of the managers claimed success in making large-scale change beyond their own department. They agreed that lack of support from their organization was the most critical barrier to learning transfer. They attributed the limited impact of their new knowledge on the overall organizational practice to an unsupportive organizational environment. Manager 1 said, "I was inspired by the strategic management course and came up with some ideas about repositioning our company in the marketplace more strategically. I shared my proposal a year ago with the CEO and his management team, but after a few months, they came back to me and said my idea was too novel to be considered." Manager 6 shared his experience, which was representative: "Shortly after I came on board as the investment manager of the group, I was asked by the president to develop an overall strategic development plan for the company. I was very excited and spent several months conducting a comprehensive feasibility study, environmental scanning, and wrote up a thirty-page report. But guess what? My report has been on the president's desk gathering dust for half a year already. I checked with the president three times, and each time he told me that he hadn't had time to read it yet."

A number of managers had similar stories regarding the limited support they received from their organizations and peers. To our surprise, none had positive experiences in this area. Repeatedly we heard similar stories from each of them and felt their frustrations. Manager 4 concluded the interview with the following statement: "With several failures in introducing some of my newly acquired knowledge to top management, I came to the realization that a small number of M.B.A. managers will never make a difference in an organization where leaders decide not to change." Much evidence has revealed the inconsistency between the organizations' claimed commitment to learning and lack of practical support on their side.

Impact on the Organization. Although we did not study the organizations each manager worked with, it was clear by the managers' stories that their organizations did benefit from their learning. Two issues stood out across the five organizations that the interviewed managers represented: shared knowledge and improved communication systems.

Sharing their acquired new management skills seemed to be a passion of all managers interviewed. They used the following terms to describe their roles within the organization: "coach," "facilitator," and "educator." Having been the head of business development for five years, Manager 6 said, "Becoming a learning organization is the vision of my company. My M.B.A. learning fits perfectly with our corporate mission. In my daily practice, I try to operationalize my newly acquired management philosophy starting within my department." Manager 7 stated, "As an HR manager, developing people has always been my mission. Now I try to take every opportunity to pass on some of my new learning to others. I believe it is beneficial to my organization."

The managers also reported improved communication systems within their organizations. For example, Manager 10 acknowledged, "It has made a huge difference spending sufficient time with your people. Communication ought to be interactive to be mutually beneficial. That was a big lesson I learned from the M.B.A. program." Similarly, after sharing a story that resulted from a lack of communication between his department and other functions, Manager 12 concluded, "It is of vital importance to have built a two-way communication system within my organization. Otherwise, we would still see many overlaps of work here."

Although the perceived outcomes reported here represented a small portion of all the data collected, the findings are significant in that they suggest that when shared within the organization, individual learning has the potential to improve organizational systems, promote learning at higher levels, and have a pervasive impact on employees and organizations.

Discussions and Implications

We made sense of the meanings formulated by the participants based on the descriptions they provided, our own experiences, and our knowledge from the literature. Our discussion focuses on five issues, mingled with our own reflections as researchers. From the discussions, we also derived three propositions.

Participation as Result of Environmental Pressure. Multiple issues were addressed by the managers and informed our understanding of why they decided to participate in M.B.A. training. Overall, these findings support the literature, particularly in the field of adult education, where issues such as skill deficiencies or discrepancies (Dechant, 1989; Mumford, 1993), developmental opportunities (Ellinger, Watkins, & Bostrom, 1999; Noe & Wilk, 1993), and socioeconomic status (Miller, 1967) are often cited as being significant triggers for participation.

However, what was noticeable in this study was that while the interviewed managers experienced intrinsic motivation such as a desire for enhancing management capability and commitment to work, they identified many more external motivators that appeared to be influential on their decision to pursue an M.B.A. In other words, participation was a decision prompted by environmental changes, which subsequently created a sense of urgency for learning.

Most of the external and internal motivators outlined by the managers, such as economic reform, global competition, higher social or family status, a need for developing management competency, and anticipated opportunities for career advancement can be related to macroenvironment change, pointing to change as the top force driving their participation in an M.B.A. program. It is this dynamic change that created the pressure on the managers and made the need for learning important.

Our finding that learning participation was prompted more by the extrinsic than intrinsic motivators seems contradictory to the commonly accepted belief that motivation comes from within first (Cheng, 2000). Furthermore, the finding that environmental change was the most significant driver in this study also contradicts our own proposition from a deductive approach based on a comprehensive review of Western literature (Wang & Wang, 2004): that environmental factors play only an indirect role in the learning participation decision through organization factors. This inconsistency reveals two implications. First, current HRD learning participation practice in China is still at a formative stage, and HRD interventions have not been integrated into the organizational strategies (Wang & Wang, 2006). Therefore, organizations do not have much of an effect on participation decision as they would at a mature stage. Second, HRD learning participation is a culture-bound phenomenon with characteristics distinctive to a specific national socioeconomic context. In this case, the prominence of the external forces in driving the twelve managers' participation in an M.B.A. training program may be explained largely by the transitional features of the Chinese socioeconomic climate and resulting changes.

Participation as Transformational Experience. Through various accounts portrayed by the managers and our thematic analysis, it was clear that the managers' participation in the M.B.A. program generally was a positive experience. They described in many ways how this experience had opened their eyes, provoked new ideas, and transformed their thinking profoundly. Such evidence includes new management knowledge and skills, increased career opportunities, changes in mind-set and ways of thinking, and new professional networks. That there was positive change in the individual manager level was clear; it was also evident that some changes occurred at the organizational level, such as shared knowledge at work and improved communications within the organization. In this sense, it may be reasonable to describe the managers' learning experience as transformational.

It was also apparent from the managers' experience that such transformational learning remained primarily at the conceptual rather than practical level. In other words, although the managers may have embraced a new perspective and a way of thinking about organizational management, their ways of working may not have changed much, if at all. This could be partially explained by the challenges the managers encountered during and after receiving their degree.

Participation as Challenging Experience. While the overall learning experience might be described as transformational, it was also reported as highly challenging. This seemingly contradictory message conveyed by the participants can be understood from two perspectives: challenges in transferring learning during the program and challenges in transferring learning at work.

Context-Based Learning. The quality and experience of instructors and instructional design–related issues, such as the appropriateness of the teaching materials and the delivery format, appeared to be some of the key elements that not only affected the managers' learning experience but also limited the influence of such training. These findings confirmed the importance of learning process factors defined by Wang and Wang (2004).

The lack of high-quality M.B.A. instructors has been documented in the literature. For example, Branine (2005) noted that the lack of qualified teaching staff has hindered the efficient implementation of Western-designed M.B.A. programs in China. Shi (2000) examined the history and current status of M.B.A. education in China and concluded that the direct transplanting of Western curriculum into China M.B.A. programs inevitably affects the learning quality of these programs because the instructors and participants are not familiar with the Western context. Shi also reasoned that most Chinese M.B.A. teachers were trained to teach socialist political economics and management techniques under the central planning system and often do not hold an M.B.A. degree themselves. Furthermore, given that the teaching materials are mainly translated textbooks of Western business schools and some subjects relating to the market economy are relatively new in China, many M.B.A. educators do not fully understand the nature of an M.B.A. program or are not familiar with the subject matter. As a result, their teaching is not satisfactory (Lau & Roffey, 2002). In fact, lack of qualified specialists (Branine, 2005; Frazer, 1999; Shi, 2000; Zhang et al., 2002) and cultural discrepancy (Fan, 1998; Lau & Roffey, 2002; Newell, 1999) are noted as two major issues influencing the quality of the M.B.A. training.

The lack of context as revealed in this study in fact presents an opportunity for international HRD practitioners. HRD professionals are obligated to develop effective learning interventions designed to bring optimal results at both the individual and organizational levels. HRD professionals can do so by playing an active role in identifying context-based learning needs, designing context-sensitive materials, and selecting appropriate instructional strategies and techniques so that learning, transfer, and impact will be maximized.

Transferring Learning at Work. The managers interviewed also extended the challenges to their work settings regarding learning transfer and impact issues. While positive impact of learning was reported by the participants, it generally occurred at the individual manager's level. The impact on the organization was quite limited. First, the managers pointed to the lack of a supportive organizational environment in which leaders encouraged new learning and behavior. Our data revealed that five of the twelve managers in this study were either partially or fully sponsored by their respective organizations. However, none of these managers reported experiencing support to apply new knowledge. The potential consequence for the organizations may be not only the lost return on human capital investment but increased turnover among trained managers. Indeed, a couple of managers interviewed expressed their intent to leave their current company soon.

In our formal and informal conversations during and after the interviews, the managers shared some of the dilemmas they faced that confirmed our analysis. For example, Manager 7 said, "The M.B.A. courses I took were truly eye-opening. I learned a great deal from the program, which is good for my personal development but not for my organization because the contexts are so different." The fact that the organizations simply went with the fad by sponsoring their managers for the M.B.A. training may turn out to be a win-lose situation for the two parties.

Second, although five of the participants were sponsored by their organizations, it was clear that these managers had participated in the M.B.A. program for their own professional development rather than initiated by their organizations as an integral part of the overall MD strategy. The managers' decision about participating in the program had little to do with the organization they worked for. Therefore, we may safely conclude that management development in this study was not incorporated into the strategic planning of the organization.

Furthermore, the immaturity and strong Western orientation of the M.B.A. program proved to be another major cause of difficulty in learning transfer. Several managers (Managers 1, 3, 5, 6, 11, and 12) shared their frustration in applying their M.B.A. knowledge to their work settings. The struggle they experienced reminds us of a well-known Chinese term, *Handan xuebu,* which originated from an ancient story about a person named Handan who mimicked the different ways of walking he observed when he traveled to a foreign country. He eventually become confused and later forgot how to walk in his own way when he returned home. The point here is that when one learns something that is not context based, the chance that the person will successfully transfer that learning becomes slim. This is the case of the managers in this study when they attempted to transplant or adapt Western management techniques in the complex and different Chinese organizational context.

Although further inference is neither impossible nor inappropriate, the combination of these findings does reinforce our recent study (Wang & Wang, 2006) in which we concluded that China's current approach to MD tends to be fragmented, generic, immature, and lacking strategic alignment and coherence. This study showed that there is also a glaring gap between what this type of training offers and what the manager's organizational reality calls for. In addition, findings in this regard have practical implications. First, organizations are facing increasing competition for limited resources, and any HRD interventions should be driven by key business objectives (Wang & Wang, 2005). HRD practitioners must take a leading role in helping organizations define their learning needs, critically assess and adopt HRD and MD interventions, strategically align selected interventions with their overall goals, and ensure that any human capital investment will generate maximized return for the organization. Meanwhile, HRD practitioners are responsible for creating a stimulating organizational culture and effective support systems that will lead to win-win situations for both individuals and organizations.

The Concept of Participation. The way the participants defined the notion of learning participation deserves further discussion. Our definition of participation confined participation to the M.B.A. program. In other words, we focused on the experiences within the learning process. In fact, all the managers gave equal (or even more) attention to their experience of applying the new learning rather than the learning itself. They led discussions around this topic when we probed for why they described their experience as "challenging" yet also "rewarding and significant." The participants' responses made it clear that their experience during the learning process could not be considered separately from their experience with the application of such learning. Instead, it should be an integral part of the learning. Without it, the learning experience would not have been completed. This point was also supported by Wang and Wang (2004) in positing that participation is an important component in learning evaluation. From this aspect, treating participation as level 0 of evaluation may make more sense (Spitzer, 2004).

The findings also have methodological implication. Instead of following the deductive approaches we used in our earlier study on HRD learning participation (Wang & Wang, 2004), we adopted an inductive approach to examine the same issue. The power of qualitative inquiry in HRD, among other things, lies in its capacity to understand particular, situated, and unfamiliar phenomena (Meyer, 1996); explore uncharted territory (Marsick, 1990); and develop new theory (Tsui & Lau, 2002; Watkins & Marsick, 1992).

As a result of the phenomenological approach we employed, unexpected information emerged during the interviews. Although this study focused on understanding the learning participation, phenomenological interviews also uncovered other related topics that proved useful in deepening our understanding of the phenomenon under study. For example, the finding on learning transfer turned out to be crucial in helping us build a complete picture of the participants' experiences. The emergent nature of phenomenological approach, as well as the openness and flexibility propelled by the phenomenologically styled interviews and the semistructured questions not only reinforced the "ultimate value of what inductive analysis will yield" (Patton, 2002, p. 44), but also contributed to an enriched understanding of the topics being studied.

Culture Context and Learning Participation. The study findings shed light on culture-oriented motivators that may have important implications yet have not been well explored in the literature. This study uncovered some interesting cultural aspects regarding learning participation. For example, the reasons that Managers 1 and 5 participated in an M.B.A. program because they felt pressure from their spouses' higher academic degrees may be understood as partially influenced by traditional Chinese culture. Hofstede (1991) defined this phenomenon as masculinity, referring to a work role model of male achievement, control, and power. Although Chinese culture has evolved in recent years into a less male-dominant one, according to Hofstede's ranking, a masculinity tendency is still reflected in this study. Therefore, it is reasonable to refer to this tendency as an individual culture orientation as specified in Wang and Wang (2004).

In culture-related studies, *guanxi* has become a focal point for understanding Chinese business operations (Chen & Chen, 2004). Wang, Wang, Ruona, and Rojewski (2005) further explored its HRD implications. Our findings from this study also support this view. It appeared from the managers' experience that exploring new *guanxi* or professional networking was one of the driving forces for participation in M.B.A. training, as explained by half of the managers interviewed.

Moreover, a few managers disclosed, pursuit for higher social status appears to be a critical motivator for learning and subsequent success. This again can be understood as rooted in Confucian culture. A representative slogan by Confucius regarding learning says, "He who excels in learning will lead a higher-ranking career and social status." In other words, traditional Chinese culture places much value on systematic learning for the purpose of gaining career opportunities and social status. This is an important way for participants to close the power distance as defined by Hofstede (1991). This perspective is apparently in line with the individual culture orientation specified by Wang and Wang (2004).

Similarly, although no definitive conclusion may be drawn from the data in this study, the managers' choice of formal versus informal training courses (in this case, a two-year program offered by a university) may also be partially explained by the Chinese cultural preference for didactic teaching and learning styles (Kirkbride, Tang, & Shae, 1989). In fact, *xue,* or learning, in the above Confucian slogan refers to systematic and formal learning rather than informal and incremental learning. The value placed on formal learning is also captured by a recent popular Chinese term, *han jin liang,* literally meaning "gold concentration," to emphasize formal and systematic learning. Obviously, the more systematic and formal a learning experience is, the higher is the "gold concentration," and thus the higher rate of participation.

Propositions: Learning Participation in Transitioning Cultural Contexts. A primary purpose for adult participation research is to assist policymakers in designing national, local, or community-based adult education programs and formulating related policies (Merriam & Caffarella, 1999). Research on HRD learning participation aims at developing strategies to encourage, motivate, and support employees' active participation in learning interventions (Wang & Wang, 2004). Hence, identifying the differences in driving forces has important policy and practical implications at the national and organizational levels.

While Wang and Wang (2004) made four distinctions related to learning participation in adult education and HRD (origin of the decision, degree of environmental influences, motivational sources, and investment sources), the findings of this study seem to have blurred those differences. First, the twelve managers' decision to participate in M.B.A. training was basically self-initiated. It had little to do with the organizations they worked in, although such decisions, as Wang and Wang (2004) would argue, should more than likely be initiated by an organization as part of its overall MD strategy. Second, almost all managers' participation was directly prompted by China's transitional socioeconomic environment. In other words, the macroenvironment influenced their participation decision to a large degree. Third, the driving forces for participation identified by the twelve Chinese managers, such as coping with environmental change, perceived benefits, and commitment to work, while supporting the HRD learning participation framework by Wang and Wang (2004) to a certain degree, were more in line with the learning motivation typology proposed by adult learning scholars (Boshier, 1971; Burgess, 1971; Houle, 1961; Morstein & Smart, 1974; Rubenson, 1977; Sheffield, 1964). Finally, among these twelve managers, only five were fully or partially sponsored by their organization to attend the M.B.A. program.

It is not clear from the findings whether this blurring of the differences in learning participation in adult learning and HRD participation was caused by the transitional context or the Chinese culture context, or a combination of the two. One possible explanation may lie in the fact that the study was situated in a unique transitioning socioeconomic context of a developing country, yet the four differences were derived largely from studies conducted in the Western countries. No definitive conclusion can be reached without investigating participation in more cultural contexts and transitioning societies. Nevertheless, it may still be safe to derive some propositions from the findings for future research. Therefore, we posit:

PROPOSITION 1. *HRD learning participation behavior in a transitioning context is likely to have a distinctive pattern that follows both general adult education models and the HRD framework defined in an organizational setting.*

This study revealed three culture-oriented elements that drove the managers to participate in the M.B.A. training: need for establishing a *guanxi* network, masculinity as represented by the *da-nan-zi-zhu-yi*, and seeking higher social status as influenced by the power distance. This finding also supported our prediction in the learning participation theory (LPT) model (Wang & Wang, 2004) that suggested culture influences the participation decision. Hence:

PROPOSITION 2. *HRD learning participation behavior is likely to have varied manifestations in different cultural contexts.*

What was made prominent by this study is the prevailing influence of external forces on the managers' participation decision. Thus, combining current literature and propositions 1 and 2, we have:

PROPOSITION 3. *HRD learning participation behavior in a transitional and culture-specific context is likely to be driven more intensively by extrinsic contextual factors than intrinsic motivators.*

Limitations. As with all other empirical studies, this study has limitations. First, this study was confined to M.B.A. programs offered by one university in one city in China. Given the size and population of the country, as well as the regional differences in the degree of economic transformation, extended inference of the findings is impossible. The findings should not be considered as representative of China M.B.A. programs in general, but a specific university's programs. Similarly, this study focused on twelve middle-level managers from five organizations. These managers do not represent the entire community of Chinese middle managers who work in many different organizational settings in different geographical locations. Therefore, the interpretation of the findings needs to be cautious and should not be extended to all middle managers in China. Nonetheless, the study paved a path to further explore and understand the phenomenon of management development and HRD learning participation in the international arena.

Conclusion

This study is one of the first in exploring the HRD participation phenomenon in an international arena. By focusing on the transitioning nature of the society and specific national cultures, the study expanded existing HRD learning participation research to a broader socioeconomic and cultural context.

Using a phenomenological approach, we explored critical issues relating participation in HRD interventions in the case of China, specifically M.B.A. programs. We conducted in-depth individual interviews with twelve middle-level managers to understand their M.B.A. experience during China's recent economic transition. The phenomenological method helped unveil the managers' learning participation experiences.

The findings of this study suggest that HRD participation in a transitioning cultural context may have features that have not been identified by previous participation studies in both HRD and adult education. In a transitional society, HRD participation behavior may represent characteristics of both HRD and adult learning, influenced by specific cultural context, and driven more by extrinsic than intrinsic motivators. In the light of the transitioning nature of the Chinese cultural context, practical implications for learning participation were discussed. As a result of our findings, we offered three propositions for future research on HRD learning participation. Given the limitations of the study, interpretations of the findings should be cautious.

References

Baldwin, T., Magjuka, R. J., & Lother, B. T. (1991). The perils of participation: Effects of choice of training on trainee motivation and learning. *Personal Psychology, 44,* 51–66.

Beddowes, P. L. (1994). Management development. *Journal of Management Development, 13* (7), 40–47.

Boisot, M., & Fiol, M. (1987). Chinese boxes and learning cubes: Action learning in a cross-cultural context. *Journal of Management Development, 6,* 8–18.

Boshier, R. (1971). Motivational orientations of adult education participants: A factor analytic exploration of Houle's typology. *Adult Education, 21* (2), 3–26.

Boshier, R. (1973). Educational participation and dropout: A theoretical model. *Adult Education, 23,* 255–282.

Boston Consulting Group and Wharton School. (2004). *China and the new rules for global business.* Philadelphia: University of Pennsylvania.

Branine, M. (1996). Observations on training and management development in the People's Republic of China. *Personnel Review, 25* (1), 25–39.

Branine, M. (2005). Cross-cultural training of managers: An evaluation of a management development programme for Chinese managers. *Journal of Management Development, 24* (5), 459–472.

Brewster, C. (2004). Developing managers in Europe. *Advances in Developing Human Resources, 6* (4), 399–403.

Bu, N., & Mitchell, V. F. (1992). Developing the PRC's managers: How can Western experts become more helpful? *Journal of Management Development, 11* (2), 42–53.

Burgess, P. (1971). Reasons for adult participation in group educational activities. *Adult Education, 22,* 3–29.

Chen, X., & Chen, C. (2004). On the intricacies of the Chinese guanxi: A process model of guanxi development. *Asia Pacific Journal of Management, 21,* 305–324.

Cheng, E.W.L. (2000). Test of the M.B.A. knowledge and skills transfer. *International Journal of Human Resource Management, 11* (4), 837–852.

Child, J. (1994). *Management in China during the age of reform.* Cambridge: Cambridge University Press.

Colaizzi, P. F. (1978). Psychological research as the phenomenologist views it. In R. Valle & M. King (Eds.), *Existential-phenomenological alternative for psychology* (pp. 8–71). New York: Oxford University Press.

Creswell, J. W. (1998). *Qualitative inquiry and research design.* Thousand Oaks, CA: Sage.

Cross, K. P. (1981). *Adults as learners: Increasing participation and facilitating learning.* San Francisco: Jossey-Bass.

Cutz, G., & Chandler, P. (2000). Emic-etic conflicts as explanation of nonparticipation in adult education among the Maya of western Guatemala. *Adult Education Quarterly, 51* (1), 64–75.

Darkenwald, G. G., & Merriam, S. B. (1982). *Adult education: Foundations of practice.* New York: HarperCollins.

Dechant, K. (1989). *Managerial change in the workplace: Learning strategies of managers.* Unpublished doctoral dissertation, Columbia University.

Ellinger, A. D., Watkins, K. E., & Bostrom, R. P. (1999). Managers as facilitators of learning in learning organizations. *Human Resource Development Quarterly, 10* (2), 105–125.

Fan, Y. (1998). The transfer of Western management to China. *Management Learning, 29* (2), 201–221.

Frazer, A. J. (1999). A scouting report on training options. *China Business Review, 1,* 44–47.

Garavan, T. N., Barnicle, B., & O'Suilleabhain, F. (1999). Management development: Contemporary trends, issues and strategies. *Journal of European Industrial Training, 23* (4/5), 191–207.

Glaser, B., & Strauss, A. (1967). *Discovery of grounded theory: Strategies for qualitative research.* Chicago: AVC.

Guest, G., Bunce, A., & Johnson, L. (2006). How many interviews are enough? An experiment with data saturation and variability. *Field Methods, 18* (1), 59–82.

Henry, G. T., & Basiel, K. C. (1994). Understanding the decision to participate in formal adult education. *Adult Education Quarterly, 44* (2), 64–82.

Hicks, W. D., & Klimoski, R. J. (1987). Entry into training programs and its effects on training outcomes: A field experiment. *Academy of Management Journal, 30,* 542–552.

Hofstede, G. (1991). *Cultures and organizations.* New York: McGraw-Hill.

Houle, C. O. (1961). *The inquiring mind.* Madison: University of Wisconsin Press.

Kirkbride, P. S., Tang, S.F.Y., & Shae, W. C. (1989). The transferability of management training and development: The case of Hong Kong. *Asia Pacific Journal of Human Resource Management, 27* (1), 7–20.

Kvale, S. (1996). *Interviews: An introduction to qualitative research interviewing.* Thousand Oaks, CA: Sage.

Lau, A., & Roffey, B. (2002). Management education and development in China: A research note. *Labour and Management in Development Journal, 2* (10), 3–10.

Lewin, K. (1947). Frontiers in group dynamics: Concept, method, and reality in social science. *Hunan Relations, 1,* 5–41.

Li, M. (2003). Qi ye jia jia zhi shi xian, guo qi gai ge zhuan zhan [Self-realization of entrepreneur and refocus of state-owned enterprise reforms]. *China Small and Medium Enterprise, 87* (2), 17–18.

Livian, Y. F., & Burgoyne, J. G. (1997). *Middle managers in Europe.* London: Routledge.

Livingstone, D. (1999). Exploring the icebergs of adult learning: Findings of the first Canadian survey of informal learning practices. *Canadian Journal for the Study of Adult Education, 13* (2), 49–72.

Luoma, M. (2005). Managers' perceptions of the strategic role of management development. *Journal of Management Development, 24* (7), 645–655.

Mabey, C. (2004). Developing managers in Europe: Policies, practices, and impact. *Advances in Developing Human Resources, 6* (4), 404–427.

Marsick, V. (1990). Altering the paradigm for theory building and research in human resource development. *Human Resource Development Quarterly, 1* (1), 5–25.

Maslow, A. H. (1954). *Motivation and personality.* New York: HarperCollins.

Maurer, T. J., & Tarulli, B. A. (1994). Investigation of perceived environment, perceived outcome, and person variables in relationship to voluntary development activity by employees. *Journal of Applied Psychology, 79* (1), 3–14.

McClelland, S. (1994). Gaining competitive advantage through strategic management development. *Journal of Management Development, 13* (5), 4–13.

Meldrum, M., & Atkinson, S. (1998). Is management development fulfilling its organizational role? *Management Decision, 36* (8), 528–532.

Merriam, S. B. (2001). *Qualitative research and case study applications in education* (rev. ed.). San Francisco: Jossey-Bass.

Merriam, S. B., & Caffarella, R. S. (1999). *Learning in adulthood.* San Francisco: Jossey-Bass.

Meyer, S. R. (1996). Mentoring and reflection: Enhancing managerial skills. In E. F. Holton (Ed.), *The Academy of Human Resource Development Conference Proceedings* (pp. 612–619). Bowling Green, OH: Academy of Human Resource Development.

Miller, H. (1967). *Participation of adults in education: A force-field analysis.* Boston: Center for the Study of Liberal Education for Adults, Boston University.

Morstein, B. R., & Smart, J. C. (1974). Reasons for participation in adult education courses: A multivariate analysis of group differences. *Adult Education, 24* (2), 83–98.

Moustakas, C. (1994). *Phenomenology research.* Thousand Oaks, CA: Sage.

Muiru, J., & Mukuria, G. (2005). Barriers to participation in adult literacy programs in Kenya. *Adult Basic Education, 15* (2), 85–102.

Mumford, A. (1993). *Management development strategies for action* (2nd ed.). London: Institute of Personnel Management.

Newell, S. (1999). The transfer of management knowledge to China: Building learning communities rather than translating Western textbooks? *Education and Training, 41* (6/7), 286–294.

Noe, R. A., & Wilk, S. L. (1993). Investigation of the factors that influence employees' participation in development activities. *Journal of Applied Psychology, 78* (2), 291–302.

O'Connell, P. J. (1999). *Adults in training: An international comparison of continuing education and training.* Paris: Organization for Economic Cooperation and Development.

Patton, M. Q. (2002). *Qualitative research and evaluation methods* (3rd ed.). Thousand Oaks, CA: Sage.

Peteraf, J. (1994). The cornerstones of competitive advantage: A resource-based view. *Strategic Management Journal, 14* (3), 179–192.

Rosen, S. (2004). The state of youth and the state in early 21st century China: The triumph of the urban rich? In P. H. Gries & S. Rosen (Eds.), *State and society in 21st-century China* (pp. 159–179). London: Routledge.

Rubenson, K. (1977). *Participation in recurrent education: A research review.* Paper presented at a meeting of national delegates on Developments in Recurrent Education, Organization for Economic Cooperation and Development, Paris.

Sargant, N. (2000). *The learning divide revisited: A report on the findings of a UK-wide survey on adult participation in education and learning.* Leicester: National Institute of Adult Continuing Education.

Seidman, I. E. (1991). *Interviewing as qualitative research.* New York: Teachers College Press.

Sheffield, S. B. (1964). The orientations of adult continuing learners. In D. Soloman (Ed.), *The continuing learner.* Chicago: Center for the Study of Liberal Education for Adults.

Shi, Y. Z. (2000). A status report on M.B.A. education in China. *International Journal of Educational Reform, 9* (4), 328–334.

Skilton-Sylvester, E. (2002). Should I stay or should I go? Investigating Cambodian women's participation and investment in adult ESL programs. *Adult Education Quarterly, 53* (1), 8–25.

Spitzer, D. R. (2004, June). *How to achieve results from learning using learning effectiveness measurement.* Paper presented at the Training Directors' Forum 2004, Phoenix, AZ.

Storey, J. (1989a). Management development: A literature review and implications for future research, part 1. *Personnel Review, 18* (6), 3–19.

Storey, J. (1989b). Management development: A literature review and implications for future research, part 2. *Personnel Review, 19* (1), 3–11.

Strauss, A. (1987). *Qualitative analysis for social scientists.* Cambridge: Cambridge University Press.

Tsui, A. S., & Lau, C. M. (2002). Research on the management of enterprises in the People's Republic of China: Current status and future directions. In A. S. Tsui & C. M. Lau (Eds.), *The management of enterprises in the People's Republic of China* (pp. 1–27). Dordrecht: Kluwer.

Van Manen, M. (1990). *Researching lived experience: Human science for an action sensitive pedagogy.* New York: State University of New York Press.

Van der Mescht, H. (1999, July 5–8). *Poetry, phenomenology, and "reality."* Paper presented at the Conference on Qualitative Research, Rand Afrikaans University, Johannesburg, South Africa.

Wang, G. G., & Wang, J. (2004). Toward a learning participation theory of HRD. *Human Resource Development Review, 4* (3), 326–353.

Wang, G. G., & Wang, J. (2005). HRD evaluation: Emerging market, barriers, and theory building. *Advances in Developing Human Resources, 7* (1), 22–36.

Wang, J., & Wang, G. G. (2006). Exploring national human resource development: A case of China management development in a transitioning context. *Human Resource Development Review, 5* (2), 176–201.

Wang, J., Wang, G. G., Ruona, W.E.A., & Rojewski, J. W. (2005). Confucian values: A review of the literature and implications for international HRD. *Human Resource Development International, 8* (3), 311–326.

Wang, X., He, W., & Yu, K. (2003, November 7). *East meets West: The dilemma of management pedagogy in China.* Paper presented at the Business Education and Emerging Market Economics: Trends and Prospects Conference Technology Square, Atlanta, GA.

Wang, Z. M. (1999). Current models and innovative strategies in management education in China. *Education and Training, 41* (6/7), 312–318.

Wang, Z. M. (2002). New research perspectives and implicit managerial competency modeling in China. In C. L. Cooper & I. T. Robertson (Eds.), *International review of industrial and organizational psychology* (Vol. 17, pp. 265–282). Hoboken, NJ: Wiley.

Watkins, K. E., & Marsick, V. J. (1992). Towards a theory of informed and incidental learning in organizations. *International Journal of Lifelong Education, 11* (4), 287–300.

Winterton, J., & Winterton, R. (1997). Does management development add value? *British Journal of Management, 8* (Special Issue), 65–76.

Wright, P. M., Dunford, B. B., & Snell, S. A. (2001). Human resources and the resource based view of the firm. *Journal of Management, 27* (6), 701–722.

Wright, P., Szeto, W. F., & Cheng, L.T.W. (2002). *Guanxi* and professional conduct in China: A management development perspective. *International Journal of Human Resource Management, 13* (1), 156–182.

Yang, B. (2004). Can adult education provide a foundation for HRD? *Advances in Developing Human Resources, 6* (2), 129–145.

Youndt, M. A., Scott, S. A., Dean, J. W., & Lepak, D. P. (1996). Human resource management, manufacturing strategy, and firm performance. *Academy of Management Journal, 39* (4), 836–867.

Zhang, D., Yang, B. Y., & Zhang, Y. C. (2002). Challenges and strategies of developing human resources in the surge of globalization: A case of the People's Republic of China. In T. M. Egan & S. A. Lynham (Eds.), *Proceedings of Academy of Human Resource Development International Research Conference* (pp. 193–200). Bowling Green, OH: Academy of Human Resource Development.

Zhao, C. L. (2005). Management of corporate culture through local managers' training in foreign companies in China: A qualitative analysis. *International Journal of Training and Development, 9* (4), 232–255.

Jia Wang is an assistant professor in the Department of Human Resource Development and Administration, Barry University, Fort Myers, Florida.

Greg G. Wang is an associate professor in the Human Resources Development Program, Old Dominion University, Norfolk, Virginia.

Mega-Trends in the American Workforce

Carl E. Van Horn

This article uses results from a series of national public opinion surveys to shed light on the views and concerns of American workers and employers. The article explores five major themes that have emerged from the surveys and then proposes ways that policymakers, employers, and workers can understand, adapt to, and accept the ever-changing labor market and economy.

For nearly a decade, Work Trends, a national public opinion series, has given American workers and employers a voice in the nation's critical and often contentious policy and economic debates.[1] Workers and employers have offered their insights and opinions on an array of subjects, including job insecurity, technology, work/life balance, discrimination, retirement, and education. Work Trends provides numerous insights into the views and concerns of American workers and employers. Overall, five major themes have emerged from over sixteen thousand interviews with American workers:

- The anxious American worker. Workers are uncertain, anxious, and stressed about the workplace and the security of their jobs. This uncertainty is demonstrated in their fear of, and experience with, layoffs, a lack of trust in employers, worries about retirement and pension security, and the difficulties of balancing work, family, and education.
- Knowledge, learning, and attitudes rule. Workers know they need to obtain more skills and credentials to succeed in the labor market. They highly value education as a tool to prepare for work and insulate them from economic

Note: This article is excerpted from a speech to the Academy of Human Resource Development, Columbus, Ohio, February 24, 2006.

HUMAN RESOURCE DEVELOPMENT QUARTERLY, vol. 17, no. 4, Winter 2006 © Wiley Periodicals, Inc.
Published online in Wiley InterScience (www.interscience.wiley.com) • DOI: 10.1002/hrdq.1186

disasters, even though they know that there is little they can do to prevent being laid off. They want to enhance their education, but often do not know what they should learn or how to get the best education and training. They are also concerned about having the time to pursue educational opportunities and need more support to do so.

• Employers demand better-prepared workers and have difficulty finding them. Employers need more skilled, qualified workers, but many are unable or unwilling to pay for education and training because they are not certain how long workers will remain with their firms.

• A work-filled retirement. As America's influential baby boom generation approaches retirement age, the typical work-free retirement is yielding to an increasingly common work-filled retirement. People want to and must work longer than before. In essence, the traditional notion of retirement—where most people stop working completely to enjoy leisure time with friends and family—is obsolete.

• Few firms or individuals understand the complex public workforce system or how to use it effectively. A substantial number of workers and employers have benefited from public workforce programs, yet many are neither aware of nor use all the government workforce development tools that are available. While both workers and employers see a role for government to play in helping them address their workforce development needs, policymakers lag behind the public in recognizing the new dynamics of the U.S. labor market.

A New Paradigm for Human Resource Development Policy and Practice

The United States needs to understand, adjust to, and even embrace the new realities of the labor market and the economy and how individuals and firms deal with human resource issues. In short, the nation requires a new paradigm for human resource policy and practice. As with any other major paradigm shift, this will have important implications for the human resource development enterprise at all levels—for private firms and, of course, for workers, students, and job seekers.

This new paradigm should incorporate the following components:

• America must do a better job of aligning workforce development programs with market needs. A key problem is that many publicly funded programs are narrowly focused on entry-level jobs and often do not adequately consider employers' immediate or long-term needs for skilled workers. In addition, many programs fail to adequately link education and workforce policies to the economic needs of states and communities.

The State of New Jersey's Ready for the Job initiative, developed in partnership with the Heldrich Center for Workforce Development, is an example of one successful approach to this dilemma. Ready for the Job used focus groups and interviews to determine the skill and education requirements of key industries in New Jersey and then to develop effective industry-education collaboratives. (Results of this work may be found at the center's Web site: www.heldrich. rutgers.edu.)

• Public education often falls short in preparing individuals for the new economy. Employers frequently complain that the nation's schools are failing to teach the basic skills needed for most jobs and that its postsecondary education institutions are not producing enough graduates with advanced math, science, and engineering degrees. Elementary, secondary, and postsecondary education should be aligned with state and national goals for economic competitiveness. Action steps include:

Ensuring the prekindergarten, elementary, secondary, and postsecondary education systems are connected and build students' skills
Strengthening math and science programs at the middle, secondary, and postsecondary school levels
Reforming high schools to improve student achievement and connect students to work and college opportunities
Promoting greater participation and choice by modifying financial aid policies
Encouraging greater use of federal and state incentives

NJNextStop (http://www.njnextstop.org), developed by the Heldrich Center and several partners and launched in October 2003, informs students, career counselors, teachers, and parents about key industries and occupations in New Jersey and the skills and education requirements needed to be successful in seventy-three occupations in eight key industries. The site, currently visited by thousands of people monthly, offers original research, labor market information, job profiles, and career advice.

• The nation must do a better job of helping workers navigate the volatile labor market and when choosing career paths. Today's economy is marked by an acceleration of high business and job turnover, a breakdown in the internal career ladders for workers, and greater worker mobility. The result is that responsibility for career advancement has shifted to individuals. Unfortunately, postsecondary education, student financial aid, training programs, and consumer information are not changing fast enough to meet the expanding needs of working adults.

Individuals must assume greater responsibility for keeping their knowledge and skills current. The public and private sectors can help by developing easier ways for people to gain necessary certifications and navigate the increasingly complex and confusing learning marketplace. Policy actions include:

Promoting the use of skill-based assessment and credentials
Increasing customer choice and strengthening consumer information systems
Working with state and federal agencies, businesses, and organized labor to improve government's role in helping people transition between jobs

The New Jersey Training Systems Web site (www.njtrainingsystems.org), also developed in partnership with the Heldrich Center, helps job seekers and students identify the training and education programs that meet their needs. The site provides wide-ranging information on forty-three hundred training programs offered by nine hundred training providers.

• The United States must more aggressively address the needs of lower-wage workers to prevent them from falling further behind. Lower-wage workers often need additional training and supports—child care, health care coverage, transportation assistance—to help them move up the job skills and wage ladder. For many, work support services are crucial to their self-sufficiency and advancement, yet the nation is not investing enough in these supports or helping employers do so.

• The new realities of a work-filled retirement must be addressed. The demographic shifts in the U.S. workforce are likely to increase pressure on the nation's political and corporate leaders to come up with creative policy solutions. The imminent retirement of the first baby boomers will put increasing strains on government retirement programs and the economy. At the same time, the growing presence of older workers in the labor force is likely to force changes in employers' policies and workplace practices. Policymakers should explore solutions that facilitate a work-filled retirement for employees who choose it, meet the needs of employers for a steady supply of qualified workers, and address the need of all workers for retirement security. Recent analysis of this critical workforce challenge, including several reports of Work Trends national surveys, may be found at the Heldrich Center's Web site.

• America must have more effective governance and accountability structures. Multiple agencies, administrative fragmentation, and a lack of systemwide accountability limit the effectiveness of the public workforce system.

Workforce policies and programs should provide customer choice with services readily accessible and customized to the needs and interests of individuals, families, and employers. This includes more flexible learning models, portable credentials for students and workers, increased e-learning opportunities, and flexible financing options.

Conclusion

The new U.S. labor market presents new realities that demand new solutions and different behaviors by government, firms, and individuals. The United States needs a fundamentally new vision for workforce and human resource development practice and policy that accommodates the new learning economy and sheds the static, mid-twentieth-century version that is based on assumptions that no longer exist: permanent jobs, early educational preparation for life, stable businesses and careers, and secure retirement without work. American workers are struggling during this economic transformation. Public policy and most private firms have not kept pace with these transforming changes.

A shared vision of the next generation of workforce development and human resource development policy and practice is urgently needed. Governments and institutions at all levels need to address the major challenges of preparing U.S. workers for high-skill, high-wage employment and help those left behind by rapid economic upheavals.

Human resource scholars and practitioners have a great deal to contribute to the solutions and to create better opportunities for the nation, its communities, its citizens, and its families. It is time to get to work.

Note

1. Since 1998, the John J. Heldrich Center for Workforce Development at Rutgers, The State University of New Jersey, and the Center for Survey Research and Analysis at the University of Connecticut have been surveying adult workers and employers about issues in the economy, the workforce, and the workplace and how workers view the policy choices made by lawmakers and employers to address these concerns. Since its inception, the Work Trends series has interviewed over sixteen thousand people. Reports detailing the survey findings are available at www.heldrich.rutgers.edu.

Carl E. Van Horn is professor and director of the John J. Heldrich Center for Workforce Development at Rutgers, The State University of New Jersey.

Why We Fail: How Hubris, Hamartia, and Anagnosis Shape Organizational Behavior

Randal Ford

This article presents three tendencies (hubris, hamartia, and anagnosis) to explain why organizational personnel are prone to fail. All people are subject to these tendencies. Few organizations or individuals understand them, however, and fewer still know how to manage them. The article employs short case studies to define them and offers solutions on how to overcome their impact.

The survival of a corporation depends on the ability of its members to shape its destiny. When an organization flounders, the stakeholders—the board of directors, the executive officers, the stockholders, management from all levels—start to analyze the failure, often pointing to a "lack of leadership" or any number of other flaws, real or imaginary. Trust goes out the window. Everyone becomes frustrated and defensive.

Making or not making a mistake in itself does not determine success. To paraphrase Viktor Frankl (1962), success depends on how we as individuals react to our failure experiences. For example, Warren Bennis and Patricia Biederman (1997) claim that in creative groups, failure is regarded as a learning experience, not a pretext for punishment. According to Peter Drucker (1993), the most important ingredient for a company's success is the members' ability to draw new knowledge from their mistakes and learn how to apply that knowledge in new and productive ways. 3M found its direction after failing in the mining business. R. W. Johnson Jr., founder of Johnson and Johnson, frequently proclaimed, "Failure is our most important product." In short, we build and maintain vital, adaptive, and resilient organizations through what we learn from "lots of failed experiments" (Collins & Porras, 1997, p. 184). It is necessary, then, that an organization understand what can and does go wrong,

HUMAN RESOURCE DEVELOPMENT QUARTERLY, vol. 17, no. 4, Winter 2006 © Wiley Periodicals, Inc.
Published online in Wiley InterScience (www.interscience.wiley.com) • DOI: 10.1002/hrdq.1187

accept responsibility for the consequences, and avoid similar circumstances in the future (Lombardo, 1986). The trick, it seems, is knowing how to fail safe.

An ultimate failure is defined as when the organization falls short of an important goal with no other recourse but to go out of business or drastically downsize to remain solvent. All of its resources have been exhausted, and in the end, the employees' sustained efforts do not fulfill a desired outcome. Failing safe and ultimate failure, however, are not the same event.

An organization fails to fail safe when its workers are unable to recover and learn from the failure experience. In the prospect of admitting to our individual mistakes, each of us is confronted with owning up to the limits of our own competence. We are not perfect. Our knowledge and personal experiences do have limits. Those members of an organization who incubate their ego and avoid learning from their failure experiences are most likely to give birth to new ones. We can never know the whole from our solitary perspective. Critical flaws in the human character, as ancient as they are pervasive, tend to preclude effective learning and produce ineffective organizations. Aristotle came to a similar conclusion over twenty-five hundred years ago.

As organizations, our collective failure is enabled by what Aristotle called our all too human tendency toward hubris, hamartia, and anagnosis. All people are subject to these tendencies. Few organizations or individuals understand them. Fewer still know how to manage them. Identifying the opportunities in the failure experience requires both knowledge of its roots and tools to change individual member behavior to better accomplish strategic goals.

To Err Is Human

Aristotle was one of the first Western philosophers to articulate three limiting characteristics that predispose humans, despite our best intentions, to fail: hubris, hamartia, and anagnosis (HH&A). Hubris and hamartia he writes about directly (see Else, 1967). Anagnosis ("without knowledge") is a term I coined for this article. Actually what Aristotle talks about is a leader experiencing *anagnorisis* (recognition) of past deeds, and always too late to do anything about them. Because people act blindly in the present, at some point in the future (though too late), they will come to recognize the full consequences of their actions. What Aristotle implies, then, is that up to the point of recognition (anagnorisis), people tend to act in a vacuum of ignorance; hence my term *anagnosis*—acting without knowledge. In short, without learning (knowledge), people are more likely to fail, either as individuals or collectively. Hence, the implication: when the organization is not able to harvest and manage knowledge gained from employees' mistakes, it has failed to fail safe.

HH&A predispose all humans and the organizations they labor in to make and repeat mistakes that lead to ultimate failure. For instance, on a broad scale, political analysts studying the consequences of institutional hubris argue that it leads to the decline and fall of world powers: from Athens, Alexandria, Antioch, Pergamon, Rome, Madrid, the Hague, and London to the atrophy of the U.S. federal government (Phillips, 1994). The ability to recognize these traits in ourselves not only increases the chances that our organizations will fail safe, but also better prepares us to minimize undesirable results and draw important lessons from the failure experience.

Hubris, an overweening pride or ego, implies the violation of a law or failure to recognize the limitations of one's knowledge by regarding oneself as equal to the gods. Hubris is an act of will and as such also suggests arrogance. We demonstrate it by behaviors and claims to our superior importance or rights.

Hamartia translates as a "flaw in character" and is essentially psychological. A person, for example, who is doggedly stubborn and exhibits a terrible temper alienates others, which leads to his or her downfall. The character flaw interpretation is accurate to a point. But hamartia has more to do with the limitation of individual perception than a psychological flaw. Hamartia derives from the Greek *hamartanien*—to miss the mark, to err. People tend to lock into a single point of view such that we often are unable to recognize or hit our intended target. We fail by a lack of ability, when left alone, to get outside our limited perspective.

For Aristotle, the limitations imposed by hubris and hamartia go hand-in-hand to undermine a person's ability to make sound decisions and act effectively. However, these tendencies are only two points in a strong triangle. The triangle is completed with *anagnosis.* We are limited despite our open-mindedness—what scholar researchers who study how decisions are made within organizations call "bounded rationality" (see Simon, 1957). Simply put, we can never know all there is to know about any endeavor or situation. Anagnosis is our lack of knowledge that creates in us an inability to make sense of how everything fits together to form the big picture. That is, if our refusal to listen (hubris) is compounded by our inability to see the whole from our limited perspective (hamartia), we are acting in a vacuum of ignorance (anagnosis), deprived of the informed knowledge we need to accomplish organizational goals.

Obvious acts of hubris include dogmatism and chauvinism. *Dogmatism* is the act of asserting an opinion in an arrogant manner without proof or evidence—in short, "My way or the highway." For example, after 350 years, the Roman Catholic church lifted its 1663 condemnation of Galileo for teaching that the earth orbited the sun, contrary to the then current dogma teaching that the sun orbited the earth. The church finally acknowledged this error in 1997 after the completion of a thirteen-year study (Cowell, 1992). Chauvinism is the unreasoning devotion to one's race, gender or sex, nationality, or class to the exclusion and with contempt for others. Prudential Insurance Co. of America permitted its agents to misrepresent its life insurance policy provisions to customers. Now, hobbled by excessive overhead, an outdated product line, and two sales scandals, there was a 50 percent decline in sales from 1991 to 1996 and another 24 percent decline in 1997. The potential cost of its market conduct settlement with policyholders could run into billions of dollars (Scism, 1997).

Hamartia is different from hubris. Hamartia is not an act of will. Instead, something obscures our vision; a mote is lodged in our eye that, left unattended, could lead to an ultimate failure. Translated, that means that if the employees are blind, the organization is blind too. For example, the crash of a ValuJet aircraft killing 110 people in the Florida Everglades in 1996 was apparently caused by a fire from the oxygen-generating canisters in the cargo hold. SabreTech cargo handlers, ValuJet maintenance, and the Federal Aviation Administration all failed to see how not designating responsibility for attaching required safety caps could lead to an ultimate failure (Greenwald, 1996). We experience failure when our circumscribed viewpoint blocks our view of the whole situation. A holistic view is impossible when we each insist our view is right, to the exclusion and devaluation of another's perspective. Our hamartia obfuscates our view of all necessary points that would give us a more complete perception of reality. Thus, when employees who are in positions of power make decisions that affect coworker lives and insist on their limited view as absolutely right, they increase the risk for an organization to go astray (see Ford, Boss, Angermeier, Townson, & Jennings, 2004).

The use of multidisciplinary and participatory forms of decision making is directed at compensating for our tendency toward hamartia. Yet more is needed. Our organizations are becoming so complex that every individual act has unexpected side effects, many of which cannot be anticipated. When systems are interdependent, actions in one area directly and immediately affect many others. The nuclear reactor failure at Chernobyl, for example, was precipitated by operators who were routinely violating safety rules because they had come to believe they knew better and considered the rules a nuisance (Dörner, 1996). We can never know all there is to know about any situation. Humans are by nature social beings and incomplete when we isolate ourselves from the collective.

Isolation creates anagnosis. For example, when we focus too intently on the isolated incident without simultaneously envisioning the end game, events remain disconnected, and we are uninformed of the driving forces antecedent to the present. Who would have predicted the World Health Organization (WHO) would be parachuting cats into Borneo to stop a bubonic plague brought on by its own extravagant use of DDT? With the best of intentions, WHO sprayed DDT to eradicate mosquitoes carrying a malaria plague. The insecticide also killed houseflies, which were eagerly eaten by geckos. Eventually, through the buildup of DDT, the geckos died too. Without the geckoes to prey on them, the population of rats rapidly expanded, resulting in an outbreak of bubonic plague. Before the thousands of cats could eat the rats, thousands of people died from the plague (Alcamo, 1991).

An increasingly popular way to view an organization is as a set of interrelated systems (see Dixon, 1994). Studies show that to understand systems-level learning, it is essential to focus on the organizational structures, processes, and systems that facilitate learning. As members of an organization, we must learn there is a lag time between the execution of a measure and its effect. We must learn to recognize patterns in time that evolve between different functional departments, with different needs and mind-sets. To do so means we must contribute to and embrace the collective knowledge of all of our members. Only then can a corporation say it is managing its knowledge well. Only then can an organization say it is acting with knowledge, not without it (Davenport & Prusak, 1998).

Creating a Credible and Open Process

A credible and open process diminishes the collusive tension of HH&A between employees and management levels within an organization (see Ford & Angermeier, 2004). Consider, for example, Nucor Corporation, one of the nation's largest steel producers. Nucor's workforce is strongly committed to build steel manufacturing facilities economically and operate them productively. It has received a great deal of attention in the business media in recent years because of its success in an industry beset by a multitude of problems.

The 1983–1984 recession that devastated the American steel industry also hit Nucor. To survive the decline in revenues, Nucor placed its employees on a two- or three-day work schedule, with a corresponding cut in pay. This policy was applied across all levels of the organization, from the CEO to the lowest maintenance worker. No employee was laid off. With this strategy, Nucor not only saved the company during economic hard times but created a network of sound working relationships and an esprit de corps that bounded back with incredible force (Iverson, 1997; for similar results in health care, see Ford & Angermeier, 2004). How?

Nucor's CEO created a credible and open process. Nucor shared with its employees the company's problem and then got them to agree to work together in constructive ways to remedy the situation. According to researchers Chrislip and Larson (1994), without these basic understandings among all participants, any attempt to define the problem, develop solutions, and implement a plan would be premature. And having involved all the stakeholders, Nucor built sound relationships that were flexible and responsive to the market.

What is the relationship between creating a credible and open process and minimizing the pernicious effect of the character flaws HH&A? If people are to collaborate effectively, they have to be able to create a shared work in common that takes shape in their mutual discussions and actions rather than from one person who acts as an authority to the others. Sharing accurate information also allows employee-stakeholders to determine where and how they fit into the greater scheme of the organization (Monge & Miller, 1988) and that allows them to effectively participate in learning how to coordinate their actions (Castrogiovanni & Macy, 1990; Lawler, 1986) and make better decisions (Brady, 1989). Nucor gave its employees a stake in a company's growth, focused on the business at hand, and kept red tape and bureaucracy to a minimum (Rodengen, 1997). This credible and open process enabled the employees at Nucor to put aside their personal agendas to embrace a larger shared goal, which created intense loyalty (Ritt, 1998a, 1998b).

Engaged in a credible and open process and keeping in mind each member's capacity for HH&A while the organization reflects on the tough questions we cannot easily answer cleanses us of our arrogance, informs our mind, and reveals our flaws. HH&A function like blinders. Once we become aware of how we are acting, we can choose to act differently. Only through a credible and open dialogue can each member's HH&A be surfaced and thus its effects minimized. The benefits for the organization increase when what is learned is captured, stored, shared, and used to improve our collaborations to create innovative systems, outcomes, and services (Ford & Angermeier, 2004; Gephart, Marsick, Van Buren, & Spiro, 1996).

At Nucor, the learning and the application of that knowledge have not stopped yet. General managers are responsible to hold annual dinners with every employee in groups of twenty-five to a hundred at one time. These meetings give employees a chance to discuss problems related to scheduling, equipment, organization, and production. The format is free and open. Topics vary widely from year to year. Sessions can last well beyond midnight. In a similar manner, the general managers meet with top management three times each year to review each facility's performance and plan for the months and years ahead (Sheridan, 1998).

Reflection and Dialogue

How can company personnel recognize HH&A, and what can they do about it once they do? A useful starting place is our underlying assumptions, beliefs, and the culture from which they stem (Argyris & Schön, 1978)—in short, our everyday interactions with our work colleagues. HH&A are inherent tendencies in the human condition that are omnipresent but mostly unconscious. The potential for HH&A to appear happens anytime people come together to work collaboratively, especially when difficult and significant decisions must be made and passions are running competitively high.

What makes the destructive aspects of HH&A so pervasive and difficult to apprehend? These dark tendencies are deeply connected to the driving passions necessary to accomplish our dreams and vision (Harris & Hogan, 1992). Yet these same tendencies, when not monitored or when we are totally unaware they exist, collude to create our own personal triangle for tragedy and undermine collective interaction with other organizational members. Trying to eliminate these tendencies, even if we could, would be sure folly. What is important is not eradication but learning when HH&A are helping the collaborative effort and when they are getting in the way.

Let us say, for instance, that several divisions of a company agree to share the same sales force in an attempt to become more horizontal and responsive to serve their market niche. However, in a vertical-functional versus a horizontal-collective environment, each district manager would be primarily concerned that the shared sales force would not give enough attention to his or her particular business and that volume would decline. Already we see each manager asserting an ego (hubris), from a perspective limited by self-interest (hamartia), that will put each at odds with the others; consequently little communication occurs (anagnosis). HH&A are driving the events toward an ultimate failure in this company. The situation calls for a credible and open process that gets each division manager to agree there is a problem, then agree they will work on it, then determine what the problem is, and together generate solutions that satisfy all their needs. The situation calls for reflective dialogue that builds sound working relationships and trust to enable all the division managers in the company to work together.

Alas, the existing culture established certain assumptions and ingrained behavior that each division manager knows from past experience works—what Peter Senge (1994) calls "mental models" or "theories-in-use." What predictably happens is that one particularly aggressive manager advises all his or her account managers to set higher sales targets than are truly needed. This way, using the reasoning of the previous culture, the shared sales force will at least give his or her division the minimum support they need. Right? Wrong. Human nature being what it is, the other divisions see this dastardly manager pushing for extra work and decide to employ the same strategy.

The new sales force's managers want to accommodate all, so they continue to accept the higher requests from the divisions. Such actions naturally create a tremendous overburden of work, which produces lower performance and increased turnover. Unable to meet its needs, soon morale and the goodwill of the sales force take a nosedive. What trust there was disintegrates. Business becomes disrupted and fouled for each division. Sore nerves and bad feelings run rampant, and vital resources are lost. And cost soars. Each division goes back to square one by maintaining its own sales force. In short, each manager's HH&A colluded with the others to create an impossible situation and an ultimate failure—misaligned, misused, and eventually squandered, resources.

The fundamental problem never addressed in this scenario is that each manager needed to amend his or her perspective on how business as usual would be accomplished with a shared sales force. But no way can do when managers are blinded by ego, a limited perspective, and lack of knowledge. Sound familiar? Now the question becomes, "What can an organization do about it?"

The skills for group reflection through dialogue are being researched and applied (Bohm, 1996; Isaacs, 1999; Senge, 1994). The purpose of group dialogue is to surface the mental models we unconsciously formulate and understand how HH&A drives the construction of our own and the group's perception, its constraints, assumptions, and beliefs, in order that we and our organizations can better recover and learn from the failure experience. Group dialogue allows each employee in the organization to clarify her or his thinking; identify and communicate values and principles; and extend the individual's perception to include the whole. Through group dialogue, employees are able to access a larger pool of meaning with each person's view bringing a unique perspective on a larger reality. And when we are able to do so, the collusive power of our personal tendency toward HH&A to create a triangle for tragedy subsides considerably.

In Closing

Peter Swartz's experience at Shell Oil illustrates an important lesson for any corporation (1991). He describes how Shell was able to minimize the negative consequences of the 1974 oil embargo through years of collective (and collected) reflection at the highest levels. Their method was the process of creating and exploring the implications of what-if future scenarios. They were not predicting the future. They were preparing their minds to comprehend it should it occur. When it did occur, they were prepared to think about it more deeply. Is it possible to achieve a breakthrough without recognizing the breakdowns? Not likely. Must we all reinvent the same broken wheel? Not always. Is there an easier way to learn from our mistakes than going through the solitary routine of trial and error? Probably, if we do not insist trying to go it alone. Individuals cannot explore all the pertinent views of a situation as well as a group, especially using a structured dialogue process. We are by nature social beings, incomplete when isolated from the collective. As organizations, our collective failure is enabled by what Aristotle called our all too human tendency toward hubris, hamartia, and anagnosis. Personnel in all companies are subject to these tendencies. Few understand them. Fewer still know how to manage them. To compensate, however, we become aware. Enlightenment begins with admitting these tendencies exist, then learning how they drive us as individuals in our organizations.

References

Alcamo, E. I. (1991). *Fundamentals of microbiology.* Boston: Benjamin Cummings.

Argyris, C., & Schön, D. (1978). *Organizational learning: A theory of action perspective.* Reading, MA: Addison-Wesley.

Bennis, W., & Biederman, P. W. (1997). *Organizing genius: The secrets of creative collaboration.* Reading, MA: Addison-Wesley.

Bohm, D. (1996). *On dialogue.* London: Routledge.

Brady, G. F. (1989). *Management by involvement: An action guide.* New York: Insight Books.

Castrogiovanni, G. J., & Macy, B. A. (1990). Organizational information with processing capabilities and degree of employee participation. *Group and Organization Studies, 15,* 313–336.

Chrislip, D., & Larson, C. E. (1994). *Collaborative leadership: How citizens and civic leaders can make a difference.* San Francisco: Jossey-Bass.

Collins, J. C., & Porras, J. I. (1997). *Built to last: The successful habits of visionary companies.* New York: HarperCollins.

Cowell, A. (1992, November 1). Church to admit error on Galileo. *Denver Post,* pp. 1A, 12A.

Davenport, T. H., & Prusak, L. (1998). *Working knowledge: How organizations manage what they know.* Boston: Harvard Business School Press.

Dixon, N. M. (1994). *The organizational learning cycle: How we learn collectively.* New York: McGraw-Hill.

Dörner, D. (1996). *The logic of failure: Recognizing and avoiding error in complex situations.* Reading, MA: Addison-Wesley.

Drucker, P. F. (1993). *Post-capitalist society.* New York: HarperCollins.

Else, G. F. (1967). *Aristotle's Poetics.* Ann Arbor: University of Michigan Press.

Ford, R., & Angermeier, I. (2004). Managing the knowledge environment: A case study from healthcare. *Knowledge Management Research and Practice, 2,* 137–146.

Ford, R., Boss, R. W., Angermeier, I., Townson, C. D., & Jennings, T. A. (2004). Adapting to change in healthcare: Aligning strategic intent and operational capacity. *Hospital Topics, 82,* 20–29.

Frankl, V. (1962). *Man's search for meaning.* Boston: Beacon Press.

Gephart, M. A., Marsick, V. J., Van Buren, M. E., & Spiro, M. S. (1996, December). Learning organizations come alive. *Training and Development, 50*(12), 35–45.

Greenwald, J. (1996, December 2). Tragedy retold: How a trail of blunders led to the ValuJet crash. *Time,* p. 57.

Harris, G., & Hogan, J. (1992, April). *Perceptions and personality correlates of managerial effectiveness.* Paper presented at the Thirteenth Annual Psychology in the Department of Defense Symposium, Colorado Springs, CO.

Iverson, K. (1997). *Plain talk: Lessons from a business maverick.* Hoboken, NJ: Wiley.

Isaacs, W. (1999). *Dialogue and the art of thinking together.* New York: Currency Books.

Lawler, E. E. (1986). *High-involvement management.* San Francisco: Jossey-Bass.

Lombardo, M. M. (1986). Questions about learning from experience. *Issues and Observations, 6,* 7–10.

Monge, P. R., & Miller, K. I. (1988). Participative processes in organizations. In G. M. Goldhaber & G. A. Barnett (Eds.), *Handbook of organizational communication* (pp. 213–229). Norwood, NJ: Ablex.

Phillips, K. (1994). *Arrogant capital: Washington, Wall Street, and the frustration of American politics.* Boston: Little, Brown.

Ritt, A. (1998a, August). Nucor's investment in loyalty. *New Steel,* p. 2.

Ritt, A. (1998b, August). Iverson's disciple. *New Steel,* p. 46.

Rodengen, J. L. (1997). *The legend of Nucor.* Fort Lauderdale, FL: Write Stuff Enterprises.

Scism, L. (1997). After the fall: Prudential's cleanup in wake of scandals hurts insurance sales. *Wall Street Journal,* pp. A1, A6.

Senge, P. M. (1994). *The fifth discipline: The art and practice of the learning organization.* New York: Doubleday.

Sheridan, J. H. (1998, June 8). Tale of a maverick. *Industry Week,* p. 22.

Simon, H. A. (1957). *Administrative behavior* (2nd ed.). New York: Free Press.

Swartz, P. (1991). *The art of the long view.* New York: Doubleday.

Randal Ford is professor of management at the Hasan School of Business, Colorado State University-Pueblo.

REVIEW

Lost Knowledge: Confronting the Threat of an Aging Workforce, by David W. DeLong. New York: Oxford University Press, 2004. 258 pages. $19.95 (hardcover).

DeLong's *Lost Knowledge* follows in the ever-widening vein of books warning of the challenges, and in some texts impending doom, certain to arrive with the crest and crash of baby boomers into retirement. Dychtwald's *AgeWave* and *AgePower* burst on the popular press scene in 1990 and 1999, respectively, and Goldberg's *Age Works* entered the fold in 2000 with her focus on the workplace. More recently, *The Aging Workforce* (Hedge, Borman, & Lammlein, 2006) and *Older Worker Advantage* (Shea & Haasen, 2005) have joined the discussion.

This book is a worthy addition to any manager's bookshelf, especially those involved in information technology and knowledge management. It is clearly written and intuitively organized for both an initial reading and future reference. According to the author, a research fellow at the Massachusetts Institute of Technology's Age-Lab and adjunct professor at Babson College, this is a solution-oriented book based in exploratory research that is broad-based but not scientific. For the human resource practitioner, Chapters Three through Six and Eleven are the most pertinent.

The author is explicit in his desire to address his fundamental premise that "the primary reason executives avoid addressing threats of lost knowledge is that they have no idea how to attack the problem" (p. 4). DeLong concentrates on strategies for retaining knowledge, whether by enticing ongoing involvement with the employee through staged retirement or contract agreement (the "human" in human capital), or by creating containers into which the employee's expertise and experience can be dumped and preserved for later retrieval (the "capital" of human capital). The author works at keeping his prose diverse, substituting a litany of terms for *knowledge,* including *intellectual capital, human capital, critical knowledge assets,* and *intellectual assets.* The dominant metaphor throughout is knowledge as money.

The book is divided into three sections, with Section One covering the problem of lost knowledge, Section Two describing retention practices, and Section Three the implementation of retention strategies. Throughout the book, DeLong uses case studies to illustrate lost knowledge consequences and successful retention practices. Chapter One is no exception. Here he provides statistics and examples demonstrating the oncoming movement of labor out of the labor force—the inevitability of huge chunks of knowledge walking out the door. In this chapter,

the author differentiates the knowledge construct into human knowledge, social knowledge, cultural knowledge, and structured knowledge. This almost appears to be an obligatory bone tossed to academics because the relevance of this break-down is unclear throughout the book. (The author does explore aspects of explicit and tacit knowledge in Chapters Five and Six.)

In Chapter Two, additional evidence is provided for the pressing need to retain employees and their knowledge as well as recruit new employees who can reuse these intellectual assets. The mismatch of supply and demand (grad-uates to jobs) is mentioned, as are potential conflicts between the generations and their perceived value differences. Because this book is about retaining and accessing knowledge, as opposed to an employee's ability to think critically or creatively, I found myself needing to substitute the term *information* for *knowledge* throughout this and other chapters. I also had to periodically remind myself that the author tends to place content over context—context requiring the additional skills of innovation and criticality.

In Chapter Three, DeLong presents an overview of his strategic framework for action, pointing to specific HR processes, policies, and practices for its suc-cessful incorporation into the business environment. The four major compo-nents are knowledge transfer practices; knowledge recovery initiatives; information technology applications to capture, store, and share knowledge; and human resource processes and practices.

Chapter Four illuminates the component of human resource processes and practices—beginning with skills inventories, building a "retention culture," and policies that affect older employees. This is not the book to consult if you want to better understand older workers, although the author does provide four actions that management might consider in retaining older employees longer.

Chapter Five, titled "Improving the Transfer of Explicit Knowledge," leads off with a definition of the terms *explicit, tacit,* and *implicit.* This dis-cussion seems misplaced, falling within a section seemingly reserved for explicit knowledge. Nonetheless, it is an important section. Explicit knowl-edge, as defined by the author, "is easily codified and can be shared inde-pendent of its human source, or it can be embedded in processes or systems" (p. 83); tacit knowledge involves craft, know-how, mental models, beliefs, images, and intuition. "But this explicit/tacit dimension is too gen-eral to be useful to managers" (p. 83), warns DeLong, who breaks down the general tacit category into implicit rule-based knowledge, implicit know-how, tacit know-how, and deep tacit knowledge. This treatment is concep-tually heavy compared to the rest of the book—possibly another attempt to engage an academic audience; however, the latter part of the chapter light-ens up with a tool kit approach to the transfer of explicit knowledge through documentation, interviews, and training.

Chapter Six continues the tool kit approach with implicit and tacit-gathering schemes including storytelling, mentoring and coaching, after-action reviews, and communities of practice. As an adult education scholar,

I found this chapter the pinnacle of the book and believe, or at least hope, that the processes outlined in this chapter will become popular practice in organizations.

Chapter Seven completes the four-component framework with an overview of the role of information technology in knowledge capture, with sections on expert systems, e-learning, Web-based repositories, knowledge mapping, and database management. Chapter Eight concludes Section Two with a discussion of recovery initiatives, including the challenges of outsourcing and rehiring employees as contractors. One aspect that is surprisingly missing throughout the book is how to manage bad knowledge emerging from erroneous translation, bad habits, or antiquated processes.

Section Three details the specific challenges an organization might encounter in implementing knowledge retention processes. Chapter Ten is a call to action—how to get started and what to pursue first. Chapter Eleven reminds readers of the complexity of human resources, including potentially contentious relationships between expert and novice and between younger and older employees. Human resource professionals will appreciate the acknowledgment of egos and the challenges these bring.

This 250-page book is packed with practical information and enlightening case studies. As long as one can hold to the view of knowledge existing outside the mind of an individual—a kind of substance flowing between individuals—this book makes perfect sense. Chapters Five and Six do introduce the concept of tacit knowledge, which tends to puncture the rigid duality of mind and world. The author seems aware of, if not slightly agitated by, this pesky epistemological elephant that has sat in the living rooms of "very smart people" since before Plato. "Any discussion about the phenomenon of 'knowledge' requires some clarification about its relationship to the concept of 'information,'" states DeLong. "Lots of very smart people have tried to articulate the differences between these two concepts. The difficulty of this task underscores the fact that knowledge and information are often overlapping constructs whose relevance is determined by the situation" (p. 22). A few "smart people" might note that the author has embodied the constructs of knowledge and information with human tendencies through his use of "whose." Finally, in the section titled "Capturing Knowledge," the author states, "Academics may argue about what's in these [organizational] documents. Is it really knowledge or just information? But from management's perspective, who cares?" (p. 132). Sometimes it is best to ignore the elephant.

REVIEWED BY
KATHY LOHR MILLER
NORTH CAROLINA STATE UNIVERSITY
RALEIGH, NORTH CAROLINA

HUMAN RESOURCE DEVELOPMENT QUARTERLY • DOI: 10.1002/hrdq

References

Dychtwald, K. (1999). *AgePower: How the 21st century will be ruled by the new old.* New York: Jeremy P. Tarcher/Putnam.

Dychtwald, K. (1990). *AgeWave: How the most important trend of our time will change your future.* New York: Bantam.

Goldberg, B. (2000). *Age works: What corporate America must do to survive the graying of the workforce.* New York: Free Press.

Hedge, J., Borman, W., & Lammlein, S. (2006). *The aging workforce: Realities, myths, and implications for organizations.* Washington, DC: American Psychological Association.

Shea, G., & Haasen, A. (2005). *Older worker advantage: Making the most of our aging workforce.* Westport, CT: Praeger.

INDEX

A

Academic journals: customer satisfaction with, 131; journal editors as managers and, 133; missions of sponsoring organizations and, 132; positioning of, in knowledge market, 132–133; as products of professional organizations, 131; Total Quality Management approach to, 133; value-oriented perspective on, 131–132

"Academic Journals Are Products of Professional Organizations," 131–133

Academy of Human Resource Development (AHRD), 242–243

Accountability, of trainers for training transfer, 352–353, 355

Action science model, of informal learning, 137

Adult education, in Africa: adult learning principles and, 359; community vs. individual contexts and, 359; environment and, 359–360; gender roles and, 360; globalization and, 360, 362; HRD implications and, 361–362; indigenous vs. traditional forms of adult education and, 359; opportunities for, 360; professional development and, 360

Adult education: definition of, 359; environment and, 359–360; globalization and, 360, 362

Adult learning participation: choice as motivating factor in, 447–448; critical factors in, definition of, 443; developing countries and, 449; HRD research on, 447–449; HRD theory/practice and, 443; individual factors and, 448; intrinsic factors and, 447; models of, 447; motivation theory and, 447; research on, 444; socialization factor model of, 447. See also Adult learning; Learning participation, in management development in China (study)

Adult learning: adult education and, 359; from artifacts/tools, 138; clusters of, 137; community vs. individual contexts and, 359; facilitating agent for, 138; HRD in workplace and, 136–137; work contexts and, 148. See also Adult education; Adult education, in Africa; Adult learning participation; Informal learning; Interactive workplace learning (study); Learning participation in management development in China (study); Workplace learning

Africa. See Adult education, in Africa

Allen, T. D., "Formal Mentoring Programs and Organizational Attraction," 43–58

Amutabi, M., Foundations of Adult Education in Africa, reviewed, 359–363

Anagnosis, 483–484

Anderson, J. E., "Influences of New Development Practices on Temporary Employee Work-Related Attitudes," 279–303

"Anyone? Anyone? Anyone?" 365–369

Articles: "Choosing Among Tests of Emotional Intelligence: What Is the Evidence?" 9–42; "Comparing the Effects of Determinants of Turnover Intentions Between Taiwanese and U.S. Hospital Employees," 403–321; "Employer Assessment of Work-Related Competencies and Workplace Adaptation," 305–324; "Formal Mentoring Programs and Organizational Attraction," 43–58; "Influence of Trainee Characteristics, Instructional Satisfaction, and Organizational Climate on Perceived Learning and Training Transfer," 85–116; "Influences of New Development Practices on Temporary Employee Work-Related Attitudes," 279–303; "Key Characteristics of Effective and Ineffective Developmental Interactions," 59–84; "Learning in Interactive Work Situations: It Takes Two to Tango: Why Not Invite Both Partners to Dance?" 135–158; "Learning to Become a Machine Operator: The Dialogical Relationship Between Context, Self, and Content," 199–221; "Making Subjective Judgments in Quantitative Studies: The Importance of Using Effect Sizes and Confidence Intervals," 159–173; "Participation in Management Training in a Transitioning Context: A Case of China," 443–473; "Roles of Informal Workplace Trainers

in Different Organizational Contexts: Empirical Evidence from Australian Companies," 175–198; "Supplier Diversity: A Missing Link in Human Resource Development," 325–341; "Survey Ranking of Job Competencies by Perceived Employee Importance: Comparing Three Regions," 371–402; "Tuition Reimbursement, Perceived Organizational Support, and Turnover Intention Among Graduate Business School Students," 423–442
Avoidance, by leaders, 366

B

Baruch, Y., "Tuition Reimbursement, Perceived Organizational Support, and Turnover Intention Among Graduate Business School Students," 423–442
Behavioral change: attitudes and, 248–250; cynicism and, 250; intentions and, 248; organizational support and, 250; perceived locus of control and, 250–252; role theory and, 247; theory of planned behavior and, 247–250, 261, 263–264. *See also* Performance improvement
Benson, G. S., "Tuition Reimbursement, Perceived Organizational Support, and Turnover Intention Among Graduate Business School Students," 423–442
Brockman, J. L., "Learning to Become a Machine Operator: The Dialogical Relationship Between Context, Self, and Content," 199–221
Burns, J. Z., "Frederick Lewis Otte (1934–2004): The Consummate Human Resource Developer," 5–8

C

Callahan, J. L., "Making Subjective Judgments in Quantitative Studies: The Importance of Using Effect Sizes and Confidence Intervals," 159–173
Capacity, leadership, 366
Career development: career advice topics and, 65, 74; developmental interactions and, 61; job/career satisfaction and, 413; multisource feedback and, 246
Career satisfaction. *See* Job/career satisfaction

Change. *See* Behavioral change; Organizational change
Chauvinism, 483
China. *See* Job skills, employee perceptions of, in China (study); Learning participation, in management development in China (study); Turnover intentions, in Taiwanese and U.S. organizations (study)
"Choosing Among Tests of Emotional Intelligence: What Is the Evidence?" 9–42
"Closing the Gap Between Research and Practice in Human Resource Development," 343–350
Coaching, learning transfer and, 180
Communities of practice, 204, 212–213
"Comparing the Effects of Determinants of Turnover Intentions Between Taiwanese and U.S. Hospital Employees," 403–321
Competitive advantage: economic theory of, 306, 320; workplace adaptation and, 305–306
Competitiveness, public education and, 477
Confidence intervals (CI): APA style manual and, 163, 170; arelational, 167; classes of, 167; definition of, 166; encouraging dialogue about, 171; history of, 166–167; HRD and, 169; implications for application of, 168–170; interpretation of, 167–168; populational value and, 167; practical meaning and, 168; quantitative studies and, 159–160; recommendations for changes in use of, 170–171; relational, 167; review of *HRDQ* and, 160; significance and, 164, 170; statistical packages and, 171; statistical significance and, 168–169; subjectivity of research and, 159, 170; as supplement to NHST, 159–160, 163; teaching methods for, 170–171; value of, 167
Conflict management, emotional intelligence and, 32
Contextual model of learning, 246–247
Credible and open process, Nucor Corporation example of, 485–486
Customer service: academic journals and, 131–133; Total Quality Management and, 133

D

D'Abate, C. P., "Key Characteristics of Effective and Ineffective Developmental Interactions," 59–84

DeLong, D. W., *Lost Knowledge: Confronting the Threat of an Aging Workforce,* reviewed, 491–494

Developmental interactions: advisee role and, 76; adviser factors (expertise, needs focus, self-discovery focus) and, 64, 72, 74–75; benefits vs. risks of, 60; career development and, 61, 65; career development issues and, 61, 65; communication factors (face-to-face vs. technology) and, 64–65, 72–73; definition of, 60; employee learning and, 60, 76–77; expanded model of, 61; factors affecting effectiveness of, 62–66; factors affecting, 62; job-/task-specific issues and, 66, 74, 76; mentoring and, 60–62; multiple forms of, 61; organizational role and, 76; personal factors (age, gender, race) and, 62–63, 69–70; relationship factors (initiation, frequency, length, duration, source) and, 64–65, 69, 71, 74–75; research on, 61–62; typology of, 61; work-life issues and, 61, 65; work-life support and, 61, 65. *See also* Developmental interactions, characteristics of (study)

Developmental interactions, characteristics of (study): advisee role and, 76; adviser factors (expertise, needs focus, self-discovery focus) and, 64, 72, 74–75; appendix, 78–81; career development advice and, 61, 65; communication factors (face-to-face vs. design/procedure, 66; discussion, 74–77; discussion topics and, 65–66, 72, 74; factors interview, 78–81; job/task-specific advice and, 66, 74, 76; measures, 67–68; method, 66–69; organizational role and, 76; participants, 67, 69; personal factors (age, gender, race) and, 62–63, 69–70; practice implications, 75–76; purpose, 60–61; relationship factors (initiation, frequency, length, duration, source) and, 64–65, 69, 71, 74–75; results, 69–74; study limitations, 77; tests of hypotheses and, 69–72; tests of topic

and, 72–74; work-life advice and, 61, 65, 74. *See also* Developmental interactions

Ding, C. G., "Comparing the Effects of Determinants of Turnover Intentions Between Taiwanese and U.S. Hospital Employees," 403–321

Dirkx, J. M., "Learning to Become a Machine Operator: The Dialogical Relationship Between Context, Self, and Content," 199–221

Diversity: manager sensitivity to, 376–377. *See also* Diversity practitioners; Supplier diversity programs

Diversity practitioners: economic considerations and, 327; educators for supplier diversity, 338–339; educator role and, 338–339; HRD practitioners and, 327–328, 332–333, 337–339; researcher role and, 339; role of, 326–327, 332–337; as strategists for supplier diversity, 337–338; strategist role and, 327–328

Dogmatism, 483

Doornbos, A. J., "Learning in Interactive Work Situations: It Takes Two to Tango: Why Not Invite Both Partners to Dance?" 135–158

E

Eddy, E. R., "Key Characteristics of Effective and Ineffective Developmental Interactions," 59–84

"Editor's Challenge to Human Resource Development, An," 1–4

Editorial: "Academic Journals Are Products of Professional Organizations," 131–133; "An Editor's Challenge to Human Resource Development," 1–4; "Frederick Lewis Otte (1934–2004): The Consummate Human Resource Developer," 5–8; "Research: The Bridge Between Human Resource Development Practitioners and Scholars," 235–243

Education: competitiveness and, 477. *See also* Adult education; Adult education, in Africa; Learning

Effect size (ES): APA style manual and, 163, 170; benchmark values and, 166; definitions of, 164; determining practical significance and, 165–166; difference indices and, 165; encouraging dialogue about, 171; group overlap indices and, 165; history of use of, 164–165; HRD and, 169; implications for application of, 168–170; interpretation of, 166; practical meaning and, 168; quantitative studies and, 159–160; recommendations for changes in use of, 170–171; relationship indices and, 165; review of *HRDQ* and, 160; significance and, 164, 170; statistical packages and, 171; statistical significance and, 168–169; subjectivity of research and, 159, 170; as supplement to NHST, 159–160, 163; teaching methods for, 170–171; types of, 165

Emotion: rationality and, 224, 226–227; social interactions and, 225–226; strategic HRD and, 224. *See also* Emotional intelligence (EI)

Emotional Competency Index (ECI-2), 12, 14–15, 19–22, 27–31, 32, 37. *See also* Emotional intelligence (EI) tests, and HRD professionals (study)

Emotional intelligence (EI): conflict management and, 32; customer service training and, 33; definition of, 11; history of, 11; of MBA students, 35; organizational change and, 32; physician training and, 32; research on application of, 36; research on development of, 34–36; research on impact of, 36–37; role of culture in, 35–36; stress management and, 33; transformational leadership and, 34

Emotional Intelligence Questionnaire (EIQ), 12, 14–15, 25–29. *See also* Emotional intelligence (EI) tests, and HRD professionals (study)

Emotional intelligence (EI) tests: construct validity and, 13; content validity and, 13; Emotional Competency Index (ECI-2) and, 12, 14–15, 19–22, 27–31, 32, 37; Emotional Quotient Inventory (EQ-i), 12, 14–15, 19, 22–25, 27–29, 37; external validity and, 14; face validity and, 13; HRD and, 9–10, 31–34; leadership development and, 33–34; Mayer-Solovey-Caruso Emotional Intelligence Test (MSCEIT), 12, 14–19, 28–31, 33, 37; organizational uses of, 10, 31–32; predictive validity and, 14; test bandwidth and, 31; test fidelity and, 31; test specificity and, 31; training

industry and, 9; training uses of, 9–10, 32–33; types of, 11; validity measures and, 13–14, 29–30

Emotional intelligence (EI) tests, and HRD professionals (study): conclusion, 37–38; definition of EI and, 11; discussion, 28–37; Emotional Competency Index (ECI-2) and, 12, 14–15, 19–22, 27–31, 32, 37; Emotional Quotient Inventory (EQ-i), 12, 14–15, 19, 22–25, 27–29, 37; focus of study and, 12–13; future directions, 37–38; HRD research and, 34–37; leadership development and, 33–34; literature review method and, 22–12; Mayer-Solovey-Caruso Emotional Intelligence Test (MSCEIT), 12, 14–19, 28–31, 33, 37; need for, 9–10; organization development and, 31–32; purpose, 10; research questions, 10; training/development and, 32–33; valid EI measurement and, 28–30; validity measures and, 13–14, 29

Emotional Quotient Inventory (EQ-i), 12, 14–15, 19, 22–25, 27–29, 37. *See also* Emotional intelligence (EI) tests, and HRD professionals (study)

Employee attitudes: behavioral change and, 248–250; HRD practices and, 281, 299; organizational socialization and, 281. *See also* New employee development (NED) practices, and temporary employee attitudes (study)

Employee development: mentoring and, 60; perceived organizational support and, 425–427, 439; turnover intention and, 413–414, 426. *See also* Developmental interactions, characteristics of (study); Employee development; Training/development; Workers

Employee learning: formal training and, 59–60; organizational success and, 59. *See also* Adult learning; Developmental interactions, characteristics of (study); Training/development

Employees: everyday problem solving by, 202–203; expertise of, 203; formal training of, 59–60; frontline, 201–203; identity development of, 203, 213–214; problem solving by, 302. *See also* Employee abilities; Employee development; Employee learning; New employee development (NED) practices, and temporary employee perceptions (study); Workers; Workforce; Workplace adaptation, and employee competencies (study)

"Employer Assessment of Work-Related Competencies and Workplace Adaptation," 305–324

Ericson, M., "Strategic HRD and the Relational Self," 223–229

Ethics: lack of, by leaders, 365–366. *See also* Leadership crisis

Everyday problem solving, 202

Experiential learning, informal learning and, 204, 218

F

Failure: hubris, hamartia, and anagnosis and, 482–483; learning from, 481; of world powers, 482–483. *See also* Organizational failure

Featured Articles: "Invited Reaction to Postfeedback Development Perceptions: Applying the Theory of Planned Behavior," 269–278; "Postfeedback Development Perceptions: Applying the Theory of Planned Behavior," 245–267

Feedback: attitudes toward behavioral change and, 248–250; contextual model of learning and, 246–247; intentions and behavioral improvement and, 248; perceived behavioral control and, 250–252; performance improvement and, 245; rater/ratee factors and, 248–249; role theory and, 247; theory of planned behavior and, 247–250, 261, 263–264; training models and, 247. *See also* Multisource feedback (MSF); Postfeedback development perceptions (study)

Ford, R., "Why We Fail: How Hubris, Hamartia, and Anagnosis Shape Organizational Behavior," 481–489

Formal mentoring programs, and applicant attraction (study): applicant attraction and, 44–45, 53–54; benefits of, 43; conclusion, 55; discussion, 52–53; future research, 53; hypotheses, 45–47, 50–51; implications, 54; individual differences and, 45–47, 53; learning goal orientation and, 46, 53; materials, 48–49; measures, 49–50; method, 48; participants, 48; proactive personality and, 47, 53; procedure, 48; research questions, 44; results, 50–52; self-efficacy and, 46–47, 53; study limitations, 54–55

"Formal Mentoring Programs and Organizational Attraction," 43–58

Formal training, employee learning and, 59–60

Forum: "Closing the Gap Between Research and Practice in Human Resource Development," 343–350; "Mega-Trends in the American Workforce," 475–479; "The New Human Resource Department: A Cross-Functional Unit," 117–123; "Strategic HRD and the Relational Self," 223–229; "Trainer Self-Loathing?" 351–357; "Why We Fail: How Hubris, Hamartia, and Anagnosis Shape Organizational Behavior," 481–489

Foundations of Adult Education in Africa, reviewed, 359–363

"Frederick Lewis Otte (1934–2004): The Consummate Human Resource Developer," 5–8

G

Garavan, T., "Postfeedback Development Perceptions: Applying the Theory of Planned Behavior," 245–267

Gender: adult education in Africa and, 360; supplier diversity programs and, 327

General Method of Theory-Building Research in Applied Disciplines model, 270–277

Gilley, J. W., "Research: The Bridge Between Human Resource Development Practitioners and Scholars," 235–243

Givens-Skeaton, S., "Key Characteristics of Effective and Ineffective Developmental Interactions," 59–84

Global competitiveness, 306. *See also* Competitive advantage

Globalization: adult education and, 360, 362; HRD practitioners and, 305–306, 321–32, 416

Greed, of leaders, 367

Greer, B. M., "Supplier Diversity: A Missing Link in Human Resource Development," 325–341

Groves, K., "Choosing Among Tests of Emotional Intelligence: What Is the Evidence?" 9–42

Gubrium, J. F., *Handbook of Interview Research*, reviewed; *Inside Interviewing: New Lenses, New Concerns*, reviewed; *Postmodern Interviewing*, reviewed, 125–129

H

Hamartia, 482–484
Handbook of Interview Research, reviewed, 125–129
Harris, R., "Roles of Informal Workplace Trainers in Different Organizational Contexts: Empirical Evidence from Australian Companies," 175–198
Hatcher, T., "An Editor's Challenge to Human Resource Development," 1–4
Holstein, J. A., *Handbook of Interview Research*, reviewed; *Inside Interviewing: New Lenses, New Concerns*, reviewed; *Postmodern Interviewing*, reviewed, 125–129
HRD, new paradigm for: addressing needs of work-filled retirement, 478; aligning education and goals for competitiveness, 477; aligning workforce development programs with market needs, 476–477; assisting lower-wage workers, 478; assisting workers in volatile labor market, 477–478; components of, 476–478; need for, 476, 478–479; workforce trends and, 475–476. *See also* Diversity practitioners
HRD activities: analysis and, 238–239; design and, 238–239; evaluation and, 238–239; implementation and, 238–239; scholar-practitioners and, 238–241; traditional research process and, 238–239
HRD practitioners: adult learning and, 359; assumptions of, about HRD, 235–236; attitudes toward training of, 235–236; diversity programs and, 327–328, 332–333, 337–339; global competitiveness and, 305–306, 321–322; HRD research and, 235, 241–243; HRD scholar-practitioners and, 235–236, 238, 243; informal workplace trainers and, 178–179; learning organizations and, 178; linking theory and practice by, 236, 242–243. *See also* Diversity practitioners; Trainers

HRD professionals. *See* Diversity practitioners; HRD practitioners; HRD scholar-practitioners
HRD research: data analysis and, 128; debate about, 235, 242–243; factors influencing interviewing and, 126–129; home-buying example and, 236–238; HRD activities and, 238–239; HRD practitioners and, 235, 241–243; linking theory and practice and, 236, organizational collaboration and, 276–277; organizational decision making and, 236–238; as process, 235; qualitative vs. quantitative, 125; recommendation for HRD scholar-practitioners about, 242; strategic decision making and, 238; technical advances and, 128; theory building and, 270; theory-building models/research and, 269–271, 276–277; Tower of Babel about, 242; trends in, 125; vulnerability of, to organizational resources, 269. *See also* HRD research-practice gap; Research
HRD research-practice gap: AHRD articles on, 343; causes of, 344–345; claims of, 343–344; conclusions, 348; definitions of, 344; forms of, 344; implications, 348; need for closing, 345–346; need for research-practice synergy and, 343; past efforts to close, 346; practice/practitioner role in, 345; research/researcher role in, 344–345; suggestions for closing, 346–348; suggestions for HRD organizations, 348; suggestions for practice/practitioners, 347; suggestions for research/researchers, 346–347
HRD scholar-practitioners: assumptions of, about HRD, 235–236; HRD practitioners and, 235–236, 238, 243; HRD research and, 235, 241–243; recommendations for HRD research for, 242; strategic thinking about HRD and, 236–237
Hubris, 482–484, 487
Hubris, hamartia, and anagnosis (HH&A): Aristotle and, 482; chauvinism and, 483; creating credible and open process and, 485–486; definitions of, 482–483; dogmatism and, 483; failure and, 482; failure of world powers and, 482–483; reflection and dialogue and, 486–488

Human resources (HR): current, 118–120; factors restricting research progress in, 119–120; global competition and, 117–118; and HR function, 118; international, 121; top priorities of, 119; transformation of, 117–118; trust and, 118; worker needs and, 118–119

Human resources department, as cross-functional unit: division of labor and, 121; internal organizational politics and, 121; model of, 122; organizational effectiveness and, 122; strategic planning and, 117–118, 120; talent management and, 119, 121; technology as enabler in, 119, 121; trust and, 119, 120; worker autonomy/freedom and, 118, 120; worker fringe benefits and, 119

Human resources development (HRD): challenge to, 1–3; expanding, theory, 2; globalization and, 4; integrity in, 4; long-term vision and, 4; as organizational value-added activity, 236, 243, 245; positive approach to, 2; professionalization of, 4; redefining, 1–2; research excellence in, 2; respecting heart in, 4; responsibility to stakeholders of, 4, 368. *See also* HRD, new paradigm for; HRD activities; HRD practitioners; HRD research; Human resources (HR); Strategic HRD

I

Identity, development of worker, 203, 213–214

"Influence of Trainee Characteristics, Instructional Satisfaction, and Organizational Climate on Perceived Learning and Training Transfer," 85–116

"Influences of New Development Practices on Temporary Employee Work-Related Attitudes," 279–303

Informal learning: action science model of, 137; characteristics of, 201; communities of practice and, 204, 212–213; contextual considerations and, 201, 304; definition of, 201; experiential learning and, 204; of frontline employees, 202; interactions and, 136–137; James Dewey and, 204;

manager as facilitator of, 216–217; as reflective process, 204; related theoretical constructs to, 204; research on, 201–202; situated learning and, 204; social context and, 137–138; social nature of, 204, 212; training programs and, 216, 218; worker identity formation and, 203; workplace expertise and, 203; workplace learning and, 136. *See also* Informal learning, in problem-solving contexts (study); Informal workplace trainers, roles of (study); Workplace learning

Informal learning, in problem-solving contexts (study): communities of practice and, 204, 212–213; data collection/analysis, 206–207; discussion, 211–218; everyday problem solving and, 202–203; findings, 207–211; future research, 217–218; learning as relational/dialogical process and, 209–213, 217; learning as social process and, 204, 212; learning in context and, 211–213; learning in job and, 213–214; learning outcomes through problem solving and, 210–211; literature review, 201–203; methods, 205–207; practical implications for HRD and, 215–217; problem solving as learning and, 208–209; purpose, 200; research questions, 203–204, 211–214; selection of site/participants, 205–206; theoretical framework, 203–205; theoretical implications for HRD and, 214–215; worker expertise/identity and, 203, 212–214

Informal workplace trainers: coaching/mentoring and, 180; formal workplace trainers and, 176–178; HRD practitioners and, 178–179; learning system of organization and, 176; learning transfer and, 180. *See also* Informal workplace trainers, roles of (study)

Informal workplace trainers, roles of (study): actions undertaken by, 184, 191, 195–196; benefits to theory of, 176–177; coaching/mentoring and, 180, 191; conclusions, 191–192; contextual factors and, 187–188, 192; formal educators/trainers and, 176–177; further research and, 194; implications for HRD and, 193–194; learning transfer and, 180, 191; literature review, 177–180;

measures, 183–184; method, 181; need for, 177; organizational learning system and, 177–180; participants, 182–183; procedure, 184; purpose of, 176–177; research background and, 177; research questions, 181; results, 184–191; role conceptions of, 186–187, 191–192; role dimensions of, 184– 186, 191–192; sampling, 181–182; theoretical background and, 177–180; trainer characteristics and, 188–192. *See also* Informal workplace trainers

Inside Interviewing: New Lenses, New Concerns, reviewed, 125–129

Intentions, and behavioral change 248

Interaction partner, defined, 137

Interactive workplace learning (study): adult learner activities and, 144–146, 150, 154–155; clusters of learning and, 137, 151; data analysis, 142–144; data collection, 141–142; definition of learning and, 137; didactic learning and, 137; discussion, 150–154; hierarchical organizational position and learning activities and, 149–150, 153; interaction partner and, 137–138, 151; interaction partners' activities and, 146–148, 151, 155–156; method, 140–144; need for, 136; negative reactions vs. compliments and, 146–147, 151; occupation-related differences/ similarities in learning activities and, 148–149, 152; participants, 140–141; power issues and, 138–139, 153; practical implications and, 153–154; purpose, 136; relationship between learning activities, work contexts, and power and, 138–139; research questions, 139, 150–153; results, 144–150; study framework, 138; theoretical background on learning and, 136–139

"Invited Reaction to Postfeedback Development Perceptions: Applying the Theory of Planned Behavior," 269–278

J

Job/career satisfaction: employee/career development programs and, 413–414, 426; leadership style and, 413; perceived organizational support and, 425; turnover intentions and, 403–404; of workers, 118; work-life support and, 65. *See also* Turnover intentions, in Taiwanese and U.S. organizations (study)

Job competencies, employee perceptions of, in China (study): age and, 381, 390; Chinese collectivist attitude and, 380, 397; Chinese ethics and, 386, 397; cultural/symbolic attributes and, 381; definition of job skills and, 372; dependent variables and, 379–381, 384; dispositional aspects and, 381, 386–388, 391, 395; dispositional qualities and, 379–380, 386; economic context and, 383; educational attainment and, 372, 374; employee attitudes and, 372; employee ranking of job competencies and, 388–393; firm ownership and, 383, 393–394; firm ranking of job competencies and, 393; firm-level characteristics and, 383; future research and, 397; generic vs. firm-specific skills and, 377, 395; hierarchical linear model and, 383–384; individual characteristics and, 381–383, 388–393; industry and, 383, 393–394; job basics and, 387, 391; job competence measurement and, 372, 374, 384, 386–388; job position/rank and, 381, 391, 396; job type and, 395, 397; market reform and, 373; measurement models and, 383–385; methods, 378–384; on-the-job training and, 378, 381–383, 392, 396; problem solving and, 387–388, 391–392; productivity and, 372; proficiency and, 382, 392; qualities for job competencies and, 384–388; region and, 383, 393; research questions, 378; resource opportunity structure and, 381; results, 384–393; sampling method, 378–379; self-knowledge and, 386; sex and, 381; socialization and, 381; sociocultural model and, 373–375, 396; study purpose, 373, 384; study questionnaire, 373, 378; teamwork and, 381; technical ability and, 387; theoretical framework, 373–378; universal vs. culture-specific skills and, 374–376, 396; workforce changes and, 372, 381; workplace attributes and, 381; workplace change and, 382, 392

Job skills: competence measures and, 372, 374; cross-cultural generalizability of,

373–376, 396; as culture-specific, 374, 376; definition of, 372; educational attainment and, 372, 374, 390; employee perceptions of, 374; frameworks of, 374–375, 387; general vs. firm-specific, 377; productivity and, 372; resource opportunity structure and, 381; sociocultural approach to, 374–375; universal vs. culture-specific, 374–376; workplace context and, 377. *See also* Job competencies, employee perceptions of, in China (study)

K

Kahnweiler, W. M., "Frederick Lewis Otte (1934–2004): The Consummate Human Resource Developer," 5–8
"Key Characteristics of Effective and Ineffective Developmental Interactions," 59–84
Kiel, F., *Moral Intelligence: Enhancing Business Performance and Leadership Success*, reviewed, 231–233
Knowledge: anagnosis and, 483; explicit, 492; organizational success and, 485; tacit, 492; types of, 492. *See also* Knowledge retention
Knowledge retention: aging workforce and, 491–492; HRD and, 492; information technology and, 493; organizational challenges and, 493; strategic action framework for, 492
Koopmans, H., "Learning in Interactive Work Situations: It Takes Two to Tango: Why Not Invite Both Partners to Dance?" 135–158
Kopp, D. M., "Trainer Self-Loathing?" 351–357

L

Leaders: avoidance by, 366; coping mechanisms of, 366–367; demands on, 366; distrust of, 367; failure of, 365; inadequacies of, 365–366; lying/cheating by, 366–367; overpayment of, 367; oversimplification by, 366. *See also* Leadership; Managers
Leadership: job/career satisfaction and, 413–415; new methods for, 366. *See also* Leaders

Leadership crisis: aspects of, 365; capacity and, 365–366; equity and, 368; HRD response to, 368; integrity and, 365–366; provoking questions about, 365; stakeholder voice and, 368; timely decision making and, 368
Leadership development, emotional intelligence and, 33–34
Learning: centrality of self in, 215; contextual model of, 246–247; definition of, 137; formal vs. informal, 60, 76–77; ongoing, 59; situated cognition theory and, 204; social nature of, 204, 212; structured vs. unstructured, 60. *See also* Adult learning; Behavioral change; Employee learning; Experiential learning; Informal learning; Interactive workplace learning (study); Organizational learning system; Situated learning; Workplace learning
Learning goal orientation, mentoring and, 46
"Learning in Interactive Work Situations: It Takes Two to Tango: Why Not Invite Both Partners to Dance?" 135–158
Learning organizations: characteristics of, 179–180; HRD practitioners and, 178–179; informal workplace trainers and, 180
Learning participation, in management development in China (study): barriers to learning and, 459; commitment to work and, 457; conclusion, 469; context-based learning and, 463–464; cultural orientation and, 457–458; data analysis, 452–454; data collection, 452; decisional context and, 454–458; defining the concept of participation and, 465–466; demand for management resources and, 444–445; discussion/implications, 462–469; economic environmental change and, 454–455; economy and, 449; findings, 454–462; formal learning and, 467; formulated meanings of learning participation and, 458–460; globalization and, 444, 446; *guanxi* model and, 466, 468; impact on individual and, 460–461; organization and, 461–462; implications, 467–468; increase in team spirit and, 459; interview and, 452, 469; lack of Chinese orientation to learning and, 459–460; lack of trainer

experience and, 460; learning beyond participation and, 460–462; learning context and, 466–467; learning experience as rewarding/significant and, 458–459; limitations, 468–469; linking of training to practice and, 459; management training/development in China and, 449; masculinity model and, 466, 468; method, 450–454; need for developing management competency and, 455–456; participant selection, 451–452; participation and cultural context and, 466–467; participation and environmental pressure and, 462–463; participation as challenging experience and, 463–465; participation as transformational experience and, 463; perceptions of M.B.A. program and, 456–457; phenomenological inquiry approach and, 450, 469; power distance and, 467–468; problems with M.B.A. programs and, 445; propositions, 467–468; purpose, 445, 450; research questions, 445–446; researchers' assumptions, 450–451; study significance, 446; theoretical perspectives, 446–449; training delivery and, 460; transferring learning at work and, 464–465

"Learning to Become a Machine Operator: The Dialogical Relationship Between Context, Self, and Content," 199–221

Learning transfer: coaching/mentoring and, 180; informal workplace trainers and, 180; supervisor and peer support and, 180; workplace factors and, 180

Lennick, D., *Moral Intelligence: Enhancing Business Performance and Leadership Success*, reviewed, 231–233

Lim, D. H., "Influence of Trainee Characteristics, Instructional Satisfaction, and Organizational Climate on Perceived Learning and Training Transfer," 85–116

Lin, C.-P., "Comparing the Effects of Determinants of Turnover Intentions Between Taiwanese and U.S. Hospital Employees," 403–321

Locus of control, and behavioral change, 250–252

Lost Knowledge: Confronting the Threat of an Aging Workforce, reviewed, 491–494

Lying/cheating, by leaders, 366–367

M

M.B.A. training/development programs. *See* Learning participation, in management development in China (study)

McCarthy, A., "Postfeedback Development Perceptions: Applying the Theory of Planned Behavior," 245–267

McEnrue, M. P., "Choosing Among Tests of Emotional Intelligence: What Is the Evidence?" 9–42

Machine operators, workplace learning by. *See* Informal learning, in problem-solving contexts (study)

"Making Subjective Judgments in Quantitative Studies: The Importance of Using Effect Sizes and Confidence Intervals," 159–173

Malthia, T. E., "Supplier Diversity: A Missing Link in Human Resource Development," 325–341

Management development (MD): adaptation to change and, 444; impact of, 444; organizational effectiveness and, 444. *See also* Learning participation, in management development in China (study); Training/development

Managers: cross-cultural approach of, 376–377, 396. *See also* Leaders

Marques, J. F., "The New Human Resource Department: A Cross-Functional Unit," 117–123

Mayer-Solovey-Caruso Emotional Intelligence Test (MSCEIT), 12, 14–19, 28–31, 33, 37. *See also* Emotional intelligence (EI) tests, and HRD professionals (study)

"Mega-Trends in the American Workforce," 475–479

Mentoring: applicant attraction and, 44–45, 53–54; benefits of, 44; employee learning and, 60; factors affecting, 62; as learning goal process, 46; learning transfer and, 180; life stage theory and, 44; organizational concern for employees and, 45; person-organization fit and, 46; publicity on, 44; research on, 43; self-efficacy and, 46–47; from symbolic action perspective, 45, 53; typology of, 61. *See also* Developmental interactions; Formal mentoring programs; Formal mentoring programs, and applicant attraction (study); Mentoring

Miller, K. L., review by, 491–494

Minority business enterprises (MBEs): definitions and, 328; demographic factors and, 325–326; economic imperative in, 326; supplier diversity programs and, 326

Moral intelligence: competencies of, 232; definition of, 231; importance of, 232; organizational applications of, 232; organizational performance and, 232; professional development planning and, 232; self-reporting inventory for, 232

Moral Intelligence: Enhancing Business Performance and Leadership Success, reviewed, 231–233

Morris, M. L., "Influence of Trainee Characteristics, Instructional Satisfaction, and Organizational Climate on Perceived Learning and Training Transfer," 85–116

Motivation: adult learning participation and, 447–448; choice and, 448; typology of, 447

Multisource feedback (MSF): accuracy and, 249; attitudes toward change and, 248–249; career development and, 246; change and development behaviors and, 246; as management development technique, 245, 269; organizational support and, 250; rater/ratee factors and, 248–249; role theory and, 247; self-awareness and, 246; studies on, outcomes, 246; theory of planned behavior and, 247–250, 261, 263–264; theory-building research and, 270–271, 276. *See also* Feedback; Postfeedback development perceptions (study)

N

Nafukho, F., *Foundations of Adult Education in Africa,* reviewed, 359–363

New employee development (NED): job satisfaction and, 283, 300; organizational commitment and, 283, 300; organizational socialization and, 281, 295–296; role of HRD and, 279; social identity and, 296; studies on employee attitudes and, 280; turnover intention and, 284

New employee development (NED) practices, and temporary employee attitudes (study): construct measurement, 286–289; control variables, 289; data collection, 286; definition of terms and, 283; discussion, 295–297; future research, 298–299; hypotheses, 283–285, 289–291; hypotheses testing and, 289–291; implications for HRD, 297–299; implications for HRD managers, 299–300; job satisfaction and, 283, 289, 291, 294–295, 297; job satisfaction and turnover intention and, 284; mediating effects of organizational commitment and job satisfaction and, 284–285, 294–295, 297; new employee development practices scale, 287–289; organizational commitment and, 283, 287, 289, 291, 294–297; organizational socialization and, 281, 295–296; purpose, 280–281; rationale for, 280; results, 289–295; sample characteristics, 285–286; sample, 285–286; social identity and, 296; study limitations, 297; study models, 281–283; testing of mediating influences of variables and, 291, 294–295; turnover intention and, 284, 287, 289, 291, 294–297;

"New Human Resource Department: A Cross-Functional Unit, The," 117–123

Null hypothesis significance testing (NHST): APA style manual and, 163, 170; confidence intervals and, 159–160, 166–168; criticisms of, 161; definition of, 161; effect size and, 159–160, 164–166; history of use of, 161–162; *HRDQ* and, 160, 163; misuse of, 161–163; *p* values and, 161, 163, 167; process of, 161; purpose of, 161; quantitative studies and, 159–160; recommendations for changes in use of, 170–171; scientific rigor and, 162–163; social science research journal editorial policy and, 163; statistical significance and, 168–169

O

O'Brien, K. E., "Formal Mentoring Programs and Organizational Attraction," 43–58

Ongoing learning, organizational success and, 59

Organizational change: emotional intelligence and, 32; learning/development activities and, 305; organizational socialization and, 277, 295, 297

Organizational commitment, turnover intentions and, 404, 409, 414–415

Organizational failure: anagnosis and, 484; analyzing, 481; chauvinism and, 483; creating credible and open process and, 485–486; dogmatism and, 483; fail safe and, 482; hamartia and, 483–484; hubris and, 483–484; as learning opportunity, 481–482; reflection and dialogue and, 486–488; ultimate, 482

Organizational learning system: definition of, 177; direct and indirect colleagues in, 177; employees as core actors in, 177; formal educators in, 177–178; HRD practitioners and, 178–179; supervisors and, 178

Organizational performance: organizational socialization and, 276; perceptions of training and, 246; performance improvement components and, 245; self-awareness and, 246; training/development and, 236, 245

Organizational socialization: employee work-related attitudes and, 281, 300; new employee development practices and, 277; organizational change and, 277, 295, 297; organizational functioning and, 276; temporary employees and, 281

Otte, F. L., 5–7

Otunga, R., *Foundations of Adult Education in Africa,* reviewed, 359–363

Oversimplification, by leaders, 366

P

Pappas, B., review by, 231–233

"Participation in Management Training in a Transitioning Context: A Case of China," 443–473

Pattie, M., "Tuition Reimbursement, Perceived Organizational Support, and Turnover Intention Among Graduate Business School Students," 423–442

Perceived organizational support (POS): employee development programs and, 426–427, 439; job satisfaction and, 425; social exchange theory and, 426; training and, 426–427; tuition reimbursement. 427; turnover intention and, 425

Performance. *See* Organizational performance

Performance appraisal instruments, and training transfer, 351–352, 354

Performance improvement: components of, 245; feedback and, 245; training and, 255. *See also* Behavioral change

Plakhotnik, M. S., review by, 125–129

Poell, R. E., "Roles of Informal Workplace Trainers in Different Organizational Contexts: Empirical Evidence from Australian Companies," 175–198

"Postfeedback Development Perceptions: Applying the Theory of Planned Behavior," 245–267

Postfeedback development perceptions (study): age and, 252, 263; applying theory-building research and praxis cycle to, 274–276; attitudes toward behavioral change and, 248–250; conclusions, 276–277; contextual model of learning and, 246–247; contributions and scholarship measures of, 274; discussion, 261–264; factor analysis and, 252–257; functionalist or postpositivist framework and, 264–275; in HRD research/practice context, 269; hypothesis 1: perceptions of MSF accuracy and postfeedback behavioral perceptions, 249–250, 258, 262–263; hypothesis 2: cynicism and postfeedback behavioral perceptions, 250, 262; hypothesis 3: perceptions of organizational support and postfeedback behavioral perceptions, 250–251, 258, 261–262; hypothesis 4: internal locus of control and postfeedback behavioral change, 251, 258; implications of, 276–277; independent variable: behavioral change and, 252; intentions and behavioral improvement and, 248; method, 252–257; MSF design/implementation and, 263; organizational culture factors and, 277; participants, 257; perceived behavioral control and, 250–252; procedure, 257; purpose, 252, 269; rater/ratee characteristics and, 248; for HRD and, 261–263; research instrument, 252–253; research model, 252–253; research variables, 253–254; results, 257–261; role theory and, 247; setting, 258; study limitations and, 263–264, 277; as theory-building research, 270–274; theoretical background and, 246–252; theory of planned behavior and, 247–250, 261, 263–264; training models and, 247; validity and, 252–253

Postmodern Interviewing, reviewed, 125–129

Power, workplace learning and, 138–139, 153

Practitioners. *See* HRD practitioners; HRD scholar-practitioners

Proactive personality, mentoring and, 47

Problem solving: everyday, 202; frontline employees and, 203; importance of, 202; informal learning and, 202–203. *See also* Problem-solving training

Problem-solving training: formal programs for, 200; for manufacturing employees, 200

Productivity: job skills and, 372; self-efficacy and, 246

R

Rationality: calculative, 224, 226–227; communicative, 225; emotion and, 224, 226–227; strategic HRD and, 224, 226–227

Reflection and dialogue: scenario of mental model and, 487; skills for, 487–488

Reio Jr., T. G., "Employer Assessment of Work-Related Competencies and Workplace Adaptation," 305–324; "Making Subjective Judgments in Quantitative Studies: The Importance of Using Effect Sizes and Confidence Intervals," 159–173

Relational self, strategic HRD and, 226–227

Research: subjectivity of quantitative, 159, 170. *See also* Confidence intervals (CI); Effect size (ES); HRD research; HRD research-practice gap; Null hypothesis significance testing (NHST)

"Research: The Bridge Between Human Resource Development Practitioners and Scholars," 235–243

Reviews: *Foundations of Adult Education in Africa,* 359–363; *Handbook of Interview Research,* 125–129; *Inside Interviewing: New Lenses, New Concerns,* 125–129; *Lost Knowledge: Confronting the Threat of an Aging Workforce,* 491–494; *Moral Intelligence: Enhancing Business Performance and Leadership Success,* 231–233; *Postmodern Interviewing,* 125–129

Robinson, G., "Key Characteristics of Effective and Ineffective Developmental Interactions," 59–84

Rocco, T. S., review by, 125–129

Role theory, and behavioral change, 247

"Roles of Informal Workplace Trainers in Different Organizational Contexts: Empirical Evidence from Australian Companies," 175–198

S

Scott, C. L., "Supplier Diversity: A Missing Link in Human Resource Development," 325–341

Self-awareness: multisource feedback and, 246; organizational performance and, 246; definition of, 46–47;

Self-efficacy: for development, 47; mentoring and, 46–47

Selvarajan, T. T., "Influences of New Development Practices on Temporary Employee Work-Related Attitudes," 279–303

Short, D. C., "Closing the Gap Between Research and Practice in Human Resource Development," 343–350

Simons, M., "Roles of Informal Workplace Trainers in Different Organizational Contexts: Empirical Evidence from Australian Companies," 175–198

Situated cognition theory, 204

Situated learning, 204

Slattery, J. P., "Influences of New Development Practices on Temporary Employee Work-Related Attitudes," 279–303

Socialization. *See* Workplace socialization

Statistical significance, NHST and, 168–169, 170

Statistical tests. *See* Confidence intervals (CI); Effect size (ES); Null hypothesis significance testing (NHST)

Storberg-Walker, J., "Invited Reaction to Postfeedback Development Perceptions: Applying the Theory of Planned Behavior," 269–278

Strategic decision making: home-buying example and, 236–238; organizational effectiveness and, 236, 238; research as basis for, 238

Strategic HRD: challenges to overly rational view of, 224; emotion and, 224, 226–227; importance of, 223–224; interactionist view and, 224–226; rationality and, 224–227; relational self and, 226–227; relational/dialogic approach to, 224–226; theory/practice challenges and, 226–227

"Strategic HRD and the Relational Self," 223–229

"Supplier Diversity: A Missing Link in Human Resource Development," 325–341

Supplier diversity programs: auto industry and, 337; charitable giving and, 336–337; community relations and, 336–337; definitions of terms, 325, 328–329; demographic factors and, 325–326; diversity issues and, 327; diversity practitioners and, 326–327; economic imperative and, 326; economic limitations and, 327; equity issues and, 335; minority business enterprises and, 326; need for, 325; organization development focus and, 335–336; organizational effectiveness and, 326; organizational role of, 320, 328–329; problems related to, 331–332; purpose of, 325, 328; qualifications and, 328; relationship building focus and, 328, 336; research on, 328–329, 333, 335; strategic positioning of, 327–328; supplier diversity initiatives and, 329, 331, 333–337; trust building and, 336. See also Supplier diversity programs, practitioner role in (study)

Supplier diversity programs, practitioner role in (study): background on, 325–328; community relations and, 336–337; conclusions, 339–340; definition of terms and, 328; diversity practitioner competencies and, 333–334; diversity practitioner goals and, 332; diversity practitioner role components and, 326–327, 332–339; educator role and, 338–339; equity issues and, 335; HRD practice implications, 337–339; HRD practitioners' role and, 327–328, 332–339;

methods, 329–331; organization development focus and, 335–336; participants, 329; problems related to supplier diversity programs and, 331–332; purpose, 329; relationship-uilding focus and, 328, 336; researcher role and, 339; results, 331–337; strategist role and, 327–328; studies on, 328–329, 333, 335; supplier diversity initiatives and, 329, 331, 333–337. See also Supplier diversity programs

"Survey Ranking of Job Competencies by Perceived Employee Importance: Comparing Three Regions," 371–402

Sutton, F. C., "Employer Assessment of Work-Related Competencies and Workplace Adaptation," 305–324

Swanson, R. A., "Anyone? Anyone? Anyone?" 365–369

Symbolic action perspective, 45, 53

T

Talent management, HR and, 119, 121

Tannenbaum, S. I., "Key Characteristics of Effective and Ineffective Developmental Interactions," 59–84

Technology, and HR, 119, 121

Temporary employees: dual organizational relationship of, 277, 296; increase in, 277; organizational socialization and, 281, 295–296; social exchange theory and, 296; social identity and, 296. See also New employee development (NED) practices, and temporary employee attitudes (study)

Theory building, 270, 273

Theory of planned behavior, 247–250, 261, 263–264

Total Quality Management (TQM): academic journals and, 133; continuous improvement goal of, 133

"Trainer Self-Loathing?" 351–357

Trainers: accountability of, in training transfer, 351–354; as managers of training transfer, 353; training of, for training transfer, 353–354. See also HRD practitioners

Training/development: accountability and, 352–353, 355; as end in itself, 236; HRD practitioner attitudes and, 236; models of, 247; organizational effectiveness and,

236; organizational performance and, 236, 245; perceived organizational support and, 426–427; performance appraisal instruments and, 351–352, 354; performance improvement and, 252; recipient perceptions of, 246; of trainers, 353–354; trainer accountability and, 351–354. *See also* Developmental interactions, characteristics of (study); Learning participation, in management development in China (study)

Training transfer: implications for HRD and, 354–355; lack of skills transfer and, 352–353; learning vs. transfer needs and, 91–92; mediating factors in, 353; organizational climate and, 90–91; organizational stake in, 354; performance appraisal instruments and, 351–352, 354; performance issues and, 353; trainee characteristics and, 88–89; trainer accountability and, 351–354; training design factors and, 89–90; transfer intervention matrix and, 106–107. *See also* Training transfer, trainee, instructional, and organizational factors and (study)

Training transfer, trainee, instructional, and organizational factors and (study): data analysis, 97–98; data collection, 94–95; differences in learning and application and, 101; discussion, 102–106; future research, 107; instruments, 95–97; learning and applicability surveys and, 108–110; learning and applications outcomes, 98–99; learning from training and, 91–92, 96–97, 101, 105; methods, 94–98; organizational climate and, 90–91, 97, 102, 105–106; organizational climate survey and, 112; population, 94; practice implications, 106–107; purpose, 92–94, 107; regression model and, 102; research design, 94–95; research questions, 91–92, 98, 101–102; study framework, 92–94; study limitations, 107; theoretical background, 86–88; trainee characteristics and, 88–89, 105; training design factors and, 89–90; training satisfaction survey and, 111; training transfer variables and, 88–92; transfer from training and, 91–92, 96–97, 101, 105; variable interrelationships and, 102. *See also* Training transfer

Transfer of training. *See* Learning transfer; Training transfer

Transformational leadership, emotional intelligence, 34

Trust, in workplace, 118, 120

Tuition reimbursement: costs of, 424, 438; funding methods for, 423; graduate education and, 424–425, 427–428; HRD theory vs. human capital theory and, 425; perceived organizational support and, 427; prevalence of programs for, 423–424, 437; retention benefits of, 424, 427, 437–439; studies on, 423–429; turnover intention and, 425–427, 437–439. *See also* Turnover intention, tuition reimbursement and organizational support and (study)

"Tuition Reimbursement, Perceived Organizational Support, and Turnover Intention Among Graduate Business School Students," 423–442

Turnover intention: actual turnover and, 427; antecedents to, 427; attractive job alternatives and, 428; conventional vs. unfolding model of, 425–426, 428; cross-cultural differences and, 404–405, 414, 416; cross-cultural research on, 403; definition of, 404; ease of movement and, 425; embeddedness and, 425; employee human capital and, 426, 428; employee-job match and, 426; graduate education and, 427–428, 438; HRD programs and, 404; HRD theory vs. human capital theory and, 425; individual differences and, 404; job alternatives and, 426; job/career satisfaction and, 403–404, 425; organizational commitment and, 404; perceived organizational support and, 425, 427; predictors of, 427; tuition reimbursement and, 425–426. *See also* Turnover intention, in Taiwanese and U.S. organizations (study); Turnover intention, tuition reimbursement and organizational support and (study)

Turnover intention, in Taiwanese and U.S. organizations (study): allocentric vs. idiocentric view of self and, 407, 415; career development programs and, 413–414; data analysis, 410; discussion, 413–416; future research, 416; hypotheses, 408, 412–415; implications for HRD and, 413–416; job/career satisfaction and, 409; measures, 409; method, 408–412; model testing, 410; moderating effect and, 411–412; networking and, 415; organizational commitment and, 407, 409, 414–415; participants, 408–409; research model, 405–406; research questions, 405; results, 412–418; study limitations, 416

Turnover intention, tuition reimbursement and organizational support and (study): analyses, 432; degree completion and, 431–432, 434, 439; discussion, 436–439; employment hours and, 431; future research and, 438; HRD implications, 436, 439; hypotheses, 425, 427–429, 432, 434, 436; implications, 438–439; job relatedness and, 431–432, 434, 436, 439; limitations, 438; literature review, 424–426; measures, 430–432; methods, 429–432; perceived organizational support and, 430, 432, 436, 438; purpose, 424; results. 432–436; salary and, 431; sample, 429–430; studies on, 423–429; tenure and, 431; tuition reimbursement and, 430, 432, 436, 438–439; turnover intention and, 430, 432, 436, 437–439

V

Validity: construct, 13; content, 13; external, 14; face, 13; predictive, 14

Van der Krogt, F. J., "Roles of Informal Workplace Trainers in Different Organizational Contexts: Empirical Evidence from Australian Companies," 175–198

van Eekelen, I. M., "Learning in Interactive Work Situations: It Takes Two to Tango: Why Not Invite Both Partners to Dance?" 135–158

Van Horn, C. E., "Mega-Trends in the American Workforce," 475–479

Vasquez-Colina, M. D., review by, 359–363

Vermulst, A. A., "Roles of Informal Workplace Trainers in Different Organizational Contexts: Empirical Evidence from Australian Companies," 175–198

W

Wang, G. G., "Participation in Management Training in a Transitioning Context: A Case of China," 443–473

Wang, J., "Participation in Management Training in a Transitioning Context: A Case of China," 443–473

"Why We Fail: How Hubris, Hamartia, and Anagnosis Shape Organizational Behavior," 481–489

Work, redefinition of, 118–119

Work-life issues: developmental interactions and, 61; types of, 65

Workers: fringe benefits for, 119, 121; job autonomy and, 118; job satisfaction of, 118; trust and, 118, 120; work environment needs of, 118.

Workers. See Employees; Employee development; Employee learning; Workforce trends

Workforce diversity: demographic factors and, 325–326. See also Minority business enterprises (MBEs); Supplier diversity programs

Workforce trends: anxious American workers, 475; employer demand for better workers, 476; inadequate understanding/use of public workforce system, 476; work-filled retirement, 476

Workplace: as learning environment, 175–176; learning potential of, 179; learning transfer systems and, 180; trust in, 118, 120. See also Informal workplace trainers, roles of (study)

Workplace adaptation: acculturation and, 307; career advancement and, 307; competitive advantage and, 305–306; establishing relationships and, 307; factors affecting, 306–309; individual demographics/background and, 308–309; job knowledge and, 307; job satisfaction and, 307; workplace competencies and, 307–308; workplace socialization/adaptation and, 306–307

Workplace adaptation, and employee competencies (study): acculturation and, 307; conclusion, 320; correlational analyses of variables and, 317–318; demographic and background variables and, 308–309, 321; demographic survey and, 314–315; discussion, 320–321; establishing relationships and, 307; future research, 320–321; hierarchical regression analyses of variables and, 318–321; HRD implications and, 321–322; hypotheses, 309, 317, 319–320; job knowledge and,

307; measures, 310–312; methods, 309–314; participants, 309–310; procedure, 312–314; purpose, 309; questionnaire, 313–314; research framework, 308; results, 314–320; validity/reliability evidence and, 315–321; workplace adaptation factors and, 306–309; workplace competencies and, 307–308, 321; workplace socialization and, 306–307

Workplace competencies: bias in assessment of, 307; definition of, 307–308. *See also* Job competencies, employee perceptions of, in China (study)

Workplace learning: formal training programs and, 200; importance of, 135; as informal/interactive, 136; informal learning and, 200; interaction as key in, 136; interaction partners and, 137–138; job context and, 148; key contributors to, 136; knowledge refinement and, 136; learning from others and, 135; power issues and, 138–139, 153; problem-solving contexts and, 200; productivity/ competitiveness and, 199, 204; social context and, 137–138; social nature of, 204, 212; workplace socialization and, 306. *See also* Informal learning

Workplace socialization: definition, 306; group-level, 306; individual-level, 306; learning and, 306; organizational-level, 306; process model of, 306–307, 320; workplace adaptation and, 306–307

X

Xiao, J., "Survey Ranking of Job Competencies by Perceived Employee Importance: Comparing Three Regions," 371–402

Y

Yang, B., "Academic Journals Are Products of Professional Organizations," 131–133

Human Resource Development Quarterly is a publication sponsored by ASTD (the American Society for Training and Development) and AHRD (the Academy of Human Resource Development). It provides a central focus for research on human resource development issues as well as the means for disseminating such research. *HRDQ* recognizes the interdisciplinary nature of the HRD field and brings together relevant research from the related fields, such as economics, education, management, sociology, and psychology. It provides an important link in the application of theory and research to HRD practice.

In general, *HRDQ* publishes scholarly work that addresses the theoretical foundations of HRD, HRD research, and evaluation of HRD interventions and contexts. Articles concerned solely with the practice of HRD are not within the scope of this journal but may be more appropriate for practitioner-oriented publications such as *T + D* (ASTD's magazine).

Authors may contribute to *HRDQ* by submitting manuscripts for peer review, for the nonrefereed forum section, and for the media reviews section.

Manuscripts for Peer Review

Manuscripts submitted for review undergo a blind peer-review process. Manuscripts are initially evaluated based on appropriateness of content and style. Appropriate manuscripts are then reviewed by three or more reviewers. Authors are informed about the results of the review through a letter from the editor and associate editor, usually within two months. Authors are also provided copies of the reviewers' comments. Manuscripts should be prepared for review in accordance with the following criteria:

- Adhere to the language and style guidelines as presented in the *Publication Manual of the American Psychological Association* (5th ed.). Double-space the entire manuscript. Margins should be at least one inch wide, with no more than 250 words per page. Use 12-point type size. Manuscript page total should be limited to approximately 25–30 pages.
- Provide a cover letter stating that the manuscript has not already been published and that it is not being considered for publication elsewhere.
- Include a title page with complete name(s) and address(es) of author(s). The first page of the text should have the title only. Subsequent pages should have a running head of the title. No author identification should appear whatsoever in the text. Include a separate page with a biography of the author(s).
- Use nondiscriminatory language throughout the text.
- Quantitative, qualitative, mixed methods, reviews of literature, and other recognized scholarly approaches are considered.
- Authors are strongly encouraged to review past volumes of *HRDQ*.

- Inquiries concerning manuscript topics and appropriateness should be addressed to Tim Hatcher, Editor, *HRDQ*, North Carolina State University, 310 Poe Hall, Campus Box 7801, Raleigh, NC 27695-7801 (tim_hatcher@ncsu.edu).

Submit manuscripts as e-mail attachments in MS Word (.doc format) to Kelley Chisholm (hrdq_ced@ncsu.edu).

Forum Section

The forum section, the nonrefereed section of *HRDQ*, provides a way to present ideas or issues related to the human resource development field, differing perspectives on specific topics, and reactions to previously published articles. As suggested by its name, the forum section is meant to encourage open discourse among scholars, who may not necessarily share the same point of view on a topic. The field as a whole should be enlivened by the varying opinions presented in forum articles. In their own limited way, forum articles often make contributions to the HRD literature, if only by the scholarly interactions that they produce as a result. Established researchers, graduate students, and senior practitioners in particular are encouraged to submit forum manuscripts. In practice, the forum section has proven an excellent way for authors to be published in *HRDQ* for the first time. Forum manuscripts should be prepared in accordance with the following criteria:

- Adhere to the language and style guidelines as presented in the *Publication Manual of the American Psychological Association* (5th ed.). Double-space the entire manuscript. Margins should be at least one inch wide, with no more than 250 words per page. Use 12-point type size.
- Indicate author's opinions where appropriate.

Submit a forum manuscript as an e-mail attachment in MS Word (.doc format) to Kelley Chisholm (hrdq_ced@ncsu.edu).

Media Review Section

The media review section of *HRDQ* provides a way to critique books, visual media, and computer software related to the human resource development field. The scholarly emphasis requires authors to have some understanding of the theoretical and practical context of the item being reviewed. In this way, the media reviews themselves can be expected to make meaningful contributions to the literature.

Media reviews can be of two types: single item or multi-item. Single-item reviews focus on one item that has recently become available. The copyright date should be within two years of the probable publication date of the review. Multi-item reviews focus on two or more items that address similar topics, issues, or lines of reasoning. One of the items should have a recent copyright date. Reviews of this type should seek to compare and contrast the items based on their perspectives, emphases, and assumptions, among other categories. Media review manuscripts should be prepared in accordance with the following criteria:

- Adhere to the language and style guidelines as presented in the *Publication Manual of the American Psychological Association* (5th ed.). Double-space the entire manuscript. Margins should be at least one inch wide, with no more than 250 words per page. Use 12-point type size.
- Provide the complete citation at the beginning of the manuscript, including the ISBN.
- Describe the purpose of the item as stated or inferred by the author. Describe the content and structure of the item. Identify the primary and secondary audiences.
- Discuss the context, theoretical bases, or unique perspectives of the item, emphasizing its relationship to the human resource development field.
- Evaluate the contributions and weaknesses of the item in terms that are relevant to HRD researchers and senior practitioners.

Submit a media review manuscript as an e-mail attachment in Word (.doc format) to Baiyin Yang (yinyang@umn.edu).

Publication Process

Once a manuscript is accepted for publication, authors are required to provide a computer file of the complete manuscript. Authors are also asked to sign a letter of agreement granting the publisher the right to copyedit, publish, and copyright the material. The editor is responsible for reviewing the copyediting and for proofreading each issue, and will only contact authors if clarification is required. Copyedited manuscripts will not be returned to authors. Authors must ensure the accuracy of all statements—particularly data, quotations, and references—before submitting manuscripts. Authors will receive complimentary copies of the completed journal issue.

Authors requiring information about a manuscript under review should e-mail the managing editor, Kelley Chisholm, at hrdq_ced@ncsu.edu. All other official submission and editorial correspondence should be submitted to Tim Hatcher, Editor, *HRDQ*, North Carolina State University, 310 Poe Hall, Campus Box 7801, Raleigh, NC 27695-7801 (tim_hatcher@ncsu.edu).

Sam Adams
DeVry University

Sonia Agut
University of Murcia

Mohammed Al-Emadi
Qatar Petroleum

Susan Awbrey
Oakland University

Timothy T. Baldwin
Indiana University

Kenneth Bartlett
University of Minnesota

Alexandra Bell
University of Connecticut

John Benson
University of Melbourne

Laura Bierema
University of Georgia

Dale Brandenburg
Wayne University

Paul Brauchle
Illinois State University

Ann K. Brooks
University of Texas, Austin

Jamie Callahan
Texas A&M University

Jennifer Calvin
Ohio State University

Shani Carter
Rhode Island College

Michael Cassidy
Marymount University

Melissa Cefkin
Institute for Research on Learning

Diane Chapman
North Carolina State University

Hsin-Chih Chen
Louisiana State University

Yuh Jia Chen
Mid Tennessee State University

Thomas Chermack
Penn State

Eunsang Cho
Korea Research Institute for Vocational Education & Training

Alan Clardy
Towson University

Rosemary B. Closson
University of South Florida

Debra J. Cohen
George Washington University

Sharon Confessore
Kaiser Permanente

Maria Cseh
Oakland University

Barbara Daley
University of Wisconsin, Milwaukee

Carol Decker
Lincoln Memorial University

Jennifer Dewey
North Central Regional Education Laboratory

Robert Dilworth
Virginia Commonwealth University

Sharon K. Drake
Iowa State University

Andrea Ellinger
University of Alabama

Michael Enos
Clark/Bardes Consulting

Kevin J. Freer
Lucent Technologies

Jo Gallagher
Florida International University

Thomas Garavan
University of Limerick, Ireland

Robert T. Golembiewski
University of Georgia

Paul J. Guglielmino
Florida Atlantic University

Rosa Grau Gumbau
Jaume University

Lynn Harland
University of Nebraska, Omaha

Clark Hickman
University of Missouri, St. Louis

Barbara Hinton
University of Arkansas

Linda M. Hite
Indiana-Purdue University

Courtney Holladay
Rice University

Elwood Holton III
Louisiana State University

Barry-Craig P. Johansen
Red Wing Shoe Company

James R. Johnson
Purdue University, Calumet

Scott D. Johnson
University of Illinois

William M. Kahnweiler
Georgia State University

Roger Kaufman
Florida State University

Marijke Kehrhahn
University of Connecticut

Scott Keller
Michigan State University

Hye Shin Kim
University of Delaware

Nell Kimberley
Monash University

Howard Klein
The Ohio State University

Judith Kolb
Pennsylvania State University

Constantine Kontoghiorghes
Cyprus International Institute of Management

Sharon Korth
Xavier University

Kenneth A. Kovach
George Mason University

K. Peter Kuchinke
University of Illinois

Joseph Lapides
University of Michigan

Chan Lee
Ohio State University

Monica Lee
Lancaster University

Sharon Leiba-O'Sullivan
University of Ottawa

Michael P. Leimbach
Wilson Learning Corporation

Brenda S. Levya-Gardner
Xavier University

Margaret C. Lohman
Penn State University, Harrisburg

Diannah Lowry
Flinders University

Germain D. Ludwig
Palm Beach Atlantic College

Susan Lynham
Texas A&M University

Susan Madsen
Utah Valley State College

Svjetlana Madzar
Gustavus Adolphus College

Victoria J. Marsick
Columbia University, Teachers College

Joseph Martelli
University of Findlay

Jennifer Martineau
Center for Creative Leadership

Joseph Martocchio
University of Illinois

Morgan W. McCall Jr.
University of Southern California

Timothy McClernon
People Architects, Inc.

Kimberly S. McDonald
Indiana-Purdue University

David McGuire
Napier University

Gary McLean
University of Minnesota

Catherine Monaghan
Cleveland State University

Max U. Montesino
Indiana-Purdue University

Hiromitsu Muta
Tokyo Institute of Technology

Claire Nackoney
Florida International University

Frederick M. Nafukho
University of Arkansas

Sharon Naquin
Louisiana State University

Teresa M. Palmer
Illinois State University

Rob Poell
Tilburg University

Janet Polach
University of Minnesota

Toni Powell
Barry University

Hallie Preskill
University of New Mexico

J. Bruce Prince
Kansas State University

Kevin Quinlan
Nova Scotia Community College

Thomas Reio Jr.
University of Louisville

Peter J. Robertson
University of Southern California

William J. Rothwell
Pennsylvania State University

Wendy Ruona
University of Georgia

Eugene Sadler-Smith
University of Surrey

Eduardo Salas
University of Central Florida

Soyeon Shim
University of Arizona

Thomas Shindell
Texas State Auditor's Office

Gilbert B. Siegel
University of Southern California

Sununta Siengthai
Asian Institute of Technology

Mark Skillings
Ohio State University

Catherine M. Sleezer
Oklahoma State University

Douglas H. Smith
Florida International University

Julia Storberg-Walker
North Carolina State University

James Tan
University of Wisconsin, Stout

Thomas Li-Ping Tang
Middle Tennessee State University

Kecia Thomas
University of Georgia

Peg Thoms
Penn State Erie

Richard Torraco
University of Nebraska

Charles M. Vance
Loyola Marymount University

Mary Vielhaber
Eastern Michigan University

Janine Waclawski
Pepsi-Cola Company

Lori Wallace
University of Manitoba

John Walton
London Guildhall University

David Wan Wai Tai
National University of Singapore

Greg Wang
Old Dominion University

Karen E. Watkins
University of Georgia

Ryan Watkins
Nova University

Rose Mary Wentling
University of Illinois

Jon M. Werner
University of Wisconsin-Whitewater

Charles S. White
University of Tennessee, Chattanooga

Saundra Williams *
North Carolina State University

JoAnne Willment
University of Calgary

Jean Woodall
Oxford Brookes University

Michael Workman
Florida State University

Phillip C. Wright
Hong Kong Baptist University

Lyle Yorks
Columbia University, Teachers College

AHRD
Academy of Human Resource Development
Leading Human Resource Development Through Research

The Academy of Human Resource Development (AHRD) is a global organization made up of, governed by, and created for the human resource development (HRD) scholarly community of academics and reflective practitioners. The Academy was formed to encourage systematic study of human resource development theories, processes, and practices; to disseminate information about HRD; to encourage the application of HRD research findings; and to provide opportunities for social interaction among individuals with scholarly and professional interests in HRD from multiple disciplines and from across the globe.

AHRD membership includes a subscription to *HRDQ*. A partial list of other benefits includes (1) membership in the only global organization dedicated to advancing the HRD profession through research, (2) annual research conference with full proceedings of research papers (900 pages), (3) reduced prices on professional books, (4) subscription to the *Forum,* the academy newsletter, and (5) research partnering, funding, and publishing opportunities.

Academy of Human Resource Development
College of Technology
Bowling Green State University
Bowling Green, Ohio 43403-0301

Phone: 419.372.9155
Fax: 419.372.8385
E-mail: office@ahrd.org
Web site: www.ahrd.org

The Value of Belonging

ASTD membership keeps you up to date on the latest developments in your field, and provides top-quality, *practical* information to help you stay ahead of trends, polish your skills, measure your progress, demonstrate your effectiveness, and advance your career.

We give you what you need most from the entire scope of workplace learning and performance:

Information

We're your best resource for research, best practices, and background support materials – the data you need for your projects to excel.

Networking

We're the facilitator who puts you in touch with colleagues, experts, field specialists, and industry leaders – the people you need to know to succeed.

Technology

We're the clearinghouse for new technologies in training, learning, and knowledge management in the workplace – the background you need to stay ahead.

Analysis

We look at cutting-edge practices and programs and give you a balanced view of the latest tools and techniques – the understanding you need on what works and what doesn't.

Competitive Edge

ASTD is your leading resource on the issues and topics that are important to you. That's the value of belonging!

For more information, or to become a member, please call 1.800.628.2783 (U.S.) or +1.703.683.8100; visit our Website at **www.astd.org**; or send an email to customercare@astd.org.

Linking People, Learning & Performance

990-31410a

HUMAN RESOURCE DEVELOPMENT QUARTERLY AND OTHER JOSSEY-BASS PERIODICALS ARE NOW AVAILABLE ONLINE AT WILEY INTERSCIENCE

WHAT IS WILEY INTERSCIENCE?

Wiley InterScience is the dynamic online content service from John Wiley & Sons delivering the full text of over 300 leading professional, scholarly, and education journals, plus major reference works, the acclaimed *Current Protocols* laboratory manuals, and even the full text of selected Wiley print books.

WHAT ARE SOME SPECIAL FEATURES OF WILEY INTERSCIENCE?

Wiley InterScience Alerts is a service that delivers the table of contents via e-mail for any journal available on Wiley InterScience as soon as a new issue is published online.

EarlyView is Wiley's exclusive service presenting individual articles online as soon as they are ready, even before the release of the compiled print issue. These articles are complete, peer reviewed, and citable.

CrossRef is the innovative multipublisher reference linking system that enables readers to move seamlessly from a reference in a journal article to the cited publication, typically located on a different server and published by a different publisher.

HOW CAN I ACCESS WILEY INTERSCIENCE?

Visit http://www.interscience.wiley.com

Guest Users can browse Wiley InterScience for unrestricted access to journal tables of contents and article abstracts, or use the powerful search engine.

Registered Users are provided with a personal home page to store and manage customized alerts, searches, and links to favorite journals and articles. Additionally, Registered Users can view free online sample issues and preview selected material from major reference works.

Licensed Customers are entitled to access full-text journal articles in PDF, with selected journals also offering full-text HTML.

HOW DO I BECOME AN AUTHORIZED USER?

Authorized Users are individuals authorized by a paying Customer to have access to the journals in Wiley InterScience. For example, a university that subscribes to Wiley journals is considered to be the Customer. Faculty, staff, and students authorized by the university to have access to those journals in Wiley InterScience are Authorized Users. Users should contact their library for information on which Wiley and Jossey-Bass journals they have access to in Wiley InterScience.

ASK YOUR INSTITUTION ABOUT WILEY INTERSCIENCE TODAY!

9 780787 988876